Power Couples of the Renaissance

Also by Jo Romero

Forgotten Women of the Wars of the Roses: The Untold History Behind the Battle for the Crown

Power Couples of the Tudor Era: Influential Duos That Shaped the History of their Time

POWER COUPLES of the RENAISSANCE

Influential Duos that Shaped the History of their Time

JO ROMERO

PEN & SWORD HISTORY

AN IMPRINT OF PEN & SWORD BOOKS LTD.
YORKSHIRE – PHILADELPHIA

First published in Great Britain in 2026 by
PEN AND SWORD HISTORY
An imprint of
Pen & Sword Books Ltd
Yorkshire – Philadelphia

Print ISBN 978 1 03610 512 9
ePUB ISBN 978 1 03610 514 3
ePPDF ISBN 978 1 03610 516 7

A CIP catalogue record for this book is available from the British Library.

Typeset in Times New Roman 11/14 by
SJmagic DESIGN SERVICES, India.
Cover images credits: *The Court of Love* (British Library, BL Royal 16fii, f1. Via Picryl), *Betrothal* (National Gallery, Denmark), *Taj Mahal* (Wellcome Collection), *Sanguine Temperament* (Rijksmuseum).
Printed and bound in the UK by CPI Group (UK) Ltd, Croydon, CR0 4YY.

The Publisher's authorised representative in the EU for product safety is Authorised Rep Compliance Ltd., Ground Floor, 71 Lower Baggot Street, Dublin D02 P593, Ireland.
www.arccompliance.com

For a complete list of Pen & Sword titles please contact:
PEN & SWORD BOOKS LIMITED
George House, Units 12 & 13, Beevor Street, Off Pontefract Road,
Barnsley, South Yorkshire, S71 1HN, England
E-mail: enquiries@pen-and-sword.co.uk
Website: www.pen-and-sword.co.uk

or

PEN AND SWORD BOOKS
1950 Lawrence Rd, Havertown, PA 19083, USA
E-mail: uspen-and-sword@casematepublishers.com
Website: www.penandswordbooks.com

MIX
Paper | Supporting responsible forestry
FSC® C013604

Contents

Acknowledgements

Thanks to Silvia Merigo, art historian at the Palazzo Ducale di Mantova, for helping me identify figures in Mantegna's paintings in the palace's Bridal Chamber at Mantua. Thank you also to Sabrina Zin for her help in translating Italian texts. I also owe thanks to staff at the V&A in South Kensington in London for their assistance on various visits and the secretary at the Basilica of San Lorenzo in Florence for helping with enquiries relating to Contessina de Bardi. Special thanks must go to Konrad Eisenbichler for his kindness and for sharing valuable comments about Margaret of Austria and Laudomia Forteguerri. I have also found huge help in the transcripts and translations of many original letters written by individuals discussed in this book. A particular mention must be made to historians of earlier times who preserved many of these for future researchers, especially Yvonne Maguire, Janet Ross and Julia Cartwright.

As always, thanks must go to Jav, Georgina, Sofia, Viv, Amy, Mark, Rob, Dave and Malcolm for their support and patience as I navigated the Renaissance world. Thanks, too, to the ever-patient Kerrin Wilkinson and the Pen and Sword team.

Every effort has been made to cross-check and eliminate any errors in the text, however, any that remain are, of course, my own.

Introduction

With its main activity spanning roughly the late fourteenth to the late seventeenth centuries, the Renaissance era was a period of revolution. Those who lived through it watched as entire modes of government were abolished and later resurrected, their ancient social structures reformed and overhauled. Startling and rapid transformation was seen in almost every aspect of life, from the religion worshipped in local churches to the ingredients that fed hungry families at the dinner table. Nakedness and excess, previously considered sinful to the medieval mind, began to be openly celebrated in art and sculpture, along with vivid expressions of love and sensuality. It was also an era of power, conspiracy and war, with families like the Medicis, Borgias and Sforzas committing often brutal and underhand tactics to achieve political and financial success. Outside of Italy, the Habsburgs, Valois, Plantagenets, Tudors and Stuarts made their own mark on the age, along with the Braganzas of Portugal and the Mughals of modern-day India.

Today we refer to the period as a 'rebirth' (from the French word *renaissance*). The early fifteenth century saw a resurgence of interest in ancient Greek and Roman culture, as classical ruins were studied and stone statues were pulled from the earth. These figures, unlike those created by earlier medieval sculptors, twisted, gestured and glared, conveying emotion, movement and a sense of drama. Chiselled in bronze and marble, they were also intricately detailed with painstakingly realistic depictions of clothing, flexed muscle and armour. Artists eagerly sketched these finds, using them to learn the basics of new concepts such as foreshortening, perspective and anatomy. Encouraged by an emphasis on realism, they also experimented with tantalisingly lifelike depictions of foliage, props and animals. In one sketch by German artist Albrecht Dürer dated 1505, a stag beetle appears, complete with spiked shadows underneath its spindly legs. Startlingly realistic even 500 years after it was painted, it appears as if you could pick it up from the page.[1]

The Renaissance era is well known for its contribution to the art world, but it also triggered major developments in education. Scholars squinted at ancient texts, learning philosophy, medicine, politics and history. Bundled into parcels and wooden trunks, these dog-eared manuscripts were shipped from Greece and Rome into the states of wider Europe and carefully pushed onto the bookshelves of public and private libraries. Soon, lectures were being held in the Greek language, while architects unfurled designs for new structures inspired by ancient architecture, mathematics and geometry. Residents of towns and cities watched as labourers raised domes, pillars and elegant courtyards within buildings that served not only as private homes and places of worship, but places to meet, conduct business and oversee political affairs.

The city of Florence in Italy is today often regarded as the era's historic centre, but it did not achieve its fame in isolation from the rest of Europe, nor was it alone in its significance to the Renaissance. Emerging as a vibrant community dedicated to craft and education, intellectuals, craftsmen and aristocrats from other nations flocked to the city to learn from its well-paid and successful masters. However, the era would not have developed as it did without the invention of the printing press in Germany in the mid-fifteenth century. Not only was it crucial to the faster and more efficient spread of information, but it led to a new wave of critique, comment and creative output as poets, historians and prose writers created new, derivative works inspired by these older, printed texts. The translation of works in different languages made them even more accessible to readers in Europe and the wider world, as homes and palaces were filled with romance stories and chivalrous tales of legendary kings and knights. Readers of the era became fascinated by the adventures of mythological and historical heroes as they adopted their moral lessons and desirable values. Others were attracted to philosophy, science and astronomy, pushing forward new developments in scientific enquiry during the age. One trailblazing work, published in the mid-sixteenth century in Siena, explored a real-life example of same-sex love between two women. Another, in the next century, investigated whether life could be sustained on the moon.

It was a period of huge creative and scholarly output. But artists, writers, scholars and other masters of their craft could not have made these significant contributions without their patrons and supporters. These financial backers employed artists for their own projects, recommending them for other lucrative commissions from within their social circles. Wealthy, influential and usually politically powerful, these patrons shaped and defined specific styles of artistic expression in their chosen commissions, filling their homes with paintings and statues created by Renaissance masters. In many cases, it is thanks to them that so many works from the period have survived for us to study and enjoy today.

It was also a period of exploration. Leather purses bulging with coins were emptied onto wooden tables, financing new voyages to distant lands and triggering a commercial revolution, the effects of which we can still see today.

Away from the cultural revival, the period sizzled with risk and danger, fuelled by relentless ambition and ego. Aristocrats and politicians were found strangled in their beds, stabbed in their homes or poisoned at dinner. Others were swiftly deposed from power by men and women more determined and ruthless. Florentine writer Niccolò Machiavelli, author of the 1532 political work *The Prince*, praised a merciless approach to ruling, arguing that it instilled fear and obedience in subjects and intimidated enemies. Many leaders of the age adopted this attitude and thousands suffered because of it. In Europe and beyond, people were enslaved or forced to follow a state-enforced faith, facing severe punishment, expulsion or even execution if they did not obey.

Women also become more visible in the historical record at this time not only as poets, playwrights, biographers and actors, but in managing their own governments. As regents, rulers and co-rulers of nations including the Netherlands, France, Castile, Aragon, Granada, Portugal, England and Mantua, they personally altered and influenced significant local and international events. Civil wars were common during the period, fought in England and Castile, while leaders were deposed in the states of Italy and in the Mughal Empire of Hindustan. Shockwaves echoed around the world as leaders learned that Charles I, anointed King of England and Scotland, had been executed by order of Parliament in January 1649. At that moment in Whitehall, London, the traditional basis of monarchical power that had existed for centuries was severed in seconds by the thud of a blood-stained axe.

Unsurprisingly, those who lived during the period knew they were experiencing a revolution. Tommaso Campanella, in *The City of the Sun*, written in the first years of the seventeenth century, wrote of the 'coming age, and of our age, that has in it more history within a hundred years than all the world had in four thousand years before'.[2] The Renaissance era did not follow a rigid timeline. Its impact can be observed throughout different periods and geographical areas, affecting not only Europe, but as far as

Asia and the Americas. Naturally, this has caused some debate between historians over where to place the age. V. H. H. Green, in *Renaissance and Reformation*, positioned it approximately between 1450–1660, while Edith Helen Sichel began her study of the English Renaissance from the sixteenth century.[3] I have stretched these dates to include biographies of prominent characters crucial to the development of the age that were active in the late fourteenth century. I have also extended the end of the era to around 1700, when Renaissance momentum began to wane, its discoveries triggering a new wave of exploration and study now known as the Enlightenment era.

With so many men and women publicly active during this time, it is interesting that many of the period's events, developments and achievements have often been acknowledged as the work of an individual. There is in fact ample evidence that many prominent personalities were working within partnerships where they were not only encouraged and supported by partners, but where the lesser-known of the duo wielded considerable influence of their own. Working behind the scenes or at their partner's side, they affected not only the success of their partner, but enhanced their combined power. These partners can be regarded as power couples.

Seventeenth-century writer and poet Katherine Phillips conveyed the notion of a power couple when she penned the lines 'Betwixt two souls, and they two friends, Whose either joys in both are fix'd, And multiply'd by being mix'd'.[4] With their advantages and skills multiplied and mixed, couples were able to delegate and allocate responsibilities and tasks between them. This increased their chances of survival in increasingly suspicious and dangerous environments, the personality of one complementing the other. Some partners were diplomatic, tactful and charming, while the other demonstrated volatile or abrasive tendencies. Others possessed efficient and meticulous administrative skills, leaving the other to conduct business and soften influential clients and politicians for the couple's gain. Both partners were therefore crucial to the couple's combined success and it is only through a fresh examination of the evidence available that their full contribution to the age can clearly be seen.

There were many reasons behind the formation of a power partnership in the Renaissance era. A carefully arranged marriage between two dominant banking families had the potential to raise their combined commercial profile as well as merge an existing client base and streamline administration. For others, a partnership offered financial and territorial benefits, with large dowries dangled in front of potential royal husbands in exchange for influence and military protection. Others simply married for love. In many cases, they grappled with imbalances of power, with one partner significantly higher in status and wealth than the other. But this did not mean that they were not powerful. Lesser-known partners were able to wield authority in more subtle ways as they demonstrated resilience, provided counsel and worked as diplomats. They were also patrons of the arts, some producing an impressive body of creative work themselves, as well as overseeing new developments in artistry, music, the theatre and study. Not everyone survived the era intact, however. For some couples, their fortunes plummeted, and care, conspiracy and often violent force were needed to regain them.

It is important to place these power couples in the context of their surroundings and specific place in time. We visit the cities in which they conducted business, where they lived and socialized. For some, we peek into their homes and wander around opulent chambers, halls and the intimate spaces they would have known. Others we will find on the battlefield, in siege tents and at the front line of fighting. Through portraiture, commissions, documents, personal items, letters and eyewitness reports, we can also piece together aspects of their private lives and individual personalities.

For such a wide expanse of time and geography, there were countless couples to choose for this analysis. Catherine de Medici and Henry II of France were prominent characters of the era whose political actions and patronage of the arts is well known. Similarly, Francis I and his queen, Claude, presided over a court rich in luxury, navigating a tense political atmosphere in the early sixteenth century. In England, Charles I and Queen Henrietta Maria made a significant contribution to the country's culture, heading a court filled with music, theatre and dance. There are also a number of Tudor monarchs who heavily contributed to the Renaissance in England; however, these have been explored in my previous book, *Power Couples of the Tudor Era: Influential Duos That Shaped the History of their Time*.

In the interests of highlighting the more 'forgotten' characters of the age, the ten power couples in this book have been chosen because one or both partners either have not widely received acknowledgement for their contributions or have not been considered in the context of their partnership. Priority was also given to couples who were rarely discussed as contributors of the Renaissance movement, whether in politics, business or the arts. It was important to bring these neglected roles and actions to the surface and regain some balance in the historical record. Many of these findings will also challenge some existing beliefs on Renaissance-era sexuality, power and patronage. I have also included characters from geographical areas often neglected in general discussions of the Renaissance, such as North America, Northern Europe and Hindustan. Finally, the chapters on each couple are not told in strict chronological order, and many of their lives overlap. In some cases, it was important to explore one couple from a future timeline before moving onto another so that their links and influence later made sense.

The Renaissance era was an exhilarating and dangerous time to be alive. It was brutal, perilous, sensual and indulgent. And within it, ten power couples emerged from different cities, backgrounds and periods to affect the lives of millions, imprinting their own indelible mark on the age.

Chapter 1

Cosimo de Medici and Contessina de Bardi of Florence

Millions of visitors flock to the Italian city of Florence every year to see Michelangelo's famous sculpture of *David* and Brunelleschi's renowned terracotta-tiled duomo. For centuries it has epitomised the Renaissance age, its churches, palaces and civic buildings filled with the work of iconic Italian masters such as Lorenzo Ghiberti, Masaccio and Sandro Botticelli. Its piazzas were once trodden by the likes of Leonardo da Vinci, Donatello and Pietro Torrigiano, as they debated, socialised and conducted business in the shade of the cathedral. It is not surprising therefore that Florence is today widely regarded as a crucial centre in the movement that triggered enormous political, cultural and social change.

At the heart of Renaissance Florence, one family influenced and controlled key events in Europe for three centuries. They are famous for poisoning, assassinating and manipulating in their relentless quest for power and supremacy, and enjoyed dominance over the continent as princes, queens, cardinals and popes. It is difficult to find a European ruler from the sixteenth century that escaped the influence and authority of an ambitious Medici. But to fully understand the family's links to the era we must go back to the husband and wife at the heart of this political dynasty. Enduring hardship and separation, they worked together to establish early Medici fortunes and shaped the future of Florence as a thriving centre of art, education and politics.

Cosimo de Medici was born on 27 September 1389, the son of Giovanni di Bicci de Medici and Piccarda Bueri. He is referred to in history books and contemporary sources as 'the Elder' to differentiate him from subsequent members of the family who adopted his name. The Medici family can be traced to the early medieval period in Florence, their names preserved in records as landowners and public servants from the twelfth century onwards. Giovanni and Piccarda had amassed a fortune in the late fourteenth century through their involvement in the mercantile and banking industries along with Giovanni's position in local government as a Gonfalonier, a prominent figure of local justice. Careful and acquisitive with his funds, he died in February 1429 leaving an impressive 179,221 scudi in the family coffers, an achievement he attributed to his wife's actions as much as his own.[1] Piccarda and Giovanni therefore left a considerable financial and social foundation for their two sons, Cosimo and Lorenzo. Aged almost 40 at the time of his father's death, the eldest, Cosimo, would have had plenty of opportunity as a young man to learn about the city's inner workings and the running of the family business from his father. He had also served in the Pisan War in his mid-twenties in 1414 and had assumed his first civic role in Florence by 1415.[2] Olive-skinned and of medium height, portraits show that Cosimo had a prominent nose, pointed chin and heavy-lidded eyes. Although he was praised for his easy-going, affable and generous nature, underneath the cordial smiles there lurked a shrewd and calculating businessman and politician.

By 1415 Cosimo had married Contessina de Bardi, the daughter of the Count of Vernio. Her specific date of birth is not recorded, but is widely believed to have occurred in around 1390–1391, making her close in age to her husband. The Bardis were powerful merchants and bankers that boasted such notable clients as English and French royalty and the leaders of the states of Italy, as well as the papacy. One of their biggest clients was the fourteenth-century King of England, Edward III, who borrowed huge sums, not only to fund his wars with Scotland and France, but also to run his royal household. The Bardis, along with another prominent banking family of Florence, the Peruzzis, propped up Edward's lavish lifestyle, funding royal funeral expenses, jewels, gifts and even the general upkeep of the leopards and lions at the Tower of London.[3]

The mid-1330s would prove disastrous for the Bardi family. Along with social and political unrest in Florence, Edward III defaulted on his repayments. The huge amounts he owed (some sources suggest it was around 100,000 florins), along with other events, reduced the Bardis' strong position and strained their financial resources.[4] However, the family continued to trade, appearing in English state records over substantial sums during the early fifteenth century. One of these, on 3 July 1427, involved a significant payment of £30, equivalent in modern terms to around £20,000. It also highlighted the recent Medici-Bardi marriage, noting carefully that a member of the Bardi family living in London was now 'of the fellowship of the Medici'.[5] That this deserved comment at all, and was important to record in English documents, suggests that the marriage was of significant financial importance, underlining the impact of Cosimo and Contessina's union on their contemporaries.

Although the Bardis' earlier influence had waned, they were still very much in business and a union with the rising Medici family promised to strengthen and further their economic interests. For the newly flourishing Medicis, the marriage offered ties with an established, traditional and well-known banking institution with access to its clients and contacts around the world. Cosimo was an outgoing and intelligent businessman, overseeing the administration of his banking enterprise and using his influence in local government. Contessina was also interested in politics and proved to be a careful administrator, confidante and organiser working alongside her husband. At the time of their marriage both partners were in their early twenties. Their union not only combined the families' commercial and political interests, but threw together two young people with skills honed from within the highest circles of powerful Florentine business and society.

According to the writer and political commentator Giovanni Cavalcanti, Giovanni di Bicci de Medici called both his sons to him as death approached and advised them to be careful with any public displays of their fortune. He warned them against being 'puffed up with pride' and told them to 'not enter into party strife'. Assuring them he had left them a legacy 'free of any stain', he requested they take care of their mother and keep her in the style of living she had been used to.[6] Although Cosimo and Contessina would make an effort to follow Giovanni's advice and tread carefully with their growing wealth, it was not long before suspicions arose that Cosimo was wielding too much influence over the city's affairs and giving preference in matters of state to his personal and business associates. This was a dangerous accusation. Florence at this time operated as a democracy with a council of men equally in control of its government. The claims made by Cosimo's enemies that he intended to 'make himself prince of the city' threatened to overturn Florence's established premise of power.[7]

In an atmosphere of jealousy, suspicion and doubt, the Medicis were abruptly toppled from their privileged position. In 1433, supporters of a Florentine nobleman and Medici opponent, Rinaldo degli Albizzi, argued that Cosimo should be removed from the city, accusing him of lending money and favouring his supporters and friends, a claim that was probably accurate. According to Cosimo's own account of the event noted in his diary, he was invited to the Signory on 7 September to discuss state business, but when he arrived, he was imprisoned in the Alberghettino, a small cell around eight feet wide inside Florence's Arnolfo Tower.[8]

According to Cosimo, the residents of Florence rebelled on hearing that he had been imprisoned, while a supporter, Niccolò da Tolentino, gathered a company of men 'intending to raise the city, so that I might be released'. Cosimo and Contessina's sons were safeguarded and taken to Venice by their uncle Lorenzo while the council tried desperately to dissuade crowds from taking military action. The next day Cosimo learned that he was to be exiled from Florence and banished to Padua.[9] Contessina's own actions during this time are unknown, but it must have been a busy and worrying time for her. The couple were in their forties and had two children: Piero, aged 17, and Giovanni, aged twelve. Later, they accompanied their father to Padua. The boys' prompt removal from Florence at Cosimo's fall indicates that they were believed to have been in some danger from their father's enemies. Removing or taking custody of both Cosimo's heirs would have given an opponent control over the family's future in government. Alternatively, they could have been used as a bartering tool to persuade Cosimo to leave Florence permanently. Another boy also lived with the family, Cosimo's illegitimate son Carlo, although it is not clear if he also travelled with his father or stayed during this time with Contessina. Conceived in around 1430, during his marriage to Contessina, he was raised in the couple's household and continued to hold a close, trusted position within it. Carlo later pursued a career in the church and was seen entertaining guests at the wedding of Cosimo and Contessina's grandson Lorenzo in June 1469.[10]

From what we know of Contessina's personality, it is very likely that during her separation from her husband and sons she was quietly gathering support for Cosimo's return to prominence. Remaining in Florence, she was well placed to gather intelligence from the city or subtly petition her husband's supporters to plot his return. Her surviving letters show that she had close contact with Cosimo's commercial contacts and displayed a mothering, but tenacious and business-like approach. She was a natural problem solver, fretting over household staff and Cosimo's clothing, diet and health while he was away from home, always offering to send supplies or follow up on business for him. She was simply not the kind of woman to do nothing during a crisis. Concrete evidence surrounding her actions during this time is scarce, though this is to be expected; discussions in the piazza with contacts, particularly those plotting his return, would have been carried out secretly and most likely by word of mouth. It would have been risky to have communicated such sensitive information by letter in case it was intercepted. As the adult daughter of a prominent and well-connected banking family with clients at the upper levels of society, it is logical that she would have had an appreciation and understanding of confidentiality and discretion.

For Cosimo's actions, there is more evidence. Political writer Niccolò Machiavelli noted that around this time he 'conducted himself in more zeal and boldness in regard to his friends than his father had done', and bribed Florence's Gonfalonier, a crucial arm of support within the Signory, with 1,000 ducats.[11] He also had followers to support him, some of them accompanying him in exile. Soon, the couple's sweetening of contacts and rallying of support paid off. By the end of summer 1434, Cosimo was restored to his former position and the Albizzis were removed from influence, and banished themselves. Popular with the people, as his father had been, Cosimo was welcomed back to Florence with open arms. As Machiavelli stated, he was later 'hailed as the benefactor of the people, and the father of his country'. Accordingly, he was later known by the nickname *Pater Patriae* (Father of the Country).[12]

Contessina's role was more subtle than that of her husband, but she was still a public figure by association and a formidable force within the Medici family. An efficient organiser and facilitator of relationships, especially among the Medici women, she could also be abrupt. In a letter to her son Giovanni on 6 June 1430 she urged him to 'Do thy best to please him [Cosimo] in all things, and see that he wants for nothing', adding that she had been told her husband, who was away from the family home, had become 'quite fat'.[13] Her letters are warm, however, as she worries over the spread of plague and fusses over sending various items of clothing. She also set out to locate missing Medici guests who were taking longer than expected to arrive and met with Cosimo's contacts in his absence. Always ready to assist her family, Contessina often repeated the line in her letters: 'if thou needest aught from here let me know.'[14] While her sons and husband were transacting business or travelling through various parts of Italy, Contessina was not only managing the household in their absence, she was fulfilling the complex role of personal assistant in business. In 1427 she chased up overdue rents and reported their successful payment to Cosimo.[15] Contessina was also well known to other families as a reliable and knowledgeable representative of her husband and sons. On 18 December 1450 she wrote from their home in Florence to her son Giovanni, complaining that 'Antonio degl' Strozzi has been to see me, and pestered me much about that business', adding that 'he could learn nothing from me: so be cautious about how thou dealest with him'.[16] On another occasion,

Contessina wrote to inform Giovanni of a political decision Cosimo had made. In August 1460, she advised that Cosimo had 'put an end to the worry of being one of the Eight, and Pier Francesco has been named in his stead: this might also be done for thee'.[17] Her mention of 'the Eight' refers to the eight members of the Signory that served in Florence's government. Both these letters show that Contessina was well aware of her husband's political developments and intentions, as well as what was worrying him. Her dangling of something they could do for Giovanni also shows that she had a good knowledge of the workings of the Signory and its power and process. Contessina also had access to confidential information that Strozzi was unable to wrest from her, demonstrating her business sense. Acting as advisor, confidante, communicator and protector, Contessina displayed professionalism and loyalty whether dealing in family, business, or more subtly, in civic affairs.

Contessina penned her surviving letters from various Medici homes including Careggi, Cafaggiolo and Florence. In many of them the maternal care and love she had for her children is evident. At the end of August 1460, Contessina and Cosimo were together at Careggi, when she wrote to her daughter-in-law Ginevra, the wife of her son Giovanni. Expressing gratitude on hearing news that the young couple had fought off a recent illness, Contessina added warmly, 'may it please God that it shall continue, in order to give these two old people joy and consolation whilst they still live.'[18] The couple were now in their early seventies and the Villa Medici at Careggi was where they spent many of these later years. The imposing pale-stone structure, nestled within wooded hills with winding tracks would have given them a sense of country isolation while being just over 2½ miles from the centre of Florence. The family villa at Cafaggiolo was further north, previously inhabited by Cosimo's earlier medieval ancestors. Comprising a central tower, it boasted an imposing outer wall, moat and leafy orchard.

Their most famous residence was the Palazzo Riccardi, just a few minutes' walk from the Cathedral di Santa Maria del Fiore in the centre of Florence. Begun in 1444, it was designed by the architect Michelozzo Michelozzi in the classical style fashionable at the time. The building included large cellars and storerooms that were essential for entertaining the couple's large family and for diplomatic events. In April 1459, the couple entertained Galeazzo Maria, the Count of Pavia and son of Francesco Sforza, Duke of Milan, at the palace. It was a diplomatic visit and the duke's son was entertained with music, dancing, poetry recitals and dinner.[19] Two courtyards dominated the space outside, with pillars, columns and sheltered areas that led to other rooms and staircases to the rest of the palace. Statues commissioned by the family also decorated this space, which would certainly have made an impression on visitors. The house had its own bakery and kitchen and a chapel where the family could worship privately. There was also a suite of apartments for the family's personal use.

Another event that would have had significance for the couple was the *Palio alla lunga*, a horse race through Florence's streets on 24 June each year. In honour of St John the Baptist, the race originated in around the thirteenth century. Goro di Stagio Dati, writing while Cosimo and Contessina lived in the city, stated that before the race began in the afternoon, women lined the streets with 'many lords and knights and foreign gentlemen', the course decked out in fresh flowers and 'rich adornments'. After three tolls of the bell, the horses raced and the first one to reach the palio (a crimson velvet banner) won.[20] With their home in the centre of the city, it's likely that Cosimo and Contessina attended the festival, particularly as public figures who wished to appear loyal aligned with Florence's regime and customs. With all of Florence attending, it would also have been an opportunity for the couple to network and make connections for the benefit of both family and business affairs. It was also a chance to make important contact with Cosimo's allies, should their support ever be needed in the future. With the contemporary account stressing the presence of 'foreign gentlemen', overseas connections would have been eagerly fostered, too.

Among the bankers, merchants and politicians who visited the couple's various homes, another group was welcomed into the Medicis' close circle. While Cosimo frowned over state affairs and Contessina tackled questions from pushy business associates, an inquisitive crowd of artists, architects and mathematicians gathered in the Piazza of Santa Maria del Fiore under the shadow of the cathedral. There, they animatedly discussed new and groundbreaking ideas in perspective, philosophy and form.

Among them were men now considered early pioneers of Renaissance art and architecture and the influence of this early Medici couple was central to many of their successes. Supporting them by personally commissioning work, they also introduced them to new clients and other lucrative opportunities from within their social sphere. Giorgio Vasari, writing in the sixteenth century, discussed a visit by Pope Eugenius to Florence in 1439. Impressed after seeing the work of the Florentine craftsman Lorenzo Ghiberti, the pope commissioned him to make a mitre of gold studded with pearls. Vasari stated that after the visit, the artist was asked by the Signory and

Guild of Merchants in Florence to make the bronze gates at the Baptistery of San Giovanni. Giving Ghiberti creative freedom in the project, it was hoped that 'even as he had surpassed all other sculptors up to his own time, he might surpass and excel all his own previous works'. Cosimo wielded political influence at this time and, as an enthusiastic supporter of the arts and prominent businessman, is likely to have been involved, if not central, to the Signory's decision to employ Ghiberti. The two men were already known to one another. A decade earlier in 1428, Cosimo and his brother Lorenzo had commissioned Ghiberti to make a bronze sarcophagus in the Church of the Monastery of the Angeli in Florence to house the remains of the martyrs Protus and Nemesius. The craftsman enjoyed a long association with the family that continued into the following generation as Ghiberti later completed work for Cosimo's younger son, Giovanni.[21]

The image of a fifteenth-century artist or philosopher working long hours alone, hunched over a candlelit desk might look good in a period drama, but it is not entirely accurate. While there was inevitably some lone working, sources show that the spread of information during the early Renaissance was driven by social and collaborative efforts, something that aligned well with the Medici couple's outgoing and accommodating approach. Giorgio Vasari's *Lives of the Most Eminent Painters, Sculptors and Architects* is a biographical collection of anecdotes relating to artists and craftsmen, many of them known to the couple. Rich in information, it is a vast work spanning many volumes. However, Vasari's reliability as a source has been questioned as his writing, in the mid-sixteenth century, came many years after the individuals concerned had died. But there is still value in his work. In his introduction, Vasari maintained that he had the help of 'friends that I have in various places', along with access to 'innumerable treasures' in the possession of the later ruler Duke Cosimo of Florence and Siena. He also insisted that he wrote with 'truth of history' in mind.[22] Among Vasari's tales we find Raphael learning form and structure from the work of Masaccio and Leonardo da Vinci, and Giovanni Manetti and Paolo Uccello discussing mathematics. We also find Filippo Brunelleschi, Donatello and other craftsmen standing in the piazza one day, enthusiastically discussing principles of architecture. Vasari also describes Donatello and Brunelleschi taking a trip to Rome to study sculpture and architecture.[23] Fifteenth-century Florence was thriving with communication, debate and inspiration, a large part of which was encouraged and aided by Medici patronage.

Spending their personal wealth on the arts not only subtly increased the perceived power of Cosimo and Contessina's family, it also elevated the reputation of Florence itself. Instead of solely topping up the purses of rich bankers and businessmen, Medici funds were diverted back into the fabric of the city and its people and is perhaps evidence that Cosimo listened carefully to the dying words of his father. Providing craftsmen with a livelihood, artists were then able to produce new work, gain further commissions and enjoy a new level of financial security.

New buildings, paid for and overseen by the Medici couple, started to rise into the skyline. It is even possible that their influence can be found in one of the city's most famous and recognisable structures, the terracotta dome of the Cathedral of Santa Maria del Fiore. According to Giorgio Vasari, when the decision was made to build the dome in 1420, Filippo Brunelleschi was chosen to design and build it, but there was anxiety over its completion. The people argued that it was safer if two craftsmen were involved, the ambitious project laying 'too great a charge on one man'. They were also nervous about any accidents that might arise in its design or building. Vasari noted that one architect in particular was 'beloved by certain men who were very powerful in the government' at that time: Lorenzo Ghiberti. It was decided by those in charge that Brunelleschi would share his commission with Ghiberti, much to the former's annoyance.[24] Is it possible that Cosimo was among these men in the government who favoured Ghiberti? We know that he later had a close relationship with the craftsman and was already exerting influence in Florentine government by this time. Brunelleschi was also elected one of the Signory in the summer of 1423, after his design for the dome was well under way. It is tempting to wonder if these men's fortunes and influence increased thanks to their association with the Medici politician. While speculative, links such as these should not be completely ignored, particularly in light of Albizzi's complaints a decade later.

Cosimo later commissioned Brunelleschi to design the Medici's Riccardi Palace. The architect created a preliminary model of the design and proudly showed it to the banker. However, on seeing it, Cosimo remembered his father's warnings about extravagance and chose not to proceed with the plans. Brunelleschi was so enraged at this rejection that he was said to have broken the model 'into a thousand pieces'.[25] The contract was given instead to the architect Michelozzo Michelozzi, who created a more understated palace with columns, courtyards and accents inspired by classical antiquity. Cosimo and Michelozzi were old friends, the architect having kept Cosimo company during his uncertain months of exile in 1433. He also designed the Convent of St Marco under Cosimo's patronage and rebuilt other Medici homes at Cafaggiolo, Careggi and Trebbio.[26]

Both Cosimo and Contessina heavily supported the sculptor Donatello, a figure who would become famous as one of the era's great masters. Cosimo used his connections to put the sculptor in touch with a Genoese merchant who, he had heard, wanted a life-sized head made of bronze.[27] Their relationship was a close one. At Cosimo's request, his son Piero granted the sculptor a farm in Cafaggiolo near the family home, but Donatello found it difficult and time-consuming to maintain and received a weekly maintenance payment instead. Vasari said the sculptor 'lived happily and free from care' for the rest of his life as a 'servant and friend' of the Medicis.[28] His close association with the family would have meant Contessina would have been known to the artist, too, and his bronze sculpture of *David* is known to have adorned their home. Mounted on a column, it acted as a centrepiece around which drinks were served at their grandson's wedding in 1469.[29] Today the statue, made in around 1440, is in the collection of the Museo Nazionale del Bargello in Florence.[30]

In 1459 Cosimo commissioned a new piece of work from the artist Benozzo Gozzoli. It was to be a depiction of a religious scene, *The Chapel of the Magi*, in the private chapel of their Florence home, the Palazzo Medici Riccardi.[31] The work, depicting a long train of worshippers on their way to greet the infant Christ, also features portraits of Cosimo and his family among them. His likeness immediately stands out to the left of the composition, his short white hair poking out from underneath a red cap. It is not known if Contessina is shown among the others in the crowd, but in such a cherished and intimate space, she would have regularly glanced up at the figures on her way to worship.

Contessina was also a patron of the arts. She hired the artist Fra Filippo Lippi to paint a *Nativity of Christ with St John the Baptist* for a hermitage cell in Camaldoli, ordering the chapel built as 'proof of her devotion'.[32] There is some evidence that she may even have modelled for their old friend Donatello. In the sixteenth century, Vasari saw a bronze bust of Contessina that he said was created by the sculptor and displayed in the household of the later Medici statesman, Duke Cosimo. This bust has not yet been identified among Donatello's surviving works and it is uncertain if it has survived at all. Yvonne Maguire, in *The Women of the Medici*, hypothesised that another likeness of her may survive, tentatively identifying Contessina as the subject of the bust of an older woman wearing a long headdress in the Museo Nazionale del Bargello in Florence.[33] There is some speculation from Maguire that the head may have been created from Contessina's death mask, placing its creation in the late fifteenth century, although any firm identification of the sitter or even the sculptor of the piece is still uncertain. For a woman who co-founded a dynasty so dedicated to artistic patronage and herself a lover of the arts, it is surprising that no definitive contemporary portrait of her survives. However, with the public's adoration centring on her husband as a well-known figure, it is understandable that fewer portraits would be made of her, as her influence was exerted 'behind the scenes'.

The couple's impact on the Renaissance did not end with artistic commissions. Cosimo was also dedicated to the spread of classical ideas and it was claimed that he imported ancient Greek texts with Indian spices in ships from around the world. He inherited 600 volumes of manuscripts on the death of his friend Niccolò de' Niccoli and distributed them among his acquaintances, keeping some for himself and adding around 400 of them to the library of San Marco. He also paid for another 200 volumes of ancient writings to be copied for the library at the Badia Fiesolana in Fiesole.[34]

Contessina's role in the sharing of knowledge and stocking of libraries is less well known, but a hint in family correspondence suggests that she was also quietly dedicated to learning. In a letter of September 1473, when the now-widowed Contessina was residing with younger members of her family, it was noted that one of the children refused to look at their book, protesting, 'I did not come into the country to read.' The author of the letter added darkly, 'This displeases Mona Contessina.'[35] She may have preferred her grandchildren to read, but for her, real-world experience was just as important as squinting at ancient manuscripts. In June 1430 she wrote to her son Giovanni asking impatiently if he and his brother Piero were working in the family bank with their father. Piero would have been around 14 years of age and Giovanni, nine.[36] In any case, the Medicis hosted several thinkers, scholars and artists at their homes over the years and no doubt Contessina, with her meticulous organisational and household skills, made them feel welcome. Cosimo once remarked that her preparations to move the family from one house to another took two weeks, revealing that she was a careful planner and project manager.

Cosimo struggled with health in his final years and family letters refer to attacks of gout, aches, fever and even plague. He and Contessina mourned the death of their younger son Giovanni in 1463, in his early forties. Cosimo died the following year on 1 August 1464 at his Careggi home with Contessina and his eldest son, the 48-year-old Piero, by his side. In her widowhood, Contessina continued to dominate family affairs and is frequently mentioned in correspondence. On 2 August 1464 she was given cloth, handkerchiefs and veils for her husband's funeral, attending with her daughters-in-law as well as her sister-in-law, Ginevra. Still a formidable influencer in her own right as she entered her eighties, she was asked to use her power to convince her grandson Lorenzo to employ a man's son as an assistant on a trip to Rome.[37]

Contessina is not named, but was very likely present at the wedding of her grandson Lorenzo and his bride Clarice Orsini on 4 June 1469, where there were banquets, dances and music. Along with Donatello's *David*, a gilded statue of a winged sprite, now in the collection of the Metropolitan Museum of Art in New York, is believed to have once graced the Medici courtyard in Florence.[38] The museum's description of the piece emphasises the statue's resemblance to the ancient Roman god Mercury, the god of commerce, communication and travel. It may be significant that these were all particularly relevant factors in the Medici's' success and the figure may have been chosen to reflect this, particularly as the palace operated a civic function as well as a personal one. The figure was also heavily inspired by the work of the Medicis' friend Donatello. Made for a fountain in 1432 during the couple's lifetime, it would have been placed into position at around the time of Cosimo's exile. With the sculptures gesturing motionlessly and adding a sense of luxury to the extravagant celebrations, it is possible that Contessina, then approaching her eighties, was seated with her daughter-in-law and mother of the groom Lucrezia, where 'on a balcony in the great room upstairs dined the women of a certain age'.[39] Generally well in her later years, she suffered from time to time with eczema and died in October 1473.

Cosimo and Contessina de Medici were a formidable partnership in fifteenth-century Florence. Patrons of artists, craftsmen and architects, they sat for emerging artists and sculptors and had their likenesses chiselled into bronze and painted onto walls. There is some evidence that both were involved in Cosimo's political rise and later survival, and although Contessina has often been forgotten in accounts of the early Medici family, she was a vital partner, personal assistant and companion to Cosimo for over fifty years.

Yvonne Maguire, in *The Women of the Medici*, was correct in stating that the character of Contessina is 'fascinating because she is the first real woman of Florence to emerge as more than the mere shadow of a name'.[40] However her legacy was far more complex and the role she fulfilled as housewife and assistant to her husband and sons in business must not be underestimated. She sent belongings to them for their necessity and comfort, dealt with Cosimo's contacts in his absence and was asked to use her influence on behalf of local families seeking to associate themselves with the powerful, growing Medicis. In her letters she always asked for errands she could run from home and kept updated with everyone's whereabouts. By taking care of all these administrative and domestic duties, Cosimo could concentrate fully on political, financial and cultural affairs.

In their personal lives, it is possible to see many similarities between the pair. Both were capable administrators and organisers, possessing energy and tenacity, seeing tasks through to completion. They were also sociable, amassing a network of useful contacts in business, politics and within the family. They were also generous. In March 1445 Contessina arranged for 'capons, spices, saffron and comfits' to be sent to local women preparing for a birth while Cosimo's nickname as 'father of the people' reveals the fondness with which Florentines remembered him after his death.[41] Vasari credited Cosimo as the 'root' of the future Medici dynasty that was to become so powerful in later years. 'Although there had been previously in the family of the Medici many men noble and distinguished in arms and in civil actions,' he wrote, '[Cosimo] was nevertheless the first founder of its extraordinary greatness, and as it were the root of that plant which has since grown so happily to such magnificence.'[42] If Cosimo was the root of the Medici fortunes and success, it was Contessina who had watered it.

Both partners were also shrewd and cautious, traits developed through observing and participating in their respective family businesses. Contessina was intensely loyal and politically intelligent, knowing when to share information and when to withhold it. Heeding his father's words, Cosimo was careful not to arouse too much jealousy from his fellow Florentines and publicly gave back to the community by building communal buildings, furthering relationships between artists and patrons and elevating the image of his city. Diplomats and leaders were welcomed into the family's palaces, where they were entertained in shows of power, wealth and trust. There is an interesting similarity in the kind of control Cosimo exercised in politics and business and how Contessina managed the home, forging lasting relationships with her daughters-in-law and grandchildren. Both devoted parents, their letters show that they worried about their adult children when they were away from home and missed them.

There were some differences, however. Cosimo seems to have been more philosophical than his wife, who comes across in correspondence as pragmatic, honest and self-assured. As he approached death, she asked him bluntly why he sat for such long periods in silence. Replying that her preparations to move the family to one of their villas kept her busy for fifteen days, he asked her, 'Dost thou not understand that I, who am leaving this life for the next one, have much to think on?'[43]

There is no question that the couple changed the lives of their contemporaries. Florentines watched as buildings, including the churches of San Marco and San Lorenzo and monasteries at Santa Verdiana, San Girolamo and the Frati Minori in the Mugello, rose into view. These all provided new establishments for religious communities to live and worship in. The hermitage cell founded by Contessina at Camaldoli provided for solitary prayer, while Lippi's religious art inspired and encouraged devotion. Machiavelli credited Cosimo with other architectural developments, as well as commissioning work on chapels, altars and providing for the furniture, utensils and ornaments within them. He was also recorded as establishing a hospital in Jerusalem for the poor and pilgrims, and paid for the rebuilding of the Abbey of the Canons-Regular of Fiesole with his own money.[44] Because of both partners, Florence and regions far beyond were equipped with new places to worship, given a financial boost and made more comfortable and attractive for religious followers.

They also encouraged Florence to become a vibrant centre of learning with the creation of a substantial library of texts and great minds collaborating and problem-solving in the city's open spaces. This communal, collaborative atmosphere encouraged other thinkers, artists and sculptors to travel to the city and learn from its famous residents. Manuscripts were collected, copied and shared under Cosimo's command, while painters and sculptors were assured a livelihood working for the Medicis and other high-profile clients associated with them. Wooden shelves groaned under the weight of hundreds of papers in libraries, while philosophical debates took place inspired by the teachings of ancient Greece. Cosimo's love of antiquity was genuine – he personally owned and read works by ancient thinkers Plato, Suetonius and Chrysostom, all mentioned in his letters to various contacts.[45]

The couple also supported the livelihoods of those in construction, with homes built, maintained and extended under their supervision. Bases at Careggi, Fiesole, Cafaggiolo and Trebbio continued to be used by subsequent Medici generations, while their Florence base, the Riccardi Palace, was developed into a luxurious Renaissance home where the family could relax, conduct business and entertain. It later housed a government base. The building still serves a civic purpose today, containing a museum and libraries, as well as the beautifully decorated chapel where Cosimo and Contessina held private prayer. The couple were among the first to enjoy the ripening fruits of Renaissance creativity with statues, paintings and homes designed by the first Italian masters. Relationships were openly forged between the couple and creatives who were given a warm welcome at their homes. Donatello was one of their closest friends, along with Marsilio Ficino. Machiavelli called Ficino 'the reviver of the Platonic philosophy' and he was entertained by the couple at their home. Eventually, the philosopher moved into a house near the Medici Palace of Careggi so that he could be closer to the family and on hand to discuss theories with Cosimo.[46] Between them, the couple also had dealings with well-known names such as Fra Filippo, Brunelleschi, Michelozzo, Niccolò de' Niccoli and Gozzoli, among many others.

It can also be argued that, through their patronage, Cosimo and Contessina shaped the specific nature and development of Renaissance art, triggering the move away from strict medieval religious depictions towards those that were more sensual and indulgent. Art historian Jonathan Jones in *The Loves of the Artists*, considered Donatello's *David*, which stood in the couple's Florence home, 'a rebellion against this Christian repugnance', and an example of 'erotic charge'.[47] As Jones argues, by choosing to patronise and make public work that explored the classical 'rebirth' of ancient sensuality and the beauty of the human body rather than as a reflection of sin, culture was set on an exciting new tangent. The era would later become known for its marble and bronze depictions of soft flesh visibly surrendering under the pressure of fingertips and facial expressions of ecstasy and sensuality. These were daring and ambitious moves, taking place at a time not only of rebirth, but of rebellion against old medieval structures and concepts, even those associated with the powerful church.

After their deaths, the couple continued to be commemorated by artists. Sandro Botticelli painted Cosimo's likeness in the 1470s, in his *Portrait of a Man with a Medal of Cosimo the Elder* now in the Uffizi Gallery in Florence.[48] In 1544, Baccio Bandinelli ran with the *Pater Patriae* theme and depicted Cosimo as a Roman leader, complete with armour and weapons. A later copy of the original survives today in the British Museum in London.[49] Contessina was also depicted as strong and powerful by later artists. A lead medal, titled *Contessina de' Bardi, died 1473, Wife of Cosimo de Medici il Vecchio*, was made by Antonio Francesco Selvi in around 1740. The medal, in the collection of the National Gallery of Art, portrays her in profile, the material of a long headdress swirling around her shoulders. On the reverse of the medal is a ship being tossed in the sea, a fortified city visible in the background. Around the edge of is the inscription *Gloriam et Opes Fero* ('I will bring glory and wealth').[50] It is interesting to wonder whether, without the couple's sustained support, patronage and friendships with founding members of the Italian Renaissance, art – and the city of Florence – might have evolved as it did.

Of course, the couple also left a political legacy. The Medici influence in Florence spanned 300 years, give or take a few years where their power was lost, and Cosimo and Contessina were its founders. While Giovanni di Bicci de Medici was the first of the family to emerge as a figure of local government, Cosimo greatly enlarged on his power. Machiavelli wrote that Cosimo 'not only preserved but increased' the family wealth, and 'laid a foundation for his descendants'.[51] Fifteenth-century residents were grateful for Cosimo's work, enhancing Florence's image around the world. Cosimo's grandson Lorenzo would marvel at the amounts spent by his father and grandfather on buildings and public works, but he wrote on coming to power, 'I do not regret this, for … it gave great honour to our State.'[52]

Contessina, too, left an enduring legacy to future Medici women. She wrote often to both her daughters-in-law, sending them personal items and insisting they barter with and complain to tradesmen and workers for poor service. A meticulous micro-manager, it is possible to see her impact on the behaviour of women in future generations. Lucrezia Tournabuoni, wife of the couple's son Piero, became an active companion to both her husband and their son, giving political advice and much-needed support. In the following generation, Clarice Orsini, the wife of Lorenzo the Magnificent, acted with dignitaries on behalf of her absent husband and was asked to intercede with him in the interests of Florence's citizens. These may have been standard practices for wives in the public eye in fifteenth- and sixteenth-century Florence, but it is possible that Contessina's subtle and continual exertion of control and encouragement during the early years of her sons' marriages formed a framework that inspired them. The twentieth-century writer Edgcumbe Staley considered this, writing that Cosimo's household 'had all the circumstances of a regal court, and his hospitalities required the co-operation of an intelligent and highly educated mistress'. Pointing to the later achievements of the couple's daughter-in-law Lucrezia Tournabuoni, he wrote that 'Contessina prepared the robes of State, but Lucrezia wore them'.[53] Later, another prolific supporter of the arts, Isabella d'Este, lodged in the Medici Palace in Florence during a trip there in 1515.[54] We can only wonder at the effect the couple's sculptures, paintings and the early Renaissance architecture had on the classics-loving marchioness, who counted Leonardo da Vinci, Michelangelo and Raphael among her contacts.

In the sixteenth century the Medici family became more politically powerful and were less careful to exert authority and attract attention, forging ties with other powerful families and states. Machiavelli wrote that through Cosimo's work (although Contessina could claim credit for this, too), the fortunes of the Tournabuoni, Benci, Portinari and Sassetti families gained new heights from their association with him.[55] The couple's descendants, with access to this greater influence and wealth, made their own mark on the era. Giovanni, son of Lorenzo the Magnificent, later became Pope Leo X, working against the rising popularity of the Protestant religion. He died in 1521. Among their other descendants was Catherine de Medici, queen to Henry II, King of France in the sixteenth century. She was the mother of future kings François II, Charles IX and Henry III. One of Cosimo and Contessina's great-grandsons made a significant decision as Pope Clement VII, ruling in 1531 that the marriage of Katherine of Aragon and Henry VIII of England was legally binding, an act that had huge consequences for Henry's realm and triggered his break with Rome in the 1530s.

Cosimo de Medici is buried in the Basilica of San Lorenzo, close to the family home in Florence. The exact location of Contessina's grave is currently unknown, but is considered likely to be near Cosimo's, within the perimeter of the Basilica.[56]

Chapter 2

Edward IV and Elizabeth Woodville of England

Nine hundred miles away from Cosimo de Medici's bedside in the Florence heat, a young couple settled quietly into newly wedded life in the south of England. Their union, solemnised in the warm Northamptonshire countryside, would soon be tested by conspiracy, personal loss and civil war.

Edward IV was the first ruler in a new line of Yorkist kings, seizing the throne from the faltering Lancastrian king, Henry VI, following a series of battles now known as the Wars of the Roses. Henry's realm had suffered with social and political unrest for over a decade, as adherents of each royal house wrestled for control of the throne. England, fractured by war and rebellion, grew tired of conflict and increasingly despondent with their monarch, who failed to regain authority. After his army's defeat at the Battle of Towton on a snowy field in Yorkshire in March 1461 Henry VI fled, and Edward, the eldest son of the Duke of York, assumed control of the realm.

Edward differed from Henry in almost every way. He was younger, decisive and more politically astute than his predecessor. He was also powerful. The son of Richard Plantagenet and Cecily Neville, Duke and Duchess of York, he was born in Rouen, France, in 1442. On the death of his father at the Battle of Wakefield in 1460, Edward became the leading Yorkist claimant and took over the cause. Descended from Edward III, he boasted an impressive family tree. In addition, he had the support of influential relatives including his uncle and aunt Richard Neville and Alice Montacute, the wealthy Earl and Countess of Salisbury. The Salisburys were strong supporters of the Yorkist cause, losing their estates and being declared traitors in the process. Their son, Richard Neville, Earl of Warwick, became Edward's senior commander and advisor, and was crucial to his early successes. Edward had three brothers who fought for the House of York, while his mother Cecily continued to support her son before and after he became king. With a strong power base of noble men and women behind him, Edward received robust and loyal support during his first years of kingship. He was also physically striking and considered brave and courageous in battle. Measurements taken of his skeleton, found during building work at Windsor in 1789, revealed that he once stood at just over six feet three inches tall, a considerable height for the medieval period.[1] With his royal lineage, a right to the throne, the backing of powerful and wealthy nobles and his imposing presence, Edward exuded power.

By the summer of 1464 he had ruled England for three years. His subjects were impatient for him to choose a queen who would provide a line of legitimate Yorkist heirs and help to secure the kingdom, freeing it from civil war. It was also important for the new government to actively forge alliances for military and political assistance in the event of a crisis. The support of a foreign king or influential prince would further strengthen Edward's budding dynasty and provide muscle should a serious Lancastrian threat emerge to challenge his power. Throughout the 1460s soldiers clashed in battles at Hedgeley Moor, Hexham and Edgecote, their deaths on blood-soaked fields starkly confirming that the civil war was still in full force.

Overseas rulers saw the new English king as an attractive ally. As word spread of his reputation, good looks and bravery, the 22-year-old was offered a string of wealthy and politically influential European brides. These women, who included Bona of Savoy and Isabella of Castile, would have provided an opportunity to tie Edward's realm to that of France or Italy, and in the latter's case, the largest kingdom in Spain. Keen to pin the king down on a decision that would benefit the kingdom politically, financially and geographically, nobles and advisors flocked to Reading Abbey in Berkshire for a Parliament meeting in late September 1464. But as Edward leaned back on his throne in the abbey's chapter house and eyed the eager assembly, he announced to a stunned silence that he had already married.

The king's new wife, Elizabeth, was not a princess or a foreign queen, but an Englishwoman, the daughter of a Northamptonshire knight named Sir Richard Woodville. Her date of birth is not certain, but is believed to be around 1437. The mother of two sons, she had recently been widowed after the death of her husband John Grey, a Lancastrian, at the Second Battle of St Albans in February 1461. However, although she was a subject of the king, she was not entirely lowly in status. Her father and grandfather had loyally served Henry V and Henry VI, while her mother Jacquetta was once part of the English royal family having married, as her first husband, Henry V's brother John, Duke of Bedford. Jacquetta also boasted an illustrious European ancestry through her father, the head of the House of Luxembourg and Count of St Pol. But Elizabeth's ties to European nobility are unlikely to have played a role in Edward's choice of her over other wealthy and powerful foreign brides. The most likely reason they married is that they simply fell in love, an almost unthinkable notion for a young medieval monarch expected to wed for the benefit of his state rather than through personal choice.

Historians agree that the couple had met by late spring of 1464 while Edward was hunting near the Woodville's home in Grafton Regis, Northamptonshire. The more intimate details vary, but two well-known versions of the event survive. In one tale given by Tudor writer Sir Thomas More in the early sixteenth century, Elizabeth refused to submit to Edward's attempts to seduce her, protecting her honour over any offer of a fleeting affair. This, wrote More, 'rather kindled his desire than quenched it'.[2] In another, she pleaded under an oak tree as the king passed by Whittlebury Forest, asking him to intervene in a property dispute.[3] Medieval marriages could be spontaneous and were not the closely documented ceremonies we witness today. A wedding between two people was considered legally binding simply by promising marriage and then consummating it. This was of course open to abuse and one or both partners could later deny that either the promise of marriage or its consummation had ever taken place. Interestingly, Edward was accused of this. In his memoirs the French diplomat Philip de Commines recorded gossip that Edward had been 'formerly in love with a beautiful young lady, and had promised her marriage, upon condition he might lie with her'. Commines then stated that after sleeping together they were married without witnesses. With Edward now sexually satisfied, it was claimed that the union was hushed up and the woman told to keep the affair secret.[4] It is possible that this was also his plan with Elizabeth Woodville. David MacGibbon, in *Elizabeth Woodville: A Life*, wondered whether Edward initially planned to take 'dishonourable advantage' of the young widow, a claim also made during her lifetime by the writer Dominic Mancini.[5] If this was the case, this time Edward entered into a marriage that even he could not undo, performed on or around 1 May 1464 in a small village church in Grafton Regis. Only a few souls were present at the nuptials, but they would be important to confirm that it had indeed taken place. In particular, there was one witness – a formidable woman who had seen her fair share of scheming kings and conspiracies during the Wars of the Roses – who stood at Elizabeth's side: Jacquetta Woodville, the bride's mother.

Just as Cecily Neville remained a prominent figure during the reign of her son, Jacquetta was a dominant figure at her daughter's court. She was seen at ceremonial events, including Elizabeth's 1466 return to public life after the birth of Elizabeth of York, escorting her daughter to Westminster Abbey with sixty of the queen's ladies.[6] Jacquetta was still considered important enough in 1469, when she found herself the subject of a slander campaign designed to remove her influence from court. She played a prominent role throughout the Wars of the Roses displaying a proactive, resilient and self-assured approach. In 1461 she was sent to approach Margaret of Anjou on behalf of the Londoners to convince her to prevent her armies attacking the city.[7] A gentlewoman of a Lancastrian queen experienced in the politics of civil conflict and with an inside working knowledge of the royal court, there was hardly anyone more qualified to help Elizabeth navigate her early years of queenship. Jacquetta was on hand to guide her daughter for her first eight years as queen, dying in 1472.

Settling into their new, now public roles as newlyweds, Elizabeth and Edward soon became models for a new trend being discussed elsewhere during the period: the power of the individual. Elizabeth had risen to her position independently of social rank. Her accession and extravagant coronation in May 1465 demonstrated that a king's subject could, under the right circumstances, become his queen. This was also underlined in the elevation of her brothers and sisters to positions of influence. The couple engineered a series of marriages that tied Elizabeth's Woodville relatives to noble English families such as the Buckinghams, Arundels and Norfolks. Woodville brides and grooms processed solemnly to churches and abbeys to become co-inheritors of great dynasties and estates of the realm. Their spouses benefitted, too, by having the king as their new in-law, with access to him and increased authority within the royal court. Elizabeth's father Richard was rewarded with new titles, while her brother, Anthony, assumed a central role at Edward and Elizabeth's side. Anthony was already known at court as the husband of Elizabeth, Lady Scales, but enjoyed more power and influence once Edward assumed the throne. In return for the Woodvilles' social elevation and security, the king was rewarded by them with loyalty, service and military support, and their heirs lived on to offer the same to the Tudor kings and queens of the next century.

Elizabeth and her family were therefore examples of a new type of social mobility no longer based solely on heritage and bloodline, but on an individual's loyalty and potential, irrespective of their born status. This can also be seen in the following century at the courts of the Tudor monarchs. Like Elizabeth, four of the king's subjects recited marriage vows to become queens of England while men such as Thomas Cromwell and Cardinal Wolsey rose from humble beginnings to important positions in government. Henry VIII's queens were eyed for their suitability for public service and perceived childbearing potential, while men were promoted based on their work in matters of state. This concept, usually attributed to the Tudors, in fact had its roots earlier, in Edward and Elizabeth's reign. In *The English Renaissance*, V. de Sola Pinto credited Edward as the inspiration behind Henry VII's practice of personally selecting those who would serve in his council, as he excluded nobles of higher birth. With everyone rewarded for behaviour that they could manipulate and control, this soon gave way to ambition, with de Sola Pinto stating that in 'Western Europe the medieval social order was beginning to crumble before the desire for personal gain, the aggrandisement of the individual at the expense of his neighbour'.[8] None felt that ambition more than those who reached for the crown. Edward, too, had achieved his position, according to Lancastrian supporters, as a usurper of the 'rightful' king, Henry VI. Historians now agree that it was Henry's grandfather Henry IV who interrupted the legitimate line of kings and Edward IV's accession restored it. Like Elizabeth and her relatives, Edward won the throne through his own hard work rather than expected hereditary right, rallying supporters, forging alliances and achieving victory in battle.

The couple made a capable team. Generally popular with his subjects, Edward struck the right balance between authority and humility and was equally at home waging war on foreign kings as he was chatting with subjects. On one occasion he called the mayor and aldermen of London to hunt with him in Windsor, regarding them with 'so friendly and so familiar cheer', and sending venison into the city, earning him 'hearty favour amongst the common people'.[9] Philip de Commines, who met him, considered Edward not of 'great management', but of 'invincible courage, and the handsomest prince my eyes ever beheld'.[10] The most well-known portraits of Edward date to after his death, but there are some contemporary images of him, including the title page of the *Dictes and Sayings of the Philosophers* created in around 1477. It depicts Edward with dark, jaw-length hair, seated on a throne and wearing state robes lined with ermine.[11]

Elizabeth was also considered beautiful, and, at 28 years old on her coronation, was still young. She had two sons, Thomas and Richard, whom she had brought with her to court from her first marriage. They were visible proof that the new queen was able to conceive and bear children, in particular sons – something that would have calmed some of her critics preoccupied with securing the Yorkist succession. Contemporary portraits show her with long, light-coloured hair, a small mouth and intelligent, sharp eyes. Politically aware, she wove in and out of adversity during the later Wars of the Roses and once queen, immediately set to work on state matters. In various entries in the Calendar of Patent Rolls, Elizabeth can be seen transferring lands and repaying sums, but also working in an advisory role within her husband's government. In 1471 she headed the list of those responsible for the upbringing of the couple's eldest son Prince Edward; and five years later appeared in a grant issued by the prince with her backing, recorded with 'the assent of his mother, Elizabeth, queen of England'.[12] The records also reveal details of the vast household she now headed, which included servants, secretaries, almoners and ushers as well as specially appointed justices who were to act in legal matters on her behalf. The cost of running Elizabeth and their children's households in 1475 was £950 annually, Edward reserving that amount for her use before leaving for war with France that year.[13] To help place this sum in modern terms, its buying power would be generally equivalent to around £651,000 today, demonstrating the medieval organisation's size and complexity.

Edward and Elizabeth ruled during one of the most turbulent eras of English history. A poem attributed to Elizabeth's brother Anthony described 'unsteadfastness; this world being of such wheeling'.[14] Loyalties changed, thousands died on battlefields and decisions were shaped by paranoia and suspicion over reason. The political climate would have taken a toll on the couple publicly, but it also affected their private lives. In their first years together, they encountered the defection of the Earl of Warwick and Edward's younger brother George, Duke of Clarence to the Lancastrian cause. Waging a new wave of the Wars of the Roses, the men, who were once close to Edward, attempted to reinstate the long-absent Henry VI on the throne in Edward's place. In 1469 there were more challenges, as Edward and Elizabeth were associated with accusations of witchcraft, Jacquetta Woodville allegedly having made wire figures of the king and her daughter to entice them into marriage under a spell.[15] Allegations of witchcraft were serious, and could potentially remove the 'culprit' from power with loss of their goods and damage to reputation. A year later, Edward was captured and held prisoner by the now-Lancastrian Warwick, but escaped and fled the realm to Burgundy. The Lancastrians celebrated victory as they now placed Henry VI back on the throne of England. Sensing danger, the heavily pregnant Elizabeth, alone in the realm, took her children and Jacquetta into sanctuary at Westminster Abbey. There, on 2 November 1470, she gave birth to a prince under difficult and uncertain circumstances. Elizabeth would have been acutely aware that the man who had deposed her husband was now on the other side of a stone wall, enthroned within the vast abbey and cheered on by his supporters. Outnumbered and alone, she must have feared for her position as the wife of a 'traitor' and the mother of a new male heir for the House of York. The following year, however, Edward returned with Burgundian aid to secure his kingdom, killing the Lancastrian prince and son of Henry VI, Edward of Westminster, at the Battle of Tewkesbury. Edward's estranged brother Clarence returned to his side, Warwick was killed during combat at the Battle of Barnet, and Margaret of Anjou was also captured at Tewkesbury and sent to France. In the meantime, Henry VI had also been seized and taken to the Tower of London, where he died in 1471. Today, visitors to the riverside fortress hear the tale of Henry's probable murder in the Wakefield Tower, carried out by representatives of Edward's regime. This act might seem brutal to us today, but while Henry lived, Edward and Elizabeth were unable to rule in peace. With the immediate threats to their power now removed, Elizabeth left the safety of sanctuary and returned to her husband's side. In just a matter of weeks, between April and May 1471, Edward had returned to England, regained his crown and eliminated all current major Lancastrian threats to his rule. Thanks to Elizabeth, he also now had a prince, his own undisputed heir who would one day succeed him as king. Appropriately, the boy was named Edward.

Other struggles faced by the couple were more personal in nature. Boastful, reckless and ambitious, Clarence would prove an unreliable ally of the king's and frequently challenged his brother's authority. He had campaigned and conspired to put Edward's enemy on the throne and showed no respect for the laws of the kingdom or his brother's wishes. In one particularly disturbing case, Clarence accused a Somerset grandmother, without evidence, of murdering his wife. His men burst into Ankarette Twynhoe's home, pushed her onto a horse and took her to Warwick to be tried for the crime. With Clarence glaring over an assembly of officials 'as though he had used [the] king's power', they 'for fear gave the verdict contrary to their conscience'. Ankarette was indicted, tried and executed within three hours.[16] There is no evidence of Elizabeth's personal opinion of her fractious brother-in-law, or whether the couple discussed his erratic behaviour. However, it is likely that some family tensions were felt, particularly after Clarence's execution in 1478.

There is also a suggestion that Edward conducted extramarital relationships. After Edward's death, Sir Thomas More claimed that the king had enjoyed a close and intimate relationship with a mistress named Jane Shore while he was married to the queen.[17] The couple also suffered the tragic deaths of three of their children: Mary, Margaret and George, along with adult family members whose lives were cut short by war.[18] Edward and Elizabeth also suffered hardship and danger directly related to their positions as heads of state during the period of civil conflict. Historically, during wartime, cultural progress is often halted while funds are diverted and steps taken to prioritise security. But even as swords clashed in the countryside, the couple was still able to lead the country into a new phase of cultural change and reform.

Edward and Elizabeth not only had personal links with men of learning and culture, but raised them to trusted and influential positions within royal government. Sir John Tiptoft, Earl of Worcester, was heavily criticised during his lifetime for the horrific execution techniques he carried out as Constable of England. But he was also well known as a scholar and advocate of humanist teaching. Cora Scofield, in *The Life and Reign of Edward IV*, discussed the earl's travels in Italy, in particular to Florence, where he purchased books and listened to a lecture on Greek.[19] During Tiptoft's visit in the 1450s, Cosimo and Contessina de Medici were wielding power and encouraging learning and the arts. But it was not just ancient manuscripts that interested the earl. The early-twentieth-century historian Lewis Einstein, in *The Italian Renaissance in England*, stated that it may also have been during these travels that Tiptoft became inspired by models of Italian absolute rule, introducing not only his 'tyrannous' system of justice but also attempts to impose Paduan law in England.[20]

Another Renaissance man with close connections to both Edward and Elizabeth was Anthony Woodville, Elizabeth's brother. Anthony was a keen supporter of literature and chivalry, but also fulfilled key duties in government and served Edward in a military capacity. While he was at Edward's side during the king's exile in Burgundy in 1470, he helped introduce, with the couple's encouragement, one of the most important cultural developments the kingdom was ever to witness.

The significance of the introduction of the printing press in England cannot be exaggerated. Up until the 1470s, books in England were expensive, hand-written and illuminated by hand. The knowledge they contained was accessible to only a select few members of society: mainly aristocrats, lawyers, scholars and clergy. Already in operation in Germany since the

1450s, the press offered a quicker and cheaper way to share information. It allowed ideas and educational material to be dispersed more rapidly and widely, leading to its broader acquisition among the people. Armed with this, readers were able to discuss subjects previously out of their reach such as religion, science, medicine, law and poetry. By the end of the sixteenth century in England, there were complaints about the 'discussion of faith in every workshop, tavern and alehouse', showing not only how far information on spiritual teachings had travelled, but readers' confidence to freely debate it in non-academic and non-religious settings.[21] And yet it all started with a meeting in the early 1470s between the king's brother-in-law, a lover of chivalry, learning and literature, and William Caxton, a merchant who owned a printing press in the city of Bruges in Belgium.

Anthony Woodville was not only a statesman, but a poet, writer and translator. At his request, William Caxton shipped his printing press to England and moved into premises at Westminster in a tenement named the Red Pale. Caxton's earliest published works in London included Anthony Woodville's own translation of *The Dictes and Sayings of the Philosophers*, a work that, in true Renaissance style, was relevant 'to the example, weal and doctrine of all kings, princes, and to people of every estate'. It also praised, among the subjects it addressed, 'virtue and science'.[22]

Caxton also published Raoul Lefèvre's *The History of Jason*. In his prologue to the work, Caxton credited the influence of Edward's sister Margaret of Burgundy for her 'commandment' in translating and publishing the work in English. But all was carried out under the steady gaze of the king and queen. Caxton acknowledged that he worked under Edward's 'protection and sufferance', while he dedicated *The History of Jason* to Prince Edward to help him learn to read, with 'the supportation of our most redoubted liege lady most excellent princess the Queen'.[23] In the title page illustration, a vividly painted scene shows the royal couple receiving a copy of *The Dictes and Sayings of the Philosophers* from Anthony Woodville. Dressed in full regalia, Edward accepts the book while Elizabeth looks on with their son, Prince Edward. Heavy with symbolism and solemnity, this contemporary depiction records the couple's public backing and patronage of the newly introduced printing industry to England. The king would also receive credits and dedications in Caxton's other early books, but it was his affiliation with the Woodvilles, via his marriage to Elizabeth, that was crucial to the dawn of this new printing age in England. Norman Blake, in *Caxton and His World* highlighted this, stating that Caxton 'owed his success as a printer at Court more to the Woodvilles than the king himself'.[24] Later in the era, scientists would look back at these first works as important inspiration to their own education and studies. Astronomer John Flamsteed, working in the late seventeenth century, remembered his teenage years reading ancient works, histories, geography and romance books.[25]

There is also compelling evidence that Edward and Elizabeth's growing collections were not just for show. They were avid readers, patrons and personal collectors of work. The king's Wardrobe Accounts reveal that he owned a copy of a work by Titus Livius, a Roman historian who lived in the first century A.D., which he paid twenty shillings in 1480 to have bound, gilded and dressed. They also identify 'The Book of Josephus', which may refer to another ancient Roman author, Flavius Josephus. 'Frossard' in the accounts likely refers to a work by Jean Froissart who wrote Arthurian romance and other texts in the late thirteenth and early fourteenth centuries. He also owned a *Book of the Holy Trinity* and a copy of the Bible. A copy of *The Governance of Kings and Princes* is also mentioned, revealing an interest in modes of political structure, as well as one titled *La Forteresse de Foy* ('The Fortress of Faith').[26] While it is possible that these works formed part of the general royal household and were not personal items of Edward's, his paying for them to be repaired and rebound does suggest they were of value to him. The copies Edward plucked from their shelves were also elaborately decorated, with Alice Claver, a London silkwoman, employed to deliver laces and tassels 'for the garnysshing of divers of the Kinges bookes'.[27] His collection was also undoubtably much larger than surviving records show. William Caxton explained that he didn't present a copy of *The History of Jason* to Edward 'as I doubt not his good grace hath it in French, which he well understandeth'.[28] Elizabeth, too, owned and bought books, and Cora Scofield, in *The Life and Reign of Edward IV,* identified a copy of the *Recueil des Histoires de Troye* in the queen's ownership, along with *The Romance of the Saint Graal.*[29]

Elizabeth's eagerness to provide her son with engaging and inspiring reading material reveals some of the qualities she and Edward wished to motivate in the 6-year-old prince. A retelling of an ancient Greek hero, *The History of Jason* highlighted qualities such as bravery, loyalty and honour, all vital for a medieval figurehead that would one day inherit a potentially turbulent realm. In Lefèvre's text, Jason was 'beheld glady' for his valiantness and performed 'so well on horseback that no man might unhorse him'.[30] The prince's own Household Ordinances state that he was to have 'read before him, such noble stories as behoveth a Prince to understand'. *The History of Jason* was just one of these, but the wording of the regulations suggests that the young prince had in his own library a collection of other 'knightly' tales at his disposal. His Ordinances also emphasised the teaching of 'virtue, honour, cunning, wisdom and deeds of worship'. Negative and anti-social behaviour around the young boy was carefully managed, with swearing, brawling and other undesirable conduct forbidden from his household.[31]

The palace might have murmured with retellings of ancient Greek and Roman histories and romantic Arthurian legends, but England still rang with the blast of cannon and the whistle of arrows. Even a decade into Edward's reign, Lancastrian supporters were still determined to undermine his authority and reassume power. To help enforce control, Edward and Elizabeth embarked on a careful and deliberate public relations campaign that linked them with popular rulers of history and legend. In Italy, attributes and tales of ancient Greek and Roman leaders were being unearthed. In England, Edward and Elizabeth called on the memory of hero kings and ancient Britons.

Establishing a sense of order within the royal household was not new. In the twelfth century, Henry II drew up a list of ordinances, and Edward III and Henry VI are other later examples. However, Edward's *Liber Niger Domus Regis Angliae* is far more detailed, longer and explicit in the contract it forms between the king and his courtiers and servants. Each position in the household is minutely described, along with the individual's responsibilities and details of any food and lodgings they could expect while at court. It also expressed the king and queen's expectations of acceptable conduct for each position, emphasising discretion, discipline and loyalty. After Edward's death, Tudor kings Henry VII and Henry VIII added to these ordinances, establishing a framework that continued into later centuries.

The *Liber Niger* is also explicit in its inspiration from ancient methods of government. Beginning with a preamble, it examines several characters from history. King Solomon is mentioned, particularly with regard to a visit by the Queen of Sheba. There is also a discussion on King Lud, the Celtic founder of London, and his brother Cassibellan. The Saxon king Harthacnut is also praised, as well as two kings from more recent memory, the twelfth-century Henry I and fourteenth-century Edward III. These rulers were celebrated for qualities such as 'wisdom, great renowned riches, welfare, and high largesse', as well as prioritising security, keeping order and issuing 'new statutes, commandments and charges'. Generosity was crucial in a king, and Edward III was well known for hosting feasts with 'disguisings, plays, minstrels and sports'.[32] Amy Licence in *Edward IV and Elizabeth Woodville: A True Romance* has extensively explored the royal couple's embodiment of the new Renaissance spirit in the context of *Liber Niger*, arguing that it was a significant document which helped reinforce order and position within a turbulent political environment.[33] But it is also possible to see the pair adopting increased sensual, indulgent and luxurious court practices, just as art and sculpture in Florence were moving towards expression depicting pleasure rather than devout ceremony and spiritual sin. They also presided over the playful, flirtatious 'rebirth' of earlier medieval chivalry, popular with Edward's ancestor, Edward III. This previous Edward was well known as a lover of the ancient tales of King Arthur and the couple encouraged echoes of the legendary Briton through their treatment of guests and courtiers.

In May 1467 the couple welcomed Antoine, the 'Bastard of Burgundy', to court. The high-profile occasion was marked by a tournament fought by him and Anthony Woodville, complete with horses dazzling in cloth of gold and silver, their trappings garnished with bells. Canopies of silk and velvet fluttered in the breeze, while on the second day Edward and Elizabeth hosted a 'great and plentiful' feast. Elizabeth was as much a fan of chivalry as her husband, overseeing her ladies while they tied a garter around Anthony's leg with a 'Flower of Souvenance'. A 'parchment rolled and closed with the little thread of gold' – a formal invitation to complete in the festivities – was also dropped into Anthony's doffed cap by the queen's women.[34]

No expense was spared on other occasions, either. In 1480, Edward's sister Margaret of Burgundy was lodged at Greenwich during a visit to England, with hangings of the Greek story of Paris and Elyn transported to the palace especially for her visit.[35] The visit of Louis de Bruges, Seigneur de la Gruthuyse, in September 1472 is another well-known example. A rare and detailed account of his lavish entertainment at Windsor Castle in Berkshire survives, rich in luxury and cultural expression. The account describes rooms hung with expensive and flowing textiles, while Elizabeth's ladies played games and performed dances. Edward walked the official through his 'Vineyard of Pleasour' before he was feasted sumptuously at a banquet. After a long day hunting, eating and gifting, Gruthuyse was then led to an opulent chamber decorated with silks and carpets. As Elizabeth and Edward looked on, Gruthuyse gazed longingly at the bed the couple had provided for his stay, which had been covered in cloth of gold furred with ermine, the tester or canopy 'shyninge clothe of golde' and the curtains white sarcenet. Before he could slip underneath its extravagant blankets, he took a warm bath with Lord Hastings and nibbled on snacks such as green ginger and comfits and sipped hippocras, a red wine drink infused with spices.[36] A visit by the Bohemian aristocrat Leo of Rozmital six years earlier, in 1466, had been treated with more of the same generosity and reverence. Eyewitnesses reported with curiosity that 'even mighty lords' knelt down before the king, while Edward shook the hands of his visitors, 'and bore himself right friendly' towards them. The king then laid on a banquet of fifty courses, afterwards knighting some of the dignitaries who were present.[37]

The couple's inspiration, taken from Italian and European courts, can be seen in these visits. From the tapestries they ordered bundled onto carts to the serene strolls through abundant vineyards, distant echoes can be seen of the ancient Greek, Roman and ancient British worlds. Previous medieval rulers held jousts, tournaments and treated guests with distinction, but there is something in Edward and Elizabeth's court that suggests a marked emphasis on luxury and pleasure. Feasts of fifty courses and extravagant fabrics were deliberately thrust onto guests, while ancient culture was acknowledged in decor and literature at court. Of course, as masters of public relations and image, Elizabeth and Edward were fully aware that rulers, nobility and diplomats from overseas would share their experiences with other kingdoms of Europe. This was multiplied by the many servants and officials who accompanied their masters and told of their travels once back home. Excited retellings of ermine-lined blankets and Arthurian jousts promoted the kingdom not only as wealthy and politically strong, but at the peak of fashionable, cultural expression. It also implied that the country's period of uncertainty and war was over and England was a secure state ready to negotiate with foreign allies.

It was also important to look the part. Edward's Wardrobe Accounts of 1480 are the only ones to survive from the reign. They reveal some of the king's expensive and cosmopolitan tastes. In that year alone, he purchased multiple pairs of shoes and boots made with Spanish leather in various colours, along with French cloth and crimson velvet from Gascony. There were also payments made for Brussels, Flemish and Holland cloth, and Bruges thread. Other purchases included silk ribbons, spangles, gold fringe, cloth of gold, purple satins and furs and a gown of green cloth of gold as a gift for Elizabeth. Embroiderers were paid to sew rose and sun designs on Edward's clothing, while his laundrywoman, Alice Shapster, ensured the king's shirts and stomachers were pristine and ready for wear.

But it was not all hosting and feasting that occupied this culture-loving royal pair. They made their impact on the age through educational and architectural projects, too. One of the first acts Elizabeth made as queen was to declare herself the new founder of Queen's College at the University of Cambridge, in place of her predecessor Margaret of Anjou. In March 1465, before her coronation, she granted its master Andrew Doket and the Fellows £200 yearly, with further gifts over the years, including the manor of Fowlmere in Cambridgeshire. She would continue to support the university during her reign until the new queen, Anne Neville, wife of Richard III, took over the college after Edward IV's death in 1483.[38]

While freshly inked books and pamphlets were pulled from printing presses, the people of medieval England squinted upwards as new and improved buildings were raised. Edward was a dedicated and enthusiastic builder, the Calendar of Patent Rolls sprinkled with royal orders for repairs and appointments of surveyors at properties in London, Greenwich and Calais. He also made improvements to the Tower of London, adding a gateway and gun tower to provide more protection to the imposing fortress.[39]

One of his most extensive projects however was at Windsor Castle, where Lord Gruthuyse had been so royally entertained. In June 1473 the king gave permission for Richard Beauchamp, Bishop of Salisbury, to demolish parts of the existing chapel originally built by Edward III inside the castle grounds. Masons gradually built up the walls and carpenters set to work chiselling stalls in the choir creating crests, closets and a carving of 'the story of St George'. The new chapel of St George was designed by Edward to be larger and grander than the one that preceded it, making his own historic mark on the ancient stronghold.[40] Once completed, it would hold services for larger numbers of people and showcase the talent and skill of the king's contractors and architects. It would also serve as another mark of the Yorks' extravagance and access to resources. The structure's improved size, grandeur and intricate decoration was appropriate, as Edward had also decided that the chapel would serve as a royal burial site.

Edward IV made his will in 1475, the year of his departure to France. In it, he gave a detailed description of the tomb he wanted built in his memory. Seven years later it was being erected, chapel expenses recording the cost of accommodation for 'masons working on the tomb of our lord the king'.[41] He wished to be laid in St George's Chapel, 'by us begun of new to be builded … low in the ground, and upon the same a stone to be laid and wrought with the figure of Deathe'. The tomb was to be inscribed with the day and year of his death and decorated with a representation of the king's armour and an effigy of Edward made from silver and gilt.[42] Edward's own concept of how his tomb would appear, with its expensive materials, replica armour and carved figure of Death reveal an appreciation and understanding of new developments in art and sculpture that had taken place during his reign. His design also stands apart from the tombs of previous medieval kings, which generally involved an effigy alone with small carved angels, saints or heraldic shields. Masons chipped away at the stone sarcophagus to begin work on the tomb in 1482. The following April, the 40-year-old king was dead.

Edward died suddenly after a short illness and was buried at St George's Chapel on 14 April 1483.[43] Elizabeth took immediate responsibility for the couple's children, among them their two young sons and heirs to the crown, Edward and Richard. As the new king, Edward V, made his way from his residence in Ludlow to his mother in London, he was met by his uncle Richard, Duke of Gloucester, Edward IV's younger brother. Anthony Woodville, so long entrusted with the boy's upbringing, was arrested and executed. Elizabeth once again demonstrated the political awareness and decisiveness that had secured her and her family's safety in 1470. She fled, once again, into sanctuary at Westminster Abbey with her younger son and daughters. Gloucester and his men convinced her to hand Prince Richard over to be with his brother Edward, who was still in the duke's custody. Shortly afterwards, Edward and Elizabeth's children were declared illegitimate. Their secret marriage, conducted in the rural grounds of a chapel in Grafton Regis in 1464 was declared legally void on the basis that Edward had already contracted himself to another woman before meeting Elizabeth.

Richard, Duke of Gloucester, ascended the throne as Richard III in the summer of 1483 and was crowned with his wife Anne. The two princes were imprisoned in the Tower of London and later presumed murdered. It was the end of Elizabeth's time in power, but she lived to see her daughter Elizabeth of York crowned queen. Henry VII acceded to the throne in 1485 following the defeat of Richard III's army at the Battle of Bosworth in Leicestershire that August. Elizabeth of York married Henry and together they established the Tudor period that ruled until the early seventeenth century. Retiring in her later years to Bermondsey Abbey, Elizabeth Woodville died in 1492 having left a short will and was buried according to her wishes, without extravagance, in St George's Chapel near her husband. The effigy and sculpture of Death on Edward's tomb was, as far as we can tell, never completed.

The early-twentieth-century writer Edith Sichel, in her discussion of the English Renaissance, began it by exploring the artists, sculptors and musicians of the sixteenth century.[44] And yet there is ample evidence that the beginning of the Renaissance era in England can be traced at least forty years earlier, to the mid-fifteenth-century court of Edward IV and Elizabeth Woodville. Through their individual backgrounds and combined ruling style, they embodied the Renaissance value of humanism, emphasising the power and potential of the individual. The son of a duke and the daughter of a knight rose to rule over a nation for almost twenty years, securing and reinforcing their hold over the throne despite conspiracy, conflict and civil war. There is evidence that they enjoyed a close and cohesive partnership, with Elizabeth eagerly and actively fulfilling religious, civil and personal roles within her husband's regime. She supported the education of her subjects and played a hands-on role in the tutoring of her son, Edward. Together, the couple were role models for a new style of leadership that they enhanced with propaganda and public image, something their predecessor Henry VI had never used to his benefit. They were also patrons of the latest developments in art and literature.

United in their aims, the couple embarked on the spread and expression of a new culture in England inspired by Arthurian romance and ancient Greek, Roman and British histories. They commissioned art and bought luxurious materials and clothing from around Europe. Even Edward's proposed tomb, with its silver and gilt work and figure of Death, shows that he had an advanced appreciation of the latest techniques his realm could offer, along with ambition and faith in his craftsmen that it could be realised. Publicly supporting and encouraging the first printing press in England, they allowed their subjects to read the first works printed in the English language, leading to the establishment of a commercial industry that continues to thrive today. Fifteenth- and early-sixteenth-century readers enjoyed romances and histories that were later used as source material by famous writers such as William Shakespeare. While it must be noted that the printing press really gained momentum as a social, religious and political tool under the Tudors, it cannot be denied that it owed its origins to Elizabeth and Edward's joint efforts in the 1470s.

Their reign triggered permanent and revolutionary change, with Tudor, Stuart and later kings and queens modelling their household ordinances on those of the *Liber Niger*, stressing safety, security and discipline. Although Edward's sons were not to inherit the throne after his death, their eldest daughter, Elizabeth of York, married Henry VII and became queen in 1486. Therefore, Edward and Elizabeth's bloodline continued into the Tudor and Stuart era, and into the royal families of later years. Through the marriages of Elizabeth's family into established houses of the nobility, they also created a new aristocracy, no longer rewarded simply because of the family they were born into, but through hard work and service. This next generation of nobles bowed, entertained and fought for the security of future kings and queens. The rise of men such as Anthony Woodville, Lord Scales and John Tiptoft, Earl of Worcester, are other examples of the couple's emphasis on work rather than birthright, arguably paving the way for non-aristocrats of the sixteenth century such as Cardinal Thomas Wolsey, Thomas Cromwell and the Boleyns to rise to power. Finally, the very building Edward commissioned, and where the couple were laid to rest, has been the site of St George's Day celebrations, worship and weddings for hundreds of years. It has also seen the funerals of many of their descendants. Henry VIII and his third wife Jane Seymour were solemnly interred here in 1547 and 1537 respectively, as well as Charles I in 1649 and later, Edward VII and George V. A little awkwardly, the body of Edward's enemy for over a decade, Henry VI, is also buried here, having been moved from its original position in Chertsey in 1484.

As partners, Edward and Elizabeth shared many things in common. Their contemporaries believed that they had married for love; in doing so Edward had risked losing the support of his advisors. Both were tenacious, dedicated and ambitious. They were also underdogs. Elizabeth, born a commoner, left a strong and visible trace of her many actions as queen and adhered strictly to ceremony when in public. Edward, too, was not brought up as a royal prince. At his birth in 1442, no one could have imagined that he would one day usurp the son of Henry V and assume the throne. Personally, they projected loyalty and devotion to one another, appearing jointly in propaganda and in person to their guests. They also birthed ten children, the last, Bridget, born in 1480, showing that they continued to be intimate long after they had secured their heir and spare for the state in 1473. They were also supported by each of their families. Their mothers, Jacquetta and Cecily, along with Elizabeth's father and each of the couple's siblings provided crucial support in aiding the couple's path to power, with their influence and assistance helping them to retain it.

A power couple in spirit as well as in authority, Edward and Elizabeth presided over a true Renaissance court that celebrated culture, generosity, luxury and learning. Any discussion of their reign should recognise the significant contribution they made together to the lives of their subjects and the impact they had on modern times.

Chapter 3

Ferdinand II of Aragon and Isabella of Castile, Spain

As Edward IV fought ankle-deep in mud at the Battle of Tewkesbury in May 1471, a 20-year-old woman in Valladolid in Spain was dealing with a complicated dynastic problem of her own. Isabella of Castile was born in Madrigal de las Altas Torres on 22 April 1451 to the King of Castile, John II and his second wife, Isabella of Portugal. Isabella had a brother, Alfonso, along with a half-brother Henry from her father's first marriage. John's first marriage to Maria of Aragon had also produced three daughters, but none of them survived to adulthood, leaving two sons and one daughter as heirs to the throne of Castile. As expected, on his death in 1454, Henry was named John's successor. Isabella, a toddler of 3 years old, was now second in line to the throne of Castile, after her brother Alfonso.

Henry IV was not a popular ruler. He presided over a court of excess, split from his first wife and leached money from the treasury. He also allowed wily and ambitious courtiers, such as the Marquis of Villena Juan Pacheco, to dominate and influence him for their own ends. In 1462, Henry's second wife, Joan of Portugal, prepared to give birth to a much-awaited heir, the couple hoping it would be a prince that would one day inherit the Kingdom of Castile.

The shrill cries ringing out from the birthing room, however, belonged to a newborn girl, who the couple named Joanna. But behind the initial congratulations and tactful smiles, there were murmurings of doubt. Philip de Commines heard rumours from various sources that the couple's 'beautiful daughter' was illegitimate. Castilians were convinced that Joanna had been 'born in adultery ... objecting impotence in King Henry, and proving it by arguments'.[1] The insinuation was that Joan, unable to conceive a child with her husband, had conducted an extramarital affair to become pregnant and maintain control over the succession, excluding his half-siblings in the process. His subjects soon voiced their anger, believing themselves to have been misled by the king and queen. Among the protestors, unsurprisingly, was 10-year-old Isabella and her 8-year-old brother, Alfonso.

Challenging the young Joanna's birthright should have been tricky. She was, after all, born within a royal marriage and Henry accepted her paternity, commanding his officials to publicly give the infant their oaths of allegiance. Some refused, branding the girl with the nickname Beltraneja, named after the man they believed to be her biological father, Beltran de la Cueva. Arguments ensued, lines were drawn and even riots broke out, as Henry was publicly denounced and Alfonso instead proclaimed king by his supporters. Castile fractured into what would become a long and bitter civil war as Henry and Alfonso fought for the crown. Alfonso's early death at the age of 14, on 5 July 1468, was a tragedy for their cause. Now it was Isabella who would become its champion.

As daughter of the King of Castile and heir to the largest kingdom in Spain, Isabella attracted a number of suitors for marriage. European courts offered up eligible royal bachelors, including Carlos of Aragon, Alfonso of Portugal and also, early in his reign, Edward IV of England.[2] It was in Castile's interest to marry Isabella to another wealthy and influential European power to elevate its own authority in wider Europe. But during their terse negotiations, Isabella had obtained from her half-brother Henry not only an agreement that she would succeed him on his death, but also the right to choose her husband. Accordingly, on 15 October 1469, a teenager with brownish-red hair slipped quietly into Isabella's apartments in Valladolid.[3]

Born on 10 March 1452, Ferdinand of Aragon had been offered as a husband for Isabella earlier during Henry's reign, but action wasn't taken and other offers had been considered. He was said to have been of average height with a calm disposition. Later, English ambassadors reported that he was 'right lusty' with a 'smiling countenance', although by then he had gained a reputation as a shrewd and calculating ruler.[4] Surviving portraits of Ferdinand show that he had a long, slim nose, full lips, five o'clock shadow and straight brown hair that rested just below his neckline. The son and heir of King John the Great of Aragon and his wife Juana Enriquez, he was dynastically powerful and in addition held the title of King of Sicily, which had been granted to him by his father.[5]

The couple would have found much in common as they talked together in secret that October evening. Their match was politically advantageous, but likely to have been fuelled by physical attraction, too, with Isabella praised for her auburn hair and blue eyes. Both heirs to great Spanish states, it was also practical. Niccolò Machiavelli, in *The Prince*, discussed the power benefits of a monarch combining forces with a similar state to their own. 'When a prince acquires the sovereignty of a country differing from his own in language, manner and intellectual organisation, great difficulties arise,' he wrote, also advising that a monarch should also physically live in the state under his or her control.[6] No one yet knew it, but the meeting of these two dynastically powerful teenagers at Valladolid in 1469 would set a series of world-changing events in motion.

Uniting the individual states of Castile and Aragon would not be easy. Isabella was especially reluctant to give up regal authority to her husband once the wedding ceremony was over. A detailed marriage agreement was painstakingly drawn up. Ferdinand was to promise to respect the laws of Castile, where he was also to live, not leaving without Isabella's knowledge or permission. No foreigners were to be appointed to public office and any new military or civic officers he wanted to recruit had to be approved by Isabella. Ferdinand also contracted himself to support Isabella in war.[7] The agreement prioritised the security of their respective realms and protected the couple's rights to their own individual power. It also formed a legal framework in which Isabella and Ferdinand would work together to run state business.

Legalities agreed on, Ferdinand and Isabella were married at the palace of Juan de Vivero in Valladolid on 19 October 1469. When news of the nuptials trickled through to Henry, he was furious. Although he had agreed that his half-sister could marry without his approval, he was offended that it had been carried out in secret and without being consulted. Seeing the marriage as an act of betrayal, in 1470 he vowed to once again actively promote his daughter Joanna's position as his successor in Isabella's place.[8] Henry died in 1474 and Isabella succeeded to the Castilian throne, but Joanna's threat as a political opponent was not extinguished until 1479, after Joanna's husband the King of Portugal waded into the war.[9]

With Isabella crowned, and the future of the Kingdoms of Castile and Aragon now united, Ferdinand and Isabella began to deliberately craft a public image of solidarity. Proclamations and letters were jointly issued, and their combined arms stitched onto banners and pressed into the royal seal. But their impact was not only visual. They also altered the administration of their government, aligning with other shifts in power already being implemented in Europe. William Hickling Prescott, writing in the mid-nineteenth century, saw the rulers working in 'the direction in which all the governments of Europe, at this period, were tending. The people, wisely preferring a single master to a multitude, sustained the crown in its efforts to recover from the aristocracy the enormous powers it so grossly abused'.[10] Machiavelli warned against a monarch surrounding themselves with members of the aristocracy 'because he is surrounded by men who, thinking themselves still his equals, submit reluctantly to his authority'. A leader raised by the common people instead, wrote the Florentine, 'stands alone and has few around him who would dare resist his measures'.[11] The careful management of nobility, which can also be seen in England under Edward IV, was not just good political practice. It also confirmed the rising importance of the individual, a continuous theme trickling through the Renaissance era. Isabella's half-brother Henry had been known for weakly indulging the arrogant and ambitious nobles who surrounded him. Lessons had been learned, and newlyweds Isabella and Ferdinand set about restoring their royal authority and placing power back into the hands of the Crown.

The couple immediately began to enforce a justice system that was governed more directly, reducing opportunities for corruption such as the offering of bribes in return for reduced punishments. The late fifteenth- and early-sixteenth-century writer Gonzalo Fernandez de Oviedo y Valdes recalled seeing Isabella and Ferdinand sitting together 'in judgement' once a week at Madrid, a practice written into law in 1480.[12] They also enforced the *hermandad*, an early type of police force with the authority to make arrests and preserve and restore order. Courts were also set up with responsibility for individual territories, all of course under the careful scrutiny of Ferdinand and Isabella. The new *Ordenanças Reales*, revised laws of the kingdom published in 1485, stated that representatives would be selected for their hard work and service rather than social status. 'When men perceive that offices of trust are not to descend by inheritance, but to be conferred on merit, they will strive to excel in virtue, that they may attain its reward,' it stated.[13] William Hickling Prescott credited the monarchs with a wide range of other moves that reduced the real and perceived power of the aristocracy, including forbidding them to quarter the royal arms with their own, placing bans on duelling and restricting the building of new castles.[14]

Both deeply pious Catholics, Peter Martyr D'Anghera, who knew the couple, stated that 'even in their sleep' they 'thought about the propagation of the Christian faith'.[15] They established several religious buildings for Catholic worship, including a chapel at Seville, the Franciscan convent of San Juan de los Reyes and the convent of Miraflores. The latter was founded in the 1480s in memory of Isabella's father, and it is where he and her brother Alfonso were buried. Monks were still living there in the nineteenth century.[16] As well as reforming abuses that had seeped into churches and monasteries, the couple also embarked on a mission to bring religion under a form of state control. These methods, at first, were gentle. Isabella, reluctant to enforce a policy of violence, encouraged Jews and Muslims in the realm to convert to Christianity.[17] Later though, harsher measures were devised, and in 1478 were enacted under the Spanish Inquisition. Designed to discover those who claimed they worshipped in the Catholic faith, but maintained another religion in private, it resulted in the interrogations of thousands of subjects, many of whom were executed. In 1492, Isabella expelled the Jews and it is estimated that 170,000 of their Jewish subjects left the realm.[18] For Machiavelli, Ferdinand's wars against Muslims in the name of religion were driven by 'a cruel piety' and were 'without doubt, barbarous'. But the Florentine also saw the effect this had on Spaniards, who were kept in 'continual suspense', claiming that it discouraged them from thinking of 'other matters, much less to engage in conspiracies against him'.[19]

The actions undertaken by Ferdinand and Isabella in trying to manage the religion of their realms can make difficult reading for us today. It is, however, important to assess them within their time and place as late medieval rulers concerned with enforcing control over their states. We have now learned, by examining policies such as theirs, that expulsion, interrogation, torture, execution and forced conversions are not only unsuccessful methods of true religious conversion, but also morally and socially detrimental. In wider Europe, religion underwent a vast upheaval during the Renaissance era as a result of the new spread of information and ideas. Religious texts and theories divided Europe, drawing many residents away from a traditional allegiance to the pope and towards Protestantism, a religion that eventually split into an increasing number of categories. A European living in the early fourteenth century would not understand the terms Calvinist, Puritan or Lutheran, but by 1600 they were established religions with followers in many countries. When faced with religious diversity, rulers often reacted with violence. The Tudors in England, for example, struggled to find an effective policy as they plunged the nation into Protestantism, then Catholicism and finally grappled with a vague solution to try and keep everyone happy. Religious persecution and related violence took place all over Europe during this period and, as Prescott has stated, it is difficult to condemn Isabella, Ferdinand and their contemporaries 'without condemning the age'.[20]

In January 1480 Ferdinand became, on the death of his father, the undisputed King of Aragon and retained his existing title of King of Sicily. Isabella had been crowned Queen of Castile in 1474, and so the couple were now uncontested rulers of Castile, León, Aragon and Sicily. Their arms visually represented their individual kingdoms, now united in one marriage. An imposing castle represented the Kingdom of Castile, a lion the Kingdom of León. Sicily was represented with eagles, and the pomegranate was the emblem of Granada. A Spanish banner from the sixteenth century survives in the collection of the Cleveland Museum of Art and is an example of propaganda promoted by the couple. Made in red and brown velvet, it is embroidered in gold thread that would have shone in the sunlight as it fluttered in the wind at battle sites and public appearances. It depicts a heraldic shield containing all the symbols of their realms gripped by the talons of a larger eagle behind it. A yoke and bundle of arrows have been added to the edges. This particular banner is also quartered with representations of the Virgin and Child, visually conveying not only the extent of the couple's united political and dynastic power, but their belief that heaven and the saints were on their side. It is identical in symbolism and structure to the arms illustrated in vivid colour in Isabella's own *Book of Hours* of around 1500, also in the collection of the Cleveland Museum of Art.[21]

The couple's adoption of the yoke and arrows is especially interesting. In another public symbol of their unity, they took the yoke, Ferdinand's symbol, and the bundle of arrows, Isabella's, and included them in their arms, along with the motto *Tanto Monta*, 'One is as good as the other'. These were all additional visual gestures which underlined the couple's intention to rule as a formidable, unbreakable partnership, their chosen motto also emphasising their balanced power and responsibility. These arms appeared abundantly throughout their kingdoms, whittled onto architecture and painted onto personal possessions.

By 1496, Ferdinand and Isabella were busy negotiating the betrothal of their daughter Katherine to the English Prince of Wales, Arthur Tudor, the son of Henry VII and Elizabeth of York. But discussions were temporarily interrupted in the summer of that year. A letter dated 6 July from the rulers to their ambassador Rodrigo González de Puebla informed him that they had been called to war. The pope had requested the couple's intervention on hearing that the King of France was assembling a 'great army' to march on Italy. 'Ferdinand has therefore gone to the frontiers of Catalonia, and there assembled a powerful army. Isabella remains near the frontiers of Navarre, in order there to superintend in person the preparations for war,' it stated.[22] By July 1496, Isabella was 45 years old, and Ferdinand 44. They were middle-aged by late medieval standards, but the speed and ease in which they assumed their roles in the midst of a military crisis revealed that this was a scene they had acted out many times before.

Ferdinand was considered a great horseman and courageous in battle. The seventeenth-century writer Baltasar Gracián celebrated his bravery, comparing him to the Greek hero Hercules for winning 'more feats than days', although Ferdinand did of course also experience defeat at the hands of his enemies.[23] Understanding the need for care in issuing commands, he wrote some of his military orders in cipher to avoid detection by the enemy. In 1862, historian G. A. Bergenroth attempted to decode some of these surviving letters, but said that one written to the Duke de Estrada in 1503, eluded him.[24] In 2018 the world's press widely reported that Ferdinand's code had finally been cracked. Ferdinand had written the sophisticated code in a letter to his military general Gonzalo Fernandez de Cordoba, using a combination of 200 characters, written without spaces.[25]

From the beginning of their marriage Ferdinand fought for his and his wife's political dominance. He battled for Isabella's supremacy at the Battle of Toro in 1476 and took decisive, but somewhat risky action at the Siege of Malaga in 1487. An eyewitness later stated that Ferdinand, eating dinner in his tent, noticed a huddle of enemy soldiers attacking a group of his men. Abandoning his food, the king leapt onto a horse and headed straight into the fight without stopping to put on his armour.[26]

He worked on state business incessantly and rarely rested. English ambassadors in 1505 reported that the king rose before six in the morning, heard two masses before eight and ate well at dinner, but 'never sits more than half an hour at table'.[27] At Granada in 1491 he was joined by Isabella, who set up camp in a village close to the siege they were conducting at the Alhambra Palace.[28] On 2 January 1492, after a decade of fighting, the building was ceremonially surrendered by its Muslim ruler to Ferdinand and Isabella. Centuries of Muslim rule in Granada were over and the couple now governed over the vast territory of Castile, Léon, Sicily, Aragon and Granada.

Isabella's role in war was not always miles away from the fight. Accounts place her not only at Granada overseeing the siege of 1491, but also close to the action in Troxillo in 1478, when her advisors expressed concern that she might be harmed. 'It was not for her,' Isabella told her worried counsellors, 'to calculate perils or fatigues in her own cause … [for] she was now resolved to remain until she had brought the war to a conclusion', ordering further sieges at Medellin, Merida and Deleitosa.[29] The idea of a 'warrior queen' was not a new one; Giles Tremlett in *Isabella of Castile, Europe's*

First Great Queen points out that Ferdinand's mother Juana Enriquez also acted as 'queen lieutenant' in Catalonia.[30] In light of this, Ferdinand might have been reminded of his mother's proactive spirit in his earliest meetings with the Castilian princess. She certainly adopted this attitude during their marriage. Issuing commands and raising troops and cash, Isabella surveyed the couple's conquered cities and remained behind to personally discuss the negotiations of their surrender. She was said to have appeared in armour at Granada although did not, of course, fight with her troops. Sets of armour exhibited in the museum of the armoury in Madrid during the early nineteenth century claimed to be those worn by the couple.[31] She was a resolute politician with an understanding of troop morale and knew that her presence among them strengthened their spirits. The pair's complementary and active military partnership deliberately mirrored the castles, eagles and pomegranates embroidered on their banners. Displaying a united front financially, geographically and politically, they would have intimidated their enemies and roused the morale of their subjects.

As the red and gold banners beat against the cool winds of the Alhambra Palace in January 1492, a dark-haired Genoese sailor watched from the crowds. Squinting up at the blocky, stone towers of the palace and then over to the victorious monarchs who now owned it, Christopher Columbus sensed that the time was right for a new enterprise. An ambitious, self-seeking explorer, he later remembered events at Granada, seeing King Boabdil 'come forth from the gates of the city and kiss the royal hands of your Highnesses, and of the Prince my Lord'. His mind wandered, he later told the monarchs, to news of the land of India, 'to see the said princes, and the cities and lands, and their disposition, with a view that they might be converted to our holy faith'.[32] If it had worked in Granada, Columbus thought, surely it would work there, too. According to Peter Martyr d'Anghiera, who knew the explorer, Columbus also promised 'to bring back pearls, spices and gold beyond anything ever imagined'.[33]

Columbus was convinced that India lay west across the Atlantic Ocean, through knowledge gained from other sailors and hours poring over ancient scripts. He was a product of the earlier Renaissance, studying old texts along with works by later writers. His son, named Ferdinand, argued in his book *The Life of the Admiral Christopher Columbus* that his father studied geography, geometry and astronomy and practised drawing after reading Ptolemy's argument that it was necessary for geographers. Columbus's son sprinkles *The Life* with the names of other ancient writers including Aristotle, Seneca, Pliny, Strabo and Ctesias, whose work inspired and led the explorer's research into the existence of new lands.[34] The discussions we saw in Cosimo de Medici's Florence taking place among new artists, sculptors and architects in the piazza of Santa Maria del Fiore is mirrored in Columbus's own story as he chatted at dockyards with navigators, physicians, courtiers, sailors and scholars in search of evidence for his voyage.

Initially, the explorer struggled to gain support for his intended expedition. John II of Portugal dismissed him, while Ferdinand and Isabella turned him away in 1484. He had no better luck at Genoa. However, now the rulers had finally hoisted their banners over the stone walls of the Alhambra, Columbus sensed a change in the wind. Negotiations were had, funding was promised and on 12 May 1492 he left Granada under Ferdinand and Isabella's flag, arming three vessels to set sail, he hoped, for India.

The three ships, *La Pinta*, *La Niña* and the *Santa Maria*, sailed from Gomera on Thursday 6 September, according to Columbus's journal. Typical of the couple's need for state eyes on important events, Ferdinand and Isabella sent along Pero Gutierrez, a gentleman of the king's bedchamber, and Rodrigo Sanchez of Segovia, who had been sent by the couple 'as inspector'. For the next few weeks, the crew saw nothing but the odd bird, floating weed or piece of debris, although on 15 September they were startled by a 'marvellous flame of fire' that fell from the sky into the sea.[35] On Friday 12 October at about 2 a.m., a cry went out that land could be seen on the horizon. Waiting for daylight, they approached a beach where a band of Natives had gathered to see their visitors. No one yet knew it, but Columbus hadn't moored his ships off the coast of India at all, but off the sandy beaches of the Caribbean. To his royal patrons he wrote describing trees, gardens, tropical fish and parrots, and hinted at the promise of large amounts of gold, worn as jewellery by the Natives.

Columbus's arrival in the New World altered the geographical and political balance of the Renaissance era and every other age after it. He wasted no time handing out Spanish names to interesting or valuable sites, such as Hispaniola, Fernandina and Isabella. But not all of this change was positive. Regrettably, although Isabella stated that her new subjects should remain under her protection, some were shipped to Spain as slaves. On finding out, she angrily ordered that they be returned to their homes on the next ship.[36] Slavery in Spain predated the couple's reign and Isabella was later known to have authorised the use of slaves of African descent in 1501 for labour in the New World. Her daughter, Katherine of Aragon, also brought women described as slaves to England on her marriage to Prince Arthur Tudor.[37] However, there is evidence that Isabella was troubled with moral aspects of slavery, adding a codicil to her will in 1504 urging her successors to treat the New World Natives with care, although she stuck firmly by her decision to continue converting them to Christianity.[38] Despite Isabella's instructions, trade in Caribbean and African slaves between Europe, Africa and the New World continued to take place during the couple's lifetimes and in the following centuries, affecting countless men, women and children. There was further trouble from inside the new colony, too, as animosity grew between Natives and newcomers and damaging attacks were carried out on both sides.

The 1492 voyage was not the last. The following year, Columbus returned to the New World with seventeen ships filled with food, cattle and foot soldiers, along with a few members of the nobility. Among these newcomers were craftsmen, labourers and carpenters, and Peter Martyr d'Anghiera estimated that 1,200 souls boarded ships that year from Spain destined for the Caribbean, a marked difference from the smaller crew that had originally set sail in 1492.[39] With this sudden increase in passengers voyaging across the seas we can see the couple's impetus in the New World swing from exploration to settlement. With the monarchs' encouragement, thousands of Spaniards embarked on establishing new colonies in the New World, marking the rapid expansion of the couple's dominions in the Americas.

Naturally, geographic discovery led to increased commercial activity, as new and interesting objects, crafts and species of animals and plants were seen for the first time. D'Anghiera compiled a series of letters he had written between 1494 and 1521. In them, he mentioned in particular 'several shiploads of scarlet wood', amber, hemp and cotton. In 1501 he wrote that 1,200 pounds of gold was sent out of the New World in just two months.[40] He also wrote of iguanas, which the Natives ate along with their eggs, a tree gum that was said to cure headaches and an unusual cotton bed used by the Natives, called a 'hammock'.[41] For the first time, medicines, previously unknown foods, household objects and other saleable commodities were making their way out of the New World and onto foreign shores.

It wasn't long before other ambitious sailors and navigators headed into the horizon chasing overseas adventures driven by wealth, glory or both. Within just a few years, their anchors plunged into the seas off Mexico, Florida and South America.[42] Columbus grumbled at the end of his life, exhausted, despondent and white-haired, that he had 'opened the gate' to the dazzling potential of new lands in the west. However, he claimed somewhat arrogantly that new explorers could not call themselves 'discoverers ... following as they do in my track'.[43]

Co-ordinating events relating to religion, local politics, war and exploration, Ferdinand and Isabella were also active on the world stage. They negotiated marriages for their children that they hoped would preserve the unification of Spain after their deaths and forged links with Portugal, England and the Netherlands. With the marriage of their daughter Juana to Philip I of Burgundy, they created the opportunity for the founding of the Habsburg Dynasty that would oversee so many world events of the sixteenth and seventeenth centuries. Their children, grandchildren and great-grandchildren would include England's first queen regnant Mary I as well as her husband Philip II of Spain. Philip's father, Charles V the Holy Roman Emperor, oversaw the growth of the Habsburg Empire in the early sixteenth century. The couple's descendants ruled states including the Netherlands, Portugal, England, France and Spain. Ferdinand and Isabella also tried, but failed, to form a marriage agreement with Scotland in 1489, and in 1495 declared themselves 'against the King of France' for his insulting the Borgia pope, Alexander VI and laying a claim to Naples along with Ferdinand's territory of Sicily.[44] Despite employing a team of ambassadors to smooth these political ties, the couple's own presence during negotiations is continuous, as evidenced by the many surviving letters. These were jointly signed, of course, and demonstrate their active and heavy role in the workings of European politics. The two teenagers who met at Valladolid in 1469 had grown, by the dawn of the sixteenth century, into astute politicians commanding the respect of their fellow rulers around the world.

There is no question that Ferdinand and Isabella were a power couple of the Renaissance era. They harnessed dynastic, political and military strength and tightened the internal administration of their realms. But what can we understand about their partnership in private, away from the glittering throne rooms and chaotic siege tents?

Although their marriage was conducted for political reasons, the couple appear to have had a genuine love and fondness for one another which continued into their later years. Married for just over three decades, they gained an intimate familiarity with one another, instinctively able to perceive the other's thoughts. After the sudden and tragic death of their heir Juan in 1497, d'Anghiera watched the couple seated together at an event. He noted that they maintained, on the outside, a professional and stately demeanour in front of spectators. But, regularly lifting their eyes to gaze into the other's, without any words spoken between them, d'Anghiera saw that 'what was hidden is revealed'.[45]

Enduring huge adversities during their relationship, both partners demonstrated a profound resilience and determination. They overcame Isabella's succession war, experienced the deaths of two of their children and were shaken by an assassination attempt on Ferdinand in December 1492 which left him injured. In war efforts, they remained focused, assuming active roles in government and in the military. While Isabella organised, oversaw and negotiated, Ferdinand led armies, formed strategy and rushed to the defence of his troops. It is likely that these roles were deliberately divided between them, the couple capitalising on each other's individual strengths. Throughout their partnership they approached joint government as a business, clearly defining and carrying out their own agreed responsibilities.

Both Isabella and Ferdinand could be charming towards diplomats, but were ruthless in ensuring that the terms agreed on were beneficial to them. Their letters to ambassadors show structure and unmistakable clarity. Isabella often receives more attention in modern times in consideration of the impressive power she wielded as a medieval woman, but Ferdinand also deserves careful consideration of his contribution. Baltasar Gracián, writing in the mid-seventeenth century, noted the harmony in which they worked. Isabella was, he wrote, 'of great capacity … of such a great King she could not only make him known, but shine'. He described their relationship as one of a 'Golden League, and a happy kingship the more they both did together'.[46]

We can also gather evidence about what the couple were like as parents. They were dedicated, with a tendency at times to be overprotective. Isabella chastised the Duke de Estrada for his overbearingness to her daughter Katherine of Aragon following her arrival in England. She 'had sent him to England as her ambassador', Isabella frowned, 'and not to rule her daughter'. English ambassadors also recorded Katherine's 'great affection to her father, who replied that she had ever loved him more than his other children'.[47] A similar protectiveness can be seen with their son, Juan. When England's Henry VII approved of a proposed match between Juan and the Duchess of Brittany, the couple responded that they 'do not like to part with their only son', although this remark could equally have been a diplomatic excuse to move away from the subject.[48] Despite Isabella's fierce nature in government, she often fulfilled a motherly role for the women in her life, taking her daughter-in-law Margaret of Austria under her wing after Juan's early death, and temporarily separating her daughter Juana from her indifferent husband, Philip of Burgundy. Some of this behaviour and protectiveness is understandable when we remember that Ferdinand and Isabella's children, as their heirs, were crucial to carrying out their vision of a united Spain. Of course, these actions can also be seen as controlling, a trait demonstrated by the pair repeatedly during their reign.

Although Machiavelli praised Ferdinand as a 'new prince' during his lifetime, both partners had attributes of what the writer considered a true Renaissance ruler. His description of Ferdinand raising himself 'from a petty state to be the most renowned monarch in Christendom' could apply equally to Isabella, as she clung to power from an early age, rising to become queen despite civil war and family conflict. Likewise, his emphasis on Ferdinand's reorganisation of the army, the victory at Granada and discipline of the nobility were in reality the work of the couple, rather than solely the king.[49]

Because of their efforts, Spaniards experienced a tightened system of justice where councillors, and sometimes the king and queen themselves, ruled on their cases. They also raised the financial stability of their realms, Castile in particular. On Isabella's death in 1504, the Crown's revenue was thirty times richer than at her accession, swelling from 885,000 reals to 2.6 million, thanks to the tightening of government administration, tax collection and improvements to the coinage.[50] They also produced a line of descendants that ruled over Europe for the next century and beyond, making new political connections, establishing dynasties, waging wars and discovering new territories of their own.

Their contemporaries praised them for rewarding hard work over born status and their reign saw rapid commercial and territorial growth. For the first time Spaniards built using Caribbean wood and imported cotton, hemp and gold from the New World. Explorers unfurled maps and released sails into the wind to claim other lands, their ports and towns given patriotic Spanish names. Like many rulers of the age, they also grappled with how to manage religious nonconformity. Ferdinand and Isabella undoubtedly believed they were acting in the interests of their realms, but there is no denying that Caribbean, African, Jewish and Muslim communities, among others, faced hostility, slavery and spiritual oppression in the couple's quest for religious, geographical and political expansion.

Isabella died at Medina del Campo on 26 November 1504, leaving Ferdinand in her will 'all my jewels, or such as he shall select, so that, seeing them, he may be reminded of the singular love I always bore him while living'. She promised she would wait for him in another world, willing her remains to be buried alongside him after his death, so 'that the union we have enjoyed in this world, and, through the mercy of God, may hope again for our souls in heaven'.[51] The following year Ferdinand married Germaine of Foix, in a last but unsuccessful bid, most writers suspect, to produce a male heir to help stabilise Spain's future. He died on 23 January 1516 and was buried with Isabella at the Alhambra in Granada. Their grandson, the Holy Roman Emperor Charles V, later moved their bodies to a specially made tomb in the Royal Chapel of Granada with intricately carved effigies of the couple.[52] They are depicted laying silently in prayer with lions at their feet, Ferdinand's effigy wears armour with a thick robe curling around his frame, while Isabella rests within the folds of a soft gown and mantle.

Chapter 4

Francesco II and Isabella d'Este of Mantua

In the late April of 1493, jewelled fingers unravelled a note sent from Florence. 'Your Highness,' it began, 'may have heard that we have had letters here telling us that the King of Spain sent some ships over the seas, which, after a voyage of thirty-six days, discovered certain islands.' The writer told of mountains, rivers and the island's residents, all recently discovered through Ferdinand and Isabella's funding. Reading slowly, the recipient noted with interest the discovery of rivers that 'run with gold' and the 'many other wonders' found in these new lands.[1] Francesco Gonzaga, the Marquis of Mantua, folded the letter and rested his eyes on the fourteenth-century towers and medieval courtyards of his ducal palace in Northern Italy.

Gonzaga, born in 1466, had enjoyed a noble upbringing as the son of the previous Marquis Federico I and his wife Margaret of Bavaria, learning war strategy, weaponry and horse riding. As a child, he would have gazed up at the walls and ceilings of the palazzo and its vividly coloured frescoes painted by the Italian master Andrea Mantegna commissioned by his grandfather. Painted into the plaster were *putti*, tiny cherubs with wings, as well as portraits of the young boy's family. In one fresco on the wall of the *Camera degli Sposi* (Bridal Chamber) in the ducal palace, his grandfather Ludovico III sits, turning to receive a message, while Francesco's grandmother Barbara tends to her young grandchildren at his side.[2] Francesco's mother died in 1479 and the young boy continued to be coached in politics by his father, assisting at important diplomatic events including a visit in 1483 from Lorenzo de Medici, the grandson of Cosimo and Contessina de Medici of Florence. The teenager led the statesman through the corridors of the palace and took him to hear Mass at the nearby church of St Francesco. Both families were highly interested in the arts and the two men took the opportunity to call on Andrea Mantegna, where they pored over his paintings and collection of antiques.[3] A year later, the sudden death of Francesco's father elevated the 17-year-old to the title of marquis, the future of this small but politically powerful realm now resting on his shoulders.

Fortunately, the matter of a bride for the young marquis had been settled before his father's death. Federico negotiated a match between his son and the daughter of the Duke and Duchess of Ferrara, Modena and Reggio: Isabella d'Este. Betrothed in childhood, the basis of the marriage was purely diplomatic. With medieval Italy a collection of individually governed states and cities it was important for smaller regions such as Mantua and Ferrara to ally with one another, particularly when loyalties between other neighbours could change without warning.

Like Francesco, Isabella had grown up at a highly cultured, wealthy court. Born on 18 May 1474, from a young age she was tutored in music and singing and could play the lute and the clavichord, a keyboard instrument similar to a harpsichord or piano. She studied the works of Virgil, Cicero and Manuel Chrysolaras, playing and running past palace walls decorated by the Ferrarese court painters Cosimo Tura, Pisanello and Piero della Francesca.[4]

In 1490, the 16-year-old Isabella prepared herself for married life and set out for Mantua. Riding slowly through the streets of Ferrara in a specially made chariot accompanied by elaborately painted wedding chests, she boarded a vessel that took her across the River Po and was greeted on her entrance to Mantua on 15 February. Thousands of citizens welcomed her to the city, along with diplomatic ambassadors and her new family, including her husband the young marquis. The serene views of the lakes and greenery from the palace towers, however, concealed the demanding and dangerous life the young newlyweds were about to lead. By the time Francesco and Isabella, pregnant with their first child, read of Ferdinand and Isabella's colonialisation of islands in the New World, the couple had already clashed with enemies and begun to target specific alliances in Italy's difficult political climate. Within the complex of buildings that formed the ducal palace they discussed strategy, shared diplomatic news and received high-status guests. This imposing structure would not only serve as a home for the couple's growing family; it was also an official building that would need to publicly reflect the era's tastes in culture, reflecting not just the wealth and power, but the sophistication and innovation of the Mantuan court. Isabella and Francesco therefore used the arts as a political tool, following in the steps of Francesco's ancestors. Alison Cole, in *Italian Renaissance Courts: Art, Pleasure and Power*, pointed out previous Gonzaga relatives who directed funds into the expression of art, education and architecture in a bid to 'improve the diplomatic standing of their court'.[5]

The earliest parts of the ducal palace where Francesco and Isabella lived during their early years of marriage were built in the fourteenth and fifteenth centuries. Later, they were renovated by generations of the Gonzaga family to include a complex of fortified buildings, some of which were ordered to be built and enlarged by Francesco. Situated near the Ponte St Giorgio, an imposing bridge that stretched over the blue lake, the site conveys beauty and tranquillity, but also immense strength in its blocky towers and walls. There were stables, drawing rooms and private chambers for the family, as well as a garden decorated with Renaissance-style classical pillars. A nineteenth-century visitor to the palace described a sprawling complex of rooms with wall and ceiling paintings, intricate stonework and carved medallions. Among the 'magnificent decaying ceilings' he viewed, four centuries after Francesco and Isabella resided there, the colourful interior was decorated with depictions of signs of the zodiac, local landscapes and portraits.[6]

The couple were united in their love of the arts and recognised its value as political propaganda. However, they did more than simply pay the salaries of creatives in return for work. Instead, they actively shaped the course of late fifteenth- and early-sixteenth-century painting, sculpture, literature and more. They encouraged the portrayal of specific themes and subjects and helped popularise the depiction of allegory, where people and objects in paintings conveyed hidden meanings to the viewer, often inspired by Greek and Roman stories and legends. They also helped pioneer one of the key differences to emerge between the medieval art form and that of the Renaissance: realism. Building on the work of earlier artists, they encouraged creatives to produce three-dimensional, anatomically correct figures with flexed muscles, flowing movement and intensity.

Francesco Gonzaga had a particular enthusiasm for the depiction of realism. In the sixteenth century, the writer Giorgio Vasari remembered an anecdote he had been told about the artist Francesco Bonsignori and the marquis. Bonsignori had been working on a painting of St Sebastian bound in rope and pierced with arrows. Gonzaga, passing by the artist's studio, looked in at his progress and questioned the position of the saint's limbs on the work. The marquis told him that there was 'no appearance of constraint' or 'that terror which one would imagine in a man who is tied up and being shot at'. Bonsignori reassured his patron that he enlisted the help of a porter at the palace, who he tied up with rope to achieve the most realistic pose.

Still not convinced, the marquis asked the painter to call for him the next time his subject was tied up and he was ready to paint, assuring him he could help improve the painting. When Bonsignori called, Francesco 'rushed into the room in a fury, with a loaded crossbow in his hand, and ran at the porter crying aloud, "Traitor, you are a dead man, I have caught you at last", and other like words'. As the terrified and practically naked porter struggled from the ropes in fear for his life, the marquis lowered his crossbow and calmly told the artist, 'There, that is how he should be; the rest you must do yourself.'[7]

One of the most prolific painters of the Mantuan court was Andrea Mantegna, who had worked for three generations of the Gonzaga family since being commissioned by Ludovico III to paint the *Camera degli Sposi*, or Bridal Chamber, at the Ducal Palace of Mantua. A pioneer in the use of foreshortening and perspective, the artist trained by sketching ancient statues from different angles to increase his understanding of the appearance of the human body. Throughout his life he continued to enjoy a passion for classical antiques.[8] Mantegna demonstrated his skill in the many cherubs who look mischievously down from the ceiling of the Bridal Chamber as well as in works such as the *Lamentation Over the Dead Christ*, painted in around 1483 and now in the collection of the Pinacoteca di Brera in Milan.[9] Mantega fully understood that the principles of perspective already being applied to architecture and landscape at this time also related to the human body. His Christ appears to recede into the canvas from our viewpoint, creating a far more realistic depiction than earlier medieval artists had achieved. The Bridal Chamber at Mantua demonstrates other examples of his talent in optical illusion, with classical stone pillars and 'marble' roundels of Roman emperors painted into the plaster. Behind the pale columns are bright blue skies, landscapes and figures silently living out events in the story of the Gonzaga family. It is no wonder that Francesco breathlessly praised the artist while he was working on a commission for him in 1492 for creating 'pictures which seem almost to live and breathe'.[10]

Mantegna's luxuriously painted Bridal Chamber at the Gonzaga palace also inspired the artistic ambitions of Francesco's new wife Isabella. After her marriage she commissioned the artist to create a portrait of her, although later considered it not an accurate likeness.[11] In 1495 Francesco appointed him to paint the *Madonna della Vittoria*, depicting the marquis kneeling in armour at the feet of the Virgin. Intended as an expression of religious and military propaganda, it celebrated a battle in which Francesco had recently claimed victory and depicted protective and avenging figures such as St George and the sword-wielding Archangel Michael. The historian Julia Cartwright has pointed out that originally Francesco intended for his wife to be depicted in the scene, but the finished result features instead the likeness of the nun Osanna dei Andreasi, also known as Beata Osanna. There is evidence of Isabella's close personal connection with Osanna. She commissioned a stand-alone portrait of the nun, named one of her daughters after her and paid for an extravagant tomb on Osanna's death in 1505. Cartwright therefore saw some collaboration between the couple as they shaped the composition of Mantegna's painting, with Isabella urging that Osanna was included in her place opposite the marquis. Osanna's presence in the painting is also particularly appropriate, the nun having prayed ardently for Francesco's safety during the battle it commemorates. In addition, Cartwright names her as a relative of the Gonzagas and so it was also through the marriage that Isabella was introduced to her.[12] As for Isabella's own dealings with Mantegna, the unsatisfactory portrait she received from him would not be the end of their relationship. Later, she commissioned him to create the allegorical *Minerva Expelling the Vices from the Garden of Virtue,* a painting created in around 1500–2 that features billowing clouds and swirling fabrics, foreshadowing the later tastes of the seventeenth-century Baroque era. Both the *Madonna della Vittoria* and *Minerva Expelling the Vices* are today housed in the Louvre in Paris.[13]

Isabella and Mantegna shared a mutual love of classical antiquity. Among a collection of ancient medals, coins and sculptures the marchioness also owned a bust of the Roman empress Faustina that she bought, with some haggling, from Mantegna just weeks before his death. Friends and artists wrote to inform her of new finds recently excavated in Greece and Rome, offering to act as agents on her behalf to close their sales. Further evidence of Isabella's classical influences can be seen in a medal designed in 1498 by a friend and favourite sculptor of the couple, Gian Cristoforo Romano. Surviving today in the collection of the Metropolitan Museum of Art in New York, it draws on ancient design, depicting Isabella in profile with braided hair gathered loosely, swirling behind her. The reverse of the medal depicts a winged figure with a lance, snake and a centaur taking aim with a bow above. A coin minted in the reign of the Roman emperor Claudius between AD 41–54 shows Minerva, goddess of wisdom, justice and the arts advancing with a shield. On the other side is the emperor depicted in profile. The iconography and design of both sides of this ancient coin are very similar to Cristoforo's rendering of Isabella's medal, hinting at both the patron and sculptor's classical influences.[14]

The list of artists and craftspeople employed by the couple is a long one, as they sourced craftsmen through personal networks or through the recommendations of others. Isabella's letters also reveal dealings with Raphael while he was painting in Rome as well as correspondence with Leonardo da Vinci while he was in Venice and Florence. During a visit to Mantua in 1499 Leonardo sketched a portrait of Isabella, later completing a painting considered 'so well done that it is not possible for it to be better'. The following year Leonardo provided the marquis with architectural sketches for a proposed house design.[15] The close timing of the couple's individual connections with Leonardo strongly suggests that Isabella and Francesco discussed and recommended artists to one another for their individual projects.

There is also evidence that Isabella influenced the appointment of Mantua's next court painter, Lorenzo Costa, contracted by the couple after Mantegna's death. In a letter of 1508, he is described as 'the Ferrara painter', and Vasari stated that he worked in Isabella's childhood home, painting the choir of the Church of St Domenico and the walls of the Duke of Ferrara's palace.[16] With this link between Lorenzo Costa and Isabella's home and family, his appointment in Mantua could have come from her suggestion. Like his predecessor, Costa was established at the couple's court in 1506 with land, a salary and a home and was granted citizenship of Mantua. He set to work painting Francesco's palace of St Sebastian and also created a number of other works for the couple including portraits of Isabella with her ladies and Francesco being led by the mythological hero Hercules.[17]

Unlike her husband, Isabella did not rely on a loaded crossbow to motivate her artists, but she did forcibly push them out of their comfort zone. In 1502 she chose the artist Pietro Perugino to create an ambitious and complicated composition of a representation of *The Battle of Love and Chastity*, something that clearly did not sit well with the artist. Perugino expressed his doubts on being able to complete the painting and kept putting off the work despite Isabella's persistence. Eventually she arranged for Leonardo da Vinci's student Salai to visit and help the exasperated artist. Meticulous in her vision of the work, she sent detailed instructions concerning the costumes of the main figures, accompanying decorations and insisted that he include 'fauns, satyrs, and thousands of little loves'. There was also the vague instruction that 'the issue of conflict between Diana and Venus must appear … doubtful'. On top of all this, in January 1504, Isabella enclosed lengths of thread to act as measurements for the finished work, having planned how they would be arranged on her wall.[18] The painting is today in the collection of the Louvre in Paris.

Isabella was a perfectionist, but she was also highly creative, able to not only visualise a complicated allegorical scene in her mind, but also convey it in detail on paper. Her many letters are examples of her tenacity to see a project through to its conclusion, negotiating with artists, solving problems in workflow and networking with her contacts to achieve the desired result. She was the equivalent of today's project manager, motivating, checking in and chasing up work. Her acquisition of art was prolific. Within a year or two of her marriage, she had collected so many artefacts and paintings that she needed a dedicated place in which to store and admire them.

Isabella mentions her studio in a letter of January 1493 to Francesco's sister, Elisabetta, who also became her close friend.[19] Francesco, keen for his wife to indulge in her passions, reserved a space for her in the Castello, which she called the *grotta*. Artists such as Leonardo da Vinci, Giovanni Bellini, Leonardo Costa and the ever-faithful Andrea Mantegna were approached specifically to adorn its walls, their work joined by antique busts, coins, statues, books, manuscripts and other collectables. Isabella also kept her musical instruments here, as well as books by Dante, Petrarch, Boccaccio and ancient writers Pliny, Seneca and Virgil.[20]

But this was not just a personal space for the marchioness to relax and escape the outside world. She invited culturally and diplomatically important guests into the *grotta*, suggesting that her collection was also used as a dazzling political tool. As well as promoting the couple's court as a fashionable centre of culture and artistic power, an invitation into this intimate space conveyed a sense of trust. It also subtly raised the perception of Mantua's military and diplomatic influence. If the Gonzagas could spare funds to commission and acquire art from all over Italy, then they likely had more at their disposal for defence or war, making them worthwhile allies. The collection also subtly emphasised their wide network of connections, with antiques having arrived not only via her contacts in the art world, but also gifted by prominent (and feared) Italian politicians. Writer Pietro Bembo (later secretary to the Medici Pope Leo X), statesman Antonio Galeazzo Bentivoglio and the Venetian Ambassador Alvise Contarini all visited Isabella's *grotta*, with the political commentator Niccolò Machiavelli paying a visit in 1505.[21]

The theatre, too, had strong diplomatic appeal for the couple. Francesco and Isabella invited envoys and state leaders to watch actors on a luxuriously decorated stage, in performances that were meticulously planned and rehearsed. One visitor in 1501 noted after one show, 'the arrangements made by this illustrious Lord Marquis have been most splendid, and deserve to be studied by all who wish to erect appropriate theatres for the performance of ancient and modern plays'. The stage at Mantua was, wrote the Ferrarese courtier Sigismundo Cantelmo, fitted out with pillars, arcades and decorated with paintings and foliage. The curtain was made from cloth of gold, the whole stage flanked by Mantegna's paintings of *The Triumphs of Caesar* and the *Triumphs of Petrarch.* Further dazzling the audience, 'hundreds of lights like shining stars' shone down from the ceiling, with representations of the sun and moon 'moving in their accustomed orbits'. The Gonzagas also used this area to publicly show their allegiance to other important rulers with the arms of the pope and emperor displayed proudly alongside their own.[22] Within their lifetimes, Isabella and Francesco were regarded as impeccable hosts, serious patrons of the theatre and a shining example for others to follow. This reputation would have been exactly what they intended and three years later there is evidence that theatrical customs from the Mantuan court had spread to other principalities. In 1504 Isabella received a letter from a member of the Ferrarese court, informing her that a play there had been 'admirably acted in perfect silence, because we have adopted the good customs learnt at Mantua, and no longer allow every rogue to come in and interrupt the performance'.[23]

There were many ways then, that the couple shaped the development of artistic expression during their lifetimes. Some they worked on together, with clear evidence of collaboration, while others were commissioned and planned individually, but with common objectives. They both worked towards elevating Mantua's status in the arts, positioning the city as a powerful political force in Italian affairs. There are clear differences in the styles and themes of the couple's commissions, however, reflecting their individual personal tastes and intentions. Both ordered religious works, although Isabella also chose complex allegorical and symbolic scenes rich in movement and visual classicism. In contrast, Francesco's commissions strongly emphasise his military position as a soldier and statesman, even when the subject was religious. In Mantegna's *Madonna della Vittoria* the marquis kneels in armour smiling up at the Virgin as she gestures down towards him, implicitly showing her holy approval and backing of his cause. In a terracotta bust now in the collection of the Mantova Museo Urbano Diffuso, he is also depicted in finely carved armour with an eagle symbol etched into his breastplate. His eyes are almost glaring, set downwards and buried under a stern frown. From 1514 the bust stared down at the hustle and bustle of the streets of Mantua from an arch situated near the Monastery of San Francesco, silently asserting his military and political power.[24]

In many respects these differences were down to medieval gender ideals, with Isabella opting for softer classical themes while Francesco focused on portrayals of his masculine power and military strength. They both commissioned portraits of themselves and loved ones and sent them to other leaders, using art as an effective tool for networking and visual propaganda. Diplomats and leaders walked through the decorated walls and ceilings of the Ducal Palace, observing the carefully curated antiques of the *grotta* bought with Gonzaga money. On their way out of the city, they would have seen Francesco's steely terracotta glare from its stone arch and considered Mantua a cultured, intelligent and powerful centre of politics and business.

All these swirling forms chiselled in marble and closely ordered theatrical performances masked the real and dangerous nature of the couple's political life. The fifteenth and sixteenth centuries were marked by turbulence in Italy through repeated conflict, and Isabella and Francesco had to tread carefully to maintain Mantua's secure position. Within the chaos and power struggles, influential men who had spoken too loudly or attracted jealous rivals were strangled in their beds or dragged, lifeless and butchered, from the river. In 1488 Girolamo Riario, ruler of Imola and Forli, was stabbed by his own guards in a planned assassination at his palace. Italian states and cities were also threatened by larger, foreign nations as French, Spanish, Turkish and Swiss rulers laid individual claims to territories including Milan, Naples, Venice and around Lake Maggiore in the north.[25]

It made good political sense for the couple to foster cautious but advantageous relationships with dominant Italian families that could serve as allies if required. The Sforzas and Borgias are well-known names of the period, both related to the Gonzagas through marriage. Isabella's sister Beatrice was married to Lodovico Sforza, Duke of Milan, while her brother Alfonso wed Lucrezia Borgia, a daughter of Pope Alexander VI. Other important characters were aligned with the couple through the birth of their children. Lorenzo de Medici of Florence wrote to congratulate them in 1493 on the birth of their daughter Leonora, while Lorenzo di Pierfrancesco de Medici was named godparent of the newborn girl, along with Lodovico Sforza, his wife Beatrice d'Este and the Doge of Venice. In 1500, on the birth of their son Federico the couple named as his godfathers the Emperor Maximilian, Cardinal Sanseverino and Lucrezia's brother, Cesare Borgia.[26] The couple can be seen carefully fostering political relationships in the adults they chose to be allied to their children. Kate Simon, in *A Renaissance Tapestry: The Gonzaga of Mantua*, has pointed out the defensive significance of the war-like Cesare Borgia being chosen as godfather, reinforcing him as their ally in order to prevent a possible future invasion of Mantua.[27] It is also possible that in selecting these allies with powerful and established figures, they were forging connections that could serve the Gonzagas in future generations.

As Francesco was often away from home on political or military business, much of the diplomatic work at Mantua fell on Isabella. Thrust into the public eye soon after their wedding she was intelligent, quick thinking and able to rapidly calm disputes. The couple wrote back and forth with confidential political news, while Isabella formally represented her husband and the House of Gonzaga in public. In 1495 she received the Venetian Ambassador in Milan and Francesco's secretary wrote to the marquis in praise of his wife, who 'does the greatest honour both to Your Excellency and herself'. In June 1498 we find her fretting over a visit from the Duke of Milan, asking about the wine he liked to drink, appropriate wall hangings for decoration and which rooms of the palace would be best to lodge him in. These arrangements were of huge importance to the couple as the duke had been negotiating with her husband over the command of the Milanese army and it was important for them to make a good impression if they wanted Francesco to gain the position. In 1506 Francesco proposed that his ally Pope Julius II visit the couple's home in Mantua, and Isabella enthusiastically agreed, also hosting talks between international powers in 1512.[28] She was always on the lookout for opportunities to gain further allies. During a visit to the town of Salò near Lake Garda, Isabella wrote to her husband discussing its residents and recommending that 'some day we may find it useful to have them for our friends'.[29] Gifts could also be sent to grease the wheels of influence and gain support, a tactic both Francesco and Isabella employed on various occasions. In 1499 the marchioness sent falcons and trout to the French king Louis XII, and in 1503 100 masks were sent to the war-loving Cesare Borgia, carefully reminding him in an accompanying letter of 'that friendship and affection which exists between you and ourselves'.[30] Isabella also showed herself an efficient organiser and administrator following her husband's capture by the Venetians in 1509. While he was imprisoned, she proclaimed their son Federico the new Marquis of Mantua and ruled as his regent, put feelers out to Louis XII and the pope for their assistance and sent musicians to play for her husband while he languished in Venice's ducal palace. Even social events gave opportunities for hushed negotiations, Isabella taking the opportunity to discuss politics with the French ambassador for almost an hour at her brother's wedding in 1501.[31]

Ambassadors were treated indulgently by the couple, who recognised their wider diplomatic power in matters of state. Just like Edward IV and Elizabeth Woodville of England, they were well aware that ambassadors wielded influence with their masters and mistresses and, if well-hosted, would spread positive accounts of the court to other European states. A description of a visit to Mantua by Venetian ambassadors in November 1515 survives, describing their tour of the 'sumptuously furnished rooms' of their son Federico and being fed 'infinite varieties of fish, eggs, tarts, confetti' all washed down with eight different types of wine. Officials also favourably remarked on the singing and music that accompanied dinner. Visiting the palace of St Sebastian, they were shown the new *Triumphs* painted by Mantegna, before being brought into Francesco's presence. The marquis was relaxing by a fireplace while being fanned by three pages, accompanied by three of his greyhounds and a variety of hunting birds on leashes. The officials dined on silver tableware, walked in the lush and fragrant gardens and of course made special trips to see the couple's own demonstrations of power: Isabella's *grotta* and Francesco's well-stocked armoury.[32]

Although Isabella wrote to her husband to advise him not to worry about Mantua while he was away fighting, she was understandably anxious when he went to war. Francesco was a brave soldier noted for his enthusiasm and fearlessness in battle. He had been interested in horses since his early years and collected breeds from Naples, Sicily, Spain, Africa and the Middle East, which he kept in a stable at the palace.[33] A variety of glittering military roles awaited him, including his appointment in 1495 of Captain of the Armies of the League against France, which consisted of the pope, the emperor, Ferdinand and Isabella of Spain, Henry VII of England and the leaders of Venice and Milan. He took fighting seriously, and sometimes struggled to communicate tactfully, clashing with the Duke of Milan on strategy and complaining to Isabella that other soldiers did not pull their weight, being only interested in 'plunder'. Isabella would play her own role in the wars when she took custody of one of her husband's prisoners of war in 1495, the French Duke of Bourbon, who was kept hospitably and under her watch at the Castello.[34]

Wartime, by its nature, is dense with suspicion, paranoia and changing allegiances, and for Francesco the Italian Wars were no different. Initially fighting for Venice against the French, he was dismissed in 1497 after the Venetians suspected him of double-dealing. Eventually, Francesco allied with France. He oversaw the Siege of Genoa in 1507, later entering Milan with Louis XII and inviting Isabella to visit and pay homage to the king. Louis created Francesco a Grand Master of the Order of St Michel, and the couple joined in the celebrations watching jousts, dancing and partaking in some diplomatic socialising, Isabella chatting with her husband's new ally 'with the greatest friendliness in the world'.[35] In 1509 troops under the marquis' command formed part of the 100,000 soldiers under the control of the Emperor Maximilian during the siege of Padua.[36]

The Gonzagas encountered a new and volatile problem, however, in Cesare Borgia, the brother of Lucrezia, Isabella's sister-in-law. Cesare, titled Duke Valentino, had a dangerous, hostile temperament and according to gossip was not beyond committing murder to seek revenge or remove his enemies. Lucrezia's second husband, the 19-year-old Alfonso, Duke of Bisceglie, suffered two attempts on his life, first being beaten and left to die and when he unexpectedly survived, was murdered in his bed. Both attacks were believed at the time to have been ordered by Cesare. Embarking on a rampage through Italy, he conquered dominions including Romagna, Forli, Pesaro and Rimini, ordering executions, murdering the nobility and looting palaces along the way.[37] As the son of the reigning pope, Cesare likely thought he was untouchable, although leaders exchanged worried letters as to where he would strike next. Soon afterwards, Lucrezia married Isabella's brother Alfonso, and the Gonzagas navigated their new family links with the Borgias cautiously. Isabella quietly and dutifully attended the wedding, while Cesare initiated talks with the pair to marry his daughter to their son.[38] In January 1502, in a move very close to home for the Gonzagas, Cesare seized the state of Urbino and seated himself on the ducal throne that was, until recently, occupied by Francesco's sister Elisabetta and her husband Guidobaldo.[39] Hearing that he had ransacked the palace there, Isabella immediately requested from Cesare, through an intermediary, the possession of statues she had seen at her sister-in-law's palace, of Venus and Cupid for her collection. Isabella's biographers have sometimes seen this as a cold-hearted move, but equally it may have been an attempt by Isabella to befriend Cesare, subtly positioning the Gonzagas as trustworthy and keeping his armies away from Mantua. Alternatively, learning that these priceless artefacts might now be destroyed by the invader, it's possible that she felt the need to safeguard them for Elisabetta or herself, noting at the time that Cesare had 'little taste for antiquities'.[40]

All of this careful manoeuvring was broken on 23 July 1502 when Isabella heard that Francesco had dangerously spoken 'angry words' against Cesare in front of Louis XII and servants of the pope, Cesare's father. Warning him that these were now likely to reach Cesare's ears, she advised him to be careful of being poisoned, remembering the violence the duke had previously levelled on other members of their own family. Isabella was deeply unsettled by this news, making enquiries as to who accompanied Francesco to dinner and the identities of his cupbearers and carvers. 'You allow all manner of persons to serve you at table,' she wrote, offering to send a 'trusted servant' from Mantua to attend him instead. 'I had rather run the risk of making you angry than that both I and our little one should be left to weep for you,' she wrote.[41] The threats posed by the unstable Cesare were soon dealt with without Isabella's intervention. The duke's power ended on the death of his father in 1503. Cesare was captured and imprisoned by Ferdinand and Isabella of Spain, but escaped, and died in 1507.

Selwyn Brinton, writing in 1927, considered Francesco Gonzaga 'a brave man and a good soldier', but thought that he could 'scarcely be considered a great general or tactician, and in his political conduct he owed much to the keener insight and untiring devotion of his wife'.[42] Isabella was certainly effective in both military and political terms, but their joint contribution to Mantua's business as partners should not go unnoticed. They were both passionate and devoted to their roles, but did not always agree with one another or carry out actions expected of them. In 1509, when offered the chance to exchange their eldest son as hostage in return for her husband's freedom in Venice, she refused, leaving her husband imprisoned. However, they presided over a lively and respected court, and each took part in negotiations, diplomacy and matters of security. Their surviving letters demonstrate that they were involved and busy rulers, writing constantly to one another to share battle results, rumours of secret negotiations and to discuss political strategy. Isabella and Francesco are discussed more often in terms of their contribution to culture during the Renaissance era, but they were also effective partners navigating a difficult age of diplomacy and war.

On 25 November 1490, Isabella signed off a letter to her husband as 'one who loves Your Highness more than herself'. Francesco replied three days later referencing the 'immense love which we both feel for each other'.[43] The newlyweds seem to have shared a strong affection during these early years, aside from their duties and professional commitment to one another. However, in their correspondence it is possible to see the interplay of their strong personalities and occasionally, tension within their relationship. Francesco was able to play the part of diplomat for a time, but could be risen quickly to temper as we have seen in his 'angry words' against Cesare Borgia. He could also act spontaneously while fighting and was known for his courage. Isabella referenced this trait in a letter of 1502, pointing out that her husband's 'natural goodness leads you to take no precautions for your safety'. He also had a tendency to disregard Isabella's worries, refusing to take them seriously. This was demonstrated in a letter from Isabella asking him not to 'laugh at my fears and say that women are cowards and always afraid'.[44]

By 1506 the couple had been married for more than fifteen years and there were signs that their initial romantic affection had waned. Isabella acknowledged to her husband that he has 'loved me little for some time past', and in 1513 was 'hardly surprised' to learn that she had upset him again.[45] Francesco was experiencing symptoms of long-term illness by this time and there are frequent references in Isabella's letters about his declining health. It is possible that during these bouts of pain and discomfort Francesco became more irritable and critical of his wife, but there is also the chance that their strong personalities clashed. Isabella was confident, self-assured and often vigorously defiant in her letters, while Francesco appears critical and bad-tempered. In one letter Isabella admitted that her husband often accused her of being 'proud'. In 1505 the couple named their newborn son Louis (sometimes written as Alvise), but as he grew older, Isabella commented to her husband how much he looked like her father, who had recently died, saying that the marquis was 'wrong not to call him Ercole'. Francesco laughed at the time and said nothing else, but in his absence, she brought the child up by her preferred name without telling him. When Francesco learned of this, he confronted his wife who defended her actions, explaining, unconvincingly, 'if you had told me your mind, I should not have made this mistake.'[46] It is possible, considering the couple's careful political approaches, that the child had been named in honour of Mantua's alliances with the French king, Louis XII. In any case, Francesco's shock at learning that his son had spontaneously been given a different name by his wife to the one they had agreed on at his birth is understandable.

Another argument between the pair simmered in March 1513 while Isabella was travelling in Piacenza in Northern Italy. Francesco wrote to advise her that during her journey he heard that she had done something to become 'the common talk of the town'. She argued that she had 'behaved as

I ought to do', haughtily adding that she 'never needed … to be controlled by others, or to be reminded how to govern my actions'. The more Francesco became angry and distant with her, she wrote, 'the more I shall always love you, because, in truth, this love is part of myself and I became your wife so young that I can never remember having been without it.' Her irritation soon subsided, and she later wrote from Salò of her travels, telling her husband that 'each time I see another lovely spot, I wish most earnestly that you may be restored to health and come here with me'.[47]

These interactions hint at marital trouble between the pair, especially when considering Isabella's strong personality and Francesco's unstable temperament. Kate Simon in *A Renaissance Tapestry: The Gonzaga of Mantua* has offered another explanation. Simon wonders whether, in line with the paranoia and deception of the age, some of their more vocal and critical letters were sent in hope of being intercepted either by allies or enemies. Francesco could therefore paint his wife in a bad light to one statesman, while the 'rebellious' Isabella gently explored alternative opportunities secretly, with a rival.[48] If Isabella's 'double-dealing' was discovered, it could then be deflected by the marquis who could claim no knowledge of it and portray his wife as careless and politically naïve, 'reprimanding' her in a letter that could be produced as evidence if needed. Simon's explanation is indeed possible. We also know that the Gonzagas were experts in diplomacy and it does explain the sudden changes between anger and affection expressed by the pair. However, we only have their written words as evidence, and the subtle meanings understood by Isabella and Francesco 500 years ago can easily be misconstrued or missed entirely by modern readers. There would also have been conversations between the pair relating to these letters, of which there is of course no surviving evidence. While they were certainly politically aware, the irritation they expressed to one another on paper is equally likely to have been the result of a clash of strong wills along with the stresses of illness and political and military business.

Their marriage was complex. Francesco had mistresses, some of whom he appeared with in public, and authors often discuss a possible sexual relationship between the marquis and his sister-in-law Lucrezia Borgia. Isabella hints at some rivalry between her and Lucrezia, rolling her eyes and complaining at how long the bride took to dress during her wedding celebrations. It was common for men of the period, particularly leaders and politicians, to have mistresses, but her husband's boldness in appearing openly with them at events must have hurt her. Francesco received a subtle reprimand from the writer Floriano Dolfo, when he wrote to the marquis telling him he was 'blessed' to have a wife, 'ever anxious to gratify your wishes, while she prudently feigns neither to see nor hear those actions of yours which must be hateful and injurious to her'.[49]

The couple though had much in common, sharing a passion for the arts and its development, Mantua's safety and promotion, and the elevation of the Gonzaga family name and its future. They enjoyed raising their children, sending touching letters to one another about their first steps and other intimate anecdotes. They also played on each other's strengths; Francesco was liable to snap, while Isabella was there to calm, charm and negotiate their way out of trouble.

Tired, irascible and in pain, Francesco wrote his will on the morning of 29 March 1519 at his palace of St Sebastian and died at around 8 o'clock that evening. He appointed Isabella his executor and their son Federico's guardian until he reached the age of twenty-two.[50] The marquis was then buried in the Gonzaga Chapel, the resting place of his father and grandfather, in the church of St Francesco in Mantua. Isabella acted as regent for her son and continued in her search for rare antiques and new art commissions, sitting for one of the foremost painters of the sixteenth century, Titian. She died on 13 February 1539 in Mantua and was buried alongside her husband.

Francesco II and Isabella d'Este changed the lives of many of their contemporaries and left an enduring legacy for generations to come. Young, exciting and dedicated rulers, their combined impact was felt not only in Mantua, but throughout the wider world. Developing new artistic themes and encouraging a more precise depiction of realism, they patronised painters who in turn inspired a new wave of artists. These newcomers perfected the depiction of flexed muscles, facial expression and posture, and were innovators of a new age in art that was to dominate the seventeenth century: the Baroque. In the work of the couple's principal painter, Andrea Mantegna, we can see the swirling fabrics and drama that typified this later style. Isabella's persistent dealings with Pietro Perugino and her complex compositions reveal the marchioness's ambition for change and progress, while her husband attempted the same, at least once, with a loaded crossbow. Mantegna is today considered one of the masters and original pioneers of the use of perspective and the family's four-decade patronage raised his profile, supported him financially and enabled him to produce the prolific body of work that can still be seen and studied today. There is evidence that the artist influenced a later master of art, the Dutch painter Rembrandt, who owned Mantegna's drawings as part of his personal collection.[51]

A long list of other artists in the pay of the couple includes Lorenzo Costa, Cristoforo Romano, Pietro Perugino and Luca Liombini. Each partner received work from Leonardo da Vinci and Isabella reached out to Raphael at least twice. The patronage of so many artists, musicians, craftspeople and writers helped support Italian livelihoods with payment in houses, land and cash. Financially supported, they were then able to produce work for other clients, growing their portfolios and further improving their skills. As suppliers to the cultured Gonzaga court of Mantua, they also gained visibility and prestige. The relationship was reciprocal and artists helped the Gonzagas elevate their own social and political standing through specially targeted propaganda that was seen and remarked on by ambassadors, citizens and rulers.

The *grotta* or studio at the palace that Isabella ensured was well stocked with artefacts, was a must-see for dignitaries visiting the couple at Mantua. Authors have often praised Isabella for building the collection, but it was only possible with effort from both partners. Isabella scouted for the latest treasures while Francesco reserved her the room for their display, demonstrating a respect for his wife's passion. Their dealings with Leonardo da Vinci and Lorenzo Costa suggest that they discussed artists and recommended them to one another. After Isabella's death, her collection remained in the palace at Mantua, but was broken up in the seventeenth century and acquired by statesmen such as Charles I of England and Cardinal Richelieu of France. Work from the fifteenth and sixteenth centuries that have been linked to the couple can be found in palaces, stately homes and galleries around the world. We have Isabella and Francesco to thank for their careful curation and safeguarding of these works between 1490 and 1539.

Working in a difficult political climate, the couple maintained their control through careful negotiation and conduct. Unlike Milan, Urbino, Venice and Padua, among others, Mantua and its inhabitants remained safe under Gonzaga rule during Isabella and Francesco's lifetimes. They both also gained the respect and co-operation of leaders and statesmen of the Italian Wars, including the Emperor Maximilian, Charles VIII and Louis XII of France, three popes and the doges and dukes of powerful Italian states. They also survived a minor clash with the Borgias and the proud and volatile Cesare.

Each of the couple's children left their mark on the history of Mantua and the Gonzaga family, and we can see some of their parents' influence in their actions. Federico II, their eldest son, was born in 1500. Inheriting the government of Mantua on his father's death, he married Maria Paleologa of Monferrato. Considered a good military commander, he defended Pavia in 1522 from an attack by the French and served as a soldier to the Emperor Charles V, who visited him at Mantua and elevated his title to that of a dukedom. The first Duke of Mantua, he maintained a love of art and architecture in the spirit of his parents and grandparents. He died in 1540, the year after his mother, and named his own son Francesco III as his heir.

While the couple's eldest son was always destined for politics, Ercole (or Louis as he had been initially named), prepared for a religious life. Born in 1505, he became Cardinal in 1526. After his brother's death, he was named regent for the young Duke Francesco III, along with the boy's mother Maria of Monferrato and Ercole's brother Ferrante. The twentieth-century historian Selwyn Brinton called Ercole a 'great statesman and great churchman' and during the regency credited him for reforming justice in Mantua, keeping the realm secure from war and regulating commerce within the state.[52] He died in 1563.

Ferrante, their third son, was born in 1507 and, like his brothers, joined the service of Charles V, successfully receiving the surrender of Florence in 1530 and making way for the subsequent return of the Medici family there. He married the heiress Isabella of Capua and bought the principality of Guastalla to rule in his name, but died fighting for Spain against France in 1557.

The couple's daughters also served as politicians and churchwomen. The eldest, Leonora, was to follow in her mother's footsteps and support her husband Francesco Maria, the Duke of Urbino, whom she married in 1509, the year her father was imprisoned in Venice. Born in 1492, she weaved through difficult political situations and represented her husband as her mother had done, dying in her late seventies in 1570. Another daughter, Ippolita, became a nun in the convent of St Vincenzo in Mantua. She was born in 1503 and also died in 1570. Her sister, Livia Osanna, who had been named after the nun her mother and father had represented in the *Madonna della Vittoria*, entered the convent of Santa Paola at a young age and kept in touch with members of her family, dying in 1569. Other descendants further down the family tree in the sixteenth and seventeenth centuries became cardinals, influencing and leading the church while others ruled over territories in Austria, France and Italy.

Chapter 5

Laudomia Forteguerri of Siena and Margaret of Austria, Duchess of Parma and Governor of the Netherlands

April 1533. A wedding party of carts and extravagantly dressed guests bumbled through the streets of Mantua, their chests laden with clothes and personal possessions.[1] The bride, a young girl approaching the age of 11, looked up as the terracotta glare of the city's previous marquis, Federico II, scowled down at her. She was on her way to meet her future husband, Alessandro de Medici, a nephew of Pope Clement VII, in a match arranged by her father to cement an alliance between their families. As the crowds waved the auburn-haired bride out of the city, they would have known that this was no ordinary wedding. The 10-year-old Margaret of Austria, daughter of the Holy Roman Emperor Charles V, was about to begin her political life as a consort of the powerful Medici family of Italy.

Margaret was born in Oudenarde in modern-day Belgium in the summer of 1522, the result of a passionate encounter between the emperor and a maid named Johanna van der Gheynst. Although a later sixteenth-century account written by Famiano Strada stated that Margaret's mother was of noble birth, this story was most likely created to artificially enhance her political legitimacy, the writer Felix Rachfahl calling it a 'romantic fairytale'. Johanna is believed to have been the eldest daughter of a carpet weaver from Nukerke. It was while she worked at Oudenarde Castle in the service of Charles of Lalaing, Baron of Montigny and Escornaix that she met the emperor.[2] Charles V immediately recognised the newborn as his own and sent Margaret to be educated in the imperial household. From an early age she was raised for a life of public service, learning Flemish, French, Italian and Spanish and was cared for by her father's female relatives. Influential and powerful Habsburg women taught the young Margaret manners and the basics of political life. First, Charles's aunt, Margaret of Savoy, an intelligent and agile ruler and then the emperor's formidable sister, Mary, Dowager Queen of Hungary.

The late-nineteenth-century writer Felix Rachfahl warned us, however, not to see the eager recognition and care Charles demonstrated for his daughter simply as an act of love. As he points out, although illegitimate, Margaret was a valuable commodity on the marriage market. Her presence was a powerful one and could assist in securing a financially or politically beneficial alliance for the Habsburgs.[3] For the nobles and princes of Europe, her hand offered them the support of the emperor and links to his growing domains across the world. The grandson of Ferdinand and Isabella, as Holy Roman Emperor, Charles would come to rule over parts of Italy, the Netherlands, Spain and Germany. Consequently, he was a valuable and important ally in this faster-paced, more ambitious world. Charles's open recognition of Margaret as his daughter, along with his care in educating her as a future stateswoman demonstrates that, from the earliest months of her life, she was deliberately being raised to play a political role in future Habsburg fortunes.

As she reached the age of 7 in 1529, an agreement was finalised for Margaret's marriage to Alessandro de Medici, Duke of Florence. The Florentine family had come a long way since Cosimo's cautious leadership of the city in the early fifteenth century. Exiled once again under the government of his great-grandson Piero de Medici, the family returned to power in 1512. By the 1530s they were not simply wealthy bankers with ties to Florentine government, but popes, dukes and rulers of powerful states. The Medicis were therefore attractive allies for the emperor, able to wield their influence in papal and state business within Italy as well as beyond.

In 1533 Margaret set off on a long journey from her home in Mechelen. Travelling through Mantua, Rome and Naples, the purpose of the trip was for her to get to know her new in-laws and the Italian people before embarking on her public duty there. She lived with the Medicis for four years before standing to recite her vows at the Church of San Lorenzo in Florence on 19 June 1536, the dark-eyed, handsome Alessandro at her side. Despite the duke's soft-eyed appearance in portraits, Alessandro de Medici had a reputation as a tyrant and womaniser. During the feasting and dancing held after their ceremony, an eyewitness noted that the new duchess seemed happy on her wedding day, 'for the Duke paid her great court', adding slyly that 'she knew not that he paid even more to other women of all grades'.[4] Alessandro was accused of ordering the poisoning of one of his opponents,

Ippolito de Medici, in 1535. Predictably, Margaret's time as a Medici wife was short. Just over six months later, on the night of 5 January 1537, her husband was brutally stabbed to death by his enemies. According to legend, he had been lured by his rivals into an ambush by the false promise of a waiting mistress.

Reeling from shock, Margaret waited for news from her father, who was already busy negotiating a second marriage for her. The emperor settled on Octavio Farnese, the 13-year-old grandson of another pope, Paul III. Now 16 years old, Margaret protested against the union. She travelled to her Rome wedding in the autumn of 1538 dressed in black and refused to say 'I do' when exchanging rings with Octavio, both silent protests against her father's political designs. Tensions between the newlyweds soon filtered into public knowledge, with Cardinal Lenoncourt calling it a 'miserable marriage'.[5] Their families interceded with the young couple to reconcile with one another, but Margaret remained obstinate, attempting to undermine the legalities of her nuptials and refusing to use her influence with her father on Octavio's behalf. Margaret's reluctance over her second marriage may have come from her dislike of the new groom or, more likely, was influenced by her relationship with the Medici family. Margaret had spent a number of years with Alessandro's relatives before her marriage and is likely to have made close and meaningful connections with many of them, in particular the women, who would have been her daily companions.

Adding to the difficulties of this second marriage, Octavio and Margaret took many years to conceive. This has sometimes been used as further evidence of the lack of affection between them with eight years passing before Margaret bore twins in 1545. Only one of the twins, Alexander, survived. In 1557, with Margaret, now Duchess of Parma following her husband's accession to the title, she enjoyed a brief trip to England staying with her younger half-brother Philip of Spain and his wife Mary I at their mid-Tudor court. It is likely that while here, Margaret and Philip discussed his plans for the future of the Netherlands. Philip had assumed control of part of his father's sprawling empire in 1556 and needed someone to head the Netherlands as regent under his authority. He clearly trusted Margaret, not only because of their close family ties, but almost certainly due to her upbringing as a Habsburg stateswoman. It also helped, he later admitted, that she had been born in the state and would, he hoped, be welcomed and trusted by the native people.

In 1559 he named Margaret Governor of the Netherlands, sending a council of Spanish advisors to assist her in her new role. Margaret often worked late into the night on state business and had to constantly balance tensions between Philip, her Spanish council and the Netherlanders, who were suspicious of the Habsburgs' foreign involvement. She was known to be pious, gave generously to the poor and oversaw military operations, mobilising thousands of troops against the French on Philip's behalf in 1562. She was also known, like other Renaissance rulers, to grant rewards based on hard work rather than social status. Praise was scribbled back to Philip in messages sent from the eagle-eyed advisors he surrounded his half-sister with. But Margaret had another admirer she had met almost thirty years before, 600 miles away in the Italian city of Siena.

Historian Konrad Eisenbichler has extensively explored the relationship between the writer Laudomia Forteguerri and Margaret of Austria, along with the impact their meeting had on literature of the Renaissance era. In *The Sword and the Pen: Women, Politics, and Poetry in Sixteenth-Century Siena*, he traced Forteguerri's birth to noble-born parents in 1515, along with her two marriages and three children.[6] The Forteguerris were an old, established family active in the city for many generations. The writer William Heywood found that a family of that name were involved in peacekeeping, conflicts and other political business in Siena in the 1270s and 1280s.[7]

In the 1530s Siena experienced a period of hardship. It had made an enemy of Florence, its commerce was in decline and robbers weaved and dodged through the city's streets. Severe outbreaks of plague also hit in 1527 and in 1529, resulting in over 40,000 deaths. The early 1530s were spent recovering, along with combating the growing influence of Margaret's father Charles V, who filled Siena with Spanish soldiers and began work on a fortress in San Prospero. Accordingly, Siena's historic city walls were destroyed and used for materials and appeals by the residents for the pope's intervention fell on deaf ears.[8]

It was against this backdrop that Laudomia Forteguerri and Margaret of Austria first met. Laudomia's friend and fellow writer Alessandro Piccolomini stated in a lecture published in 1541 that the two young women met in Siena in 1536, but Konrad Eisenbichler in *The Sword and the Pen* argues that a date of 1533 seems more likely when considering Margaret's movements.[9] Felix Rachfal's placement of Margaret's travels through Italy in this year also supports this date.

A view of Siena published by Luca Bonetti in 1574 gives us some idea of the appearance of the city during the time of Margaret and Laudomia's meeting. The city's circular stone walls snake around a hive of closely packed buildings, the skyline punctuated with tall, slim towers sprawling into the sky. Clustered within them are the rooftops of houses and businesses, along with the dome of Siena's medieval cathedral.[10] Laudomia would have known the cathedral's ornate façade, completed by the end of the fourteenth century, as well as its striking, striped marble columns inside. Within, the terracotta busts of deceased popes stared down, as outside, challenges were being made to the religious and political structures of the medieval world they had once ruled over.

Despite its social and political setbacks, Siena was dedicated to the development of Renaissance culture. Its residents included the prominent botanist Pier Antonio Mattioli and historians Orlando Malavolti and Antonio Bellarmati. Another sixteenth-century Sienese thinker, Bernardino Ochino, published works on theology and philosophy.[11] Religious works depicted saints shining with gold, while richly painted tiles were pressed into the floors of the palaces and homes of the nobility. A series of frescoes depicting mythological characters and cherubs, one named *The Rape of Proserpine*, are today in the collection of the Metropolitan Museum of Art in New York, completed by the artist Pinturicchio in around 1509. They were removed in the nineteenth and twentieth centuries, but as crowds stretched their necks to see the young Margaret of Austria and her entourage pass by, they would have been firmly in place in the ceiling of Siena's Palazzo del Magnifico.[12]

At the height of the Sienese calendar was the Palio, a horse race similar to the one held in Florence, conducted twice a year in July and August. In a custom dating to at least the thirteenth century, horses were blessed with holy water while riders waved banners and marched to music. Fierce racing then took place through Siena's streets in a display of local competitiveness, pomp and historic tradition.[13] It is unlikely that Margaret watched the Palio during her first stay in Siena, as her visit does not seem to correspond with the dates on which it was held, but Laudomia, as a native of the city, would have been familiar with the custom and seen it on various occasions. With the Forteguerris an established, noble-born Sienese family they, like the Medicis, would have used these public opportunities to network, socialise and discuss business.

Margaret was around 10 years old when she first met Laudomia, who was then 17. The two hit it off instantly, says Piccolomini in his 1541 lecture, the *Lettura del S. Alessandro Piccolomini Infiammato fatta nell' Accademia degli Infiammati*. Piccolomini described Laudomia as 'a young woman of very noble blood and of great form', praising her judgement, prudence, wisdom and natural ability to express herself eloquently. As soon as they met, said Piccolomini, 'immediately the flames of love burned within them'. They met again, said the writer, in the late 1530s, when they 'renewed their most sweet loves, and today, more than ever … they warmly confer, as I could adduce to you in testimony, many Sonnets, and some Cantons'.[14] One of these Laudomia penned shortly after Margaret left Siena for Rome and Piccolomini chose to make it the subject of his lecture. He also tells us that there was a longing between the two young women when they were apart, stating that Forteguerri, 'although she is always far from her does not fail to see her with her mind, and to have her dearly in her heart'.[15] In one of her other poems Forteguerri asks 'must I Live without my love? ... O cruel fortune, why do you not let my body go where my heart goes? ... I want nothing else, Hail, that my Goddess may hold me dear'.[16]

Same-sex love was frowned upon in the Renaissance era and there were harsh penalties for those conducting homosexual relationships, although these generally applied more severely to men. But that is not to say that they never happened. There is ample evidence that homosexual and bisexual relationships were conducted by artists, sculptors, aristocrats and rulers during the age. Some were just more open about it than others. The painter Giovanni Antonio Bazzi was known to have 'about him boys and beardless youths, whom he loved more than was decent', according to Vasari. While he lived in Siena, Bazzi wrote songs and poems about his lovers and sang them while strumming along with his lute. Famously, he also took the nickname Sodoma.[17]

At first glance Laudomia's poems, like Bazzi's songs, convey a passionate and romantic love for Margaret. However, Margaret was just 10 years old at their meeting, with Laudomia in her late teens, making it far more likely that they instead experienced a strong, but purely platonic connection. The Florentine poet Agnolo Firenzuola, in his *Dialogue On The Beauty of Women* published in 1548, used their relationship to differentiate between different types of Renaissance-era same-sex love. 'Those which had been female in both halves, or are descended from such, love each other's beauty, some in purity in holiness, as the fair Laodamia Forteguerra [sic] loved the illustrious Margaret of Austria', he wrote.[18] Firenzuola clearly places this love in the context of a warm platonic attraction, actually stating that it was not based on sexual attraction, contrasting it with the love demonstrated by the 'Lesbian among the ancients', Sappho. Their bond was reciprocal, according to Piccolomini, who stated that Laudomia and Margaret wrote poems to one another and later 'renewed their most sweet loves'. Conducted openly, and commented on during their lifetimes, it is clear that their contemporaries considered the girls' relationship more significant at least than a regular friendship.

Their relationship had also been swayed by contemporary descriptions of the duchess. Sixteenth-century writers made a conscious effort to emphasise Margaret's perceived masculine qualities, particularly when describing her manner and pastimes. She loved to hunt, although this was not unusual for a woman of status and her Habsburg female relatives had also enjoyed the sport. But Famiano Strada, the biographer of her second husband's Farnese family, wrote that Margaret's 'body was so lively in spirit and her gait such that she did not so much seem a woman born with a man's spirit, but as a man in a woman's dress'.[19] No authenticated portraits of Laudomia survive, but in one of Margaret painted by Antonis Mor in 1562, in the collection of the Gemäldegalerie in Berlin, she is dressed in black, her outfit accentuated with white pearls and gold. She wears a small veil at the top of her head secured with a headband of jewels. Her auburn-brown hair is braided and gathered up underneath, and she looks out at us with a confident gaze, plump lips and a small mouth.[20] Strada carefully noted the downy hair Margaret allowed to grow on her upper lip and chin, something that he says 'gave her the appearance of a man, but also much authority'.[21] The duchess' behaviour in ruling may also have contributed to her perception as 'manly'. Determined and strong-willed, she occasionally resisted Philip of Spain's orders, organised the military and secretly devised the fall from power of a representative Philip had sent to guide her, Antoine de Granvelle, Bishop of Arras. Margaret was not a coy Renaissance woman with a soft gaze and tumbling locks, but a Habsburg and Medici-trained enforcer of Machiavellian statecraft, even if events did not always unravel the way she had planned.

All of this, along with the unconventionally long wait for her pregnancy, has sometimes been offered as evidence that Margaret may have been attracted to women, or at least did not find men very romantically appealing. Strada wrote that despite their earlier difficulties, she and Octavio were seized in 1544 by a period of 'rare love and happiness' when he returned from a long absence, which is when their twins were conceived.[22] This is also dubious, as the couple were known to have struggled with their personal lives before and after the birth. Octavio backed Margaret on some state and family business against Philip of Spain, but privately they bickered, with one particularly visible and emotional confrontation between them at their son's wedding in 1565 leaving Margaret in tears.[23] It was also in Strada's interests to portray the birth of his patron, Alexander, the couple's son, in a romantic and lovingly intentional light. Strada was born in 1572 and would have been around 14 years of age on Margaret's death. Writing to enhance the power of the Farnese using state records, it's possible that he chose to portray the duchess positively as a strong ruler with a masculine nature, implying that his patron, her son, had inherited these desirable mannerisms. In any case, no evidence from Margaret's appearance, walk, political behaviour, favourite pastimes or the date of conception of her children can definitively support any modern claims around Margaret's preferred sexual orientation. It would be interesting, however, if any of Margaret's letters or sonnets to Laudomia, mentioned by Piccolomini, ever surfaced.

A stateswoman and a poet, the two women were destined to play different roles in the Renaissance era. But it is possible to see how they would have become close and enjoyed one another's company in the otherwise turbulent 1530s. Piccolomini wrote of Laudomia's 'witty and grave arguments', her interest in astronomy and aptitude for philosophical thought. Margaret would have found interesting and lively conversation with her, perhaps inspired by the older girl's eagerness for learning and her skill in writing verse, all things Margaret would have identified with after years of education at the cultured Habsburg court. Both women also had bold personalities. Margaret's protests against Philip of Spain and her father are well known, while Laudomia physically defended her city at the Siege of Siena in the 1550s. Her historical trace disappears, according to Konrad Eisenbichler in *The Sword and the Pen* in around 1555 and it is possible that she died during related military action, although this cannot be confirmed without further evidence coming to light.[24]

Throughout the 1560s, Margaret continued to govern the Netherlands under Philip's steady gaze, wrestling with religious conformity, stabilising the economy and regulating tensions between the native council and Spanish rulers. Earlier historians saw Margaret's initial years of governing as lucrative, providing a boost in trade, commerce and navigation. The writer Thomas Colley Grattan in 1831 credited her with overseeing a period of 'considerable prosperity', noting that millions of florins worth of wool, fish and other items were exported from the states under her watch.[25] But it was hard work. Exhausted and often frustrated, Margaret frequently asked for permission to abdicate, something Philip refused to grant until October 1567. Leaving Brussels the following December, she travelled to Italy, settling there until 1577 when she returned to the Netherlands to assist her son during his own political service there. She left for Italy once again in

1583 and died at the coastal town of Ortona on 18 January 1586. She lies buried in the Chiesa di San Sisto in Piacenza, Italy.

There is no doubt that some meaningful relationship, however brief or sporadic, existed between Laudomia Forteguerri and Margaret of Austria. Those known to the pair discussed it openly and praised them as a couple based on the affection they showed to one another, while Laudomia's surviving sonnets ardently compare the duchess to the sun and call her a 'goddess'. Those known to the pair described their connection as reciprocal and based on a form of love. However, while it is tempting to classify the pair today with what we might consider a lesbian relationship, we should be cautious. Both girls were promised to husbands at the time of their meeting and there is no evidence that their association was anything more than platonic, even if it was romantic in a sense. Even Piccolomini's descriptions surrounding the pair can be read as an exuberant and flattering account of a strong friendship with an emotional bond. Their ages also support this, with Margaret in particular especially young for a relationship with a woman seven years older than her. In addition, Margaret was the daughter of one of the most powerful men in Europe and would have been closely watched and guarded while in Siena and in the other cities and towns she visited. It is surprising then that more anecdotes of their interactions do not survive, particularly when considering Piccolomini's claim that Margaret returned to visit Laudomia in the late 1530s. Margaret, about to embark on her adult life in Italy, was probably simply struck by the visible confidence, intelligence and creativity of the older Forteguerri. This is even more likely when we consider that Margaret's reason for visiting Italy in the first place was to learn from and show herself among the Italian people, a motivation that ultimately created the opportunity for her to meet the poet Laudomia and her like-minded friends.

Other writers have also urged care in seeing Forteguerri's poems as evidence of a genuine romantic love for Margaret. Diana Maury Robin, in *Publishing Women: Salons, the Presses and the Counter-Reformation in Sixteenth-Century Italy*, argued that Laudomia's poetry may instead reflect political aims and that she had plenty of motivation to flatter the emperor's daughter to gain imperial influence.[26] This is further supported by the strong presence of symbols of authority in the poet's work, such as references to the 'sceptre' and 'empire'.[27] Charles V was certainly active in Siena at the time of the girls' first meeting and had already met with some resistance from the city's natives. It is significant that Piccolomini, the relationship's main promoter during the women's lifetimes, was also Sienese and motivated to protect his city. When they met, Margaret was preparing to marry a powerful Medici nobleman. She may have been welcomed into the cultural and exciting Sienese community in the hope that she would use her influence with either her father, future husband or other family members for the benefit of the city. Looking at the relationship from this point of view also explains why Laudomia's professions of love for the duchess survive, while any from Margaret so far have not. It is possible that Margaret, either realising that she was being flattered for political gain or simply unable to do anything for them, chose not to maintain contact with her friends in Siena. Until further evidence emerges, this seems a likely explanation.[28]

It is also possible to view the women's relationship in the context of a public expression of new Renaissance culture. The early twentieth-century writer Theodore Child discussed Firenzuola's *Dialogue on the Beauty of Women* which praises Margaret and Laudomia's bond as an example of the leap from the Middle Ages stance that was 'exclusively moral … too disdainful of beauty', towards the Renaissance love of attractiveness, luxury and excess.[29] Firenzuola used the relationship between Margaret and Laudomia to explore ways in which a form of intense love between two women could be accepted and admired in sixteenth-century society.

Whatever the nature of their relationship, they were considered a couple during their lifetimes, even if it was in terms of a platonic romance between two friends. Their bond was a force for lasting change, triggering events that would alter the progress of the Renaissance, encourage debate and inspire new works. Piccolomini, who had spoken to a room of fellow creatives and academics about the women, mentioned in his lecture that Forteguerri's sonnet to the duchess inspired him to create a similar work of his own. Not only had poetry based on same-sex female love now been introduced to the academic population, but it had motivated one of its writers to create a derivative work that would never have existed without it.

The work was also responsible for a number of firsts. Diana Maury Robin, in *Publishing Women: Salons, the Presses and the Counter-Reformation in Sixteenth-Century Italy*, called Piccolomini's lecture the 'first work of criticism on the poetry of a woman author ever published'.[30] Eisenbichler, in *The Sword and the Pen*, also wrote that Forteguerri may have been the 'first "lesbian" poet in the Italian vernacular tradition', although also emphasises that the same-sex love described may have been politically influenced.[31] If Laudomia was the first known female poet to explore romantic affection between women, others followed. Marie Maitland wrote expressing love between women in the 1580s, while Margaret Cavendish discussed two female characters in a work of 1666 whose 'meeting did produce such an intimate friendship between them, that they became Platonic Lovers, although they were both Females'.[32] Importantly, people were now talking about same-sex love as a thing of beauty and indulgence, inspiring other creatives to add their own works to the wider discussion.

As friends, lovers or as a poet and her muse, Laudomia and Margaret held power in different spheres. Margaret later governed the Netherlands and ruled over an army, a council and a state. The daughter of one of the most powerful men in Europe, she was known to princes, kings, popes and queens and knew first-hand how brutal and sudden the twists of sixteenth-century power could be. In contrast, Laudomia was a noble-born Sienese poet and intellectual, whose surviving verses left an enduring mystery surrounding the affection she bore to the Netherlands' future governess, as well as a trace of the power the 10-year-old Margaret had the potential to wield. Their bond inspired academics and other writers of their time, sparking new discussions on same-sex love and its place in an ever-changing Renaissance world.

Chapter 6

John Rolfe and Pocahontas of Virginia, North America

During the 1490s, details of Spain's lucrative expeditions to the New World continued to trickle into the correspondence of European rulers. Soon after Francesco Gonzaga and Isabella d'Este learned of an exotic land in the west filled with gold, 800 miles away a charismatic sailor from Bristol enthusiastically outlined his intention for a similar journey. A thoughtful man in his late thirties sat very still, listening as the sailor gesticulated in front of him. Henry VII of England was about to wade into the exploration of the Americas.

Four years after Columbus arrived off the shores of the Caribbean, word reached Ferdinand and Isabella of a voyage authorised by the Tudor king, Henry VII. Writing a bristling note to their ambassador Gonzales de Puebla on 28 March 1496, they fretted that Henry was being 'deceived' by the French with 'the premeditated intention of distracting him from his other business'. In a warning, they wrote that journeys like these were 'very uncertain enterprises, and must not be gone into at present', adding that 'they cannot be executed without prejudice to us and to the King of Portugal'.[1] But even as de Puebla unfurled the letter, preparations were being made to set sail. Early the following year, sacks and barrels were rolled onto the deck of *The Matthew*, a small wooden ship docked at Bristol, in readiness for its voyage. Headed by the Venetian sailor John Cabot, its crew of eighteen men left the southwestern port in May 1497 and landed on the sands of North America on 24 June.[2]

The Tudor monarchs led an ambitious and later, almost frantic campaign to establish overseas colonies and encourage further exploration of the Americas. Voyages set out in 1498, 1527 and 1536, but rapidly accelerated under Elizabeth I. In 1584, the crew of two ships captained by Philip Amadas and Arthur Barlowe under Sir Walter Raleigh's direction proclaimed that they had discovered a new land. The Natives, they said, called it Wingandacoa, but as the Englishmen stood proudly on its beach that July, they proclaimed that it would now be named Virginia, in honour of their red-haired Virgin Queen.[3]

Unsuccessful attempts to establish a colony on the site were made in July 1585. Settlers had arrived that summer only to complain to Francis Drake, during a chance visit, of lack of supplies from England. On a return voyage, the settlement was found empty. It was under the next monarch, James I of England and VI of Scotland, that a new and more successful phase in New World exploration would begin.

In April 1607, a wooden ship creaked unsteadily into Chesapeake Bay. As the Virginian coast slowly lurched into view, its crew prepared to disembark for a new life in what would be called Jamestown, in honour of their king. The new settlers had endured a long voyage hampered by storms and bad weather, but hostility of a different kind waited for them once they anchored. As they unloaded barrels of food and supplies and looked for a place to build shelter, the wary eyes of members of the nearby Powhatan community registered their arrival and reported the newcomers to their leader.

Records made by the Virginia settlers describe Natives swimming with bows in their mouths, shooting poisoned darts and engaging in 'devilish' worship. There were also attacks from both sides with food and supplies robbed and residents kidnapped. The two communities regarded their obvious differences with curiosity, distaste and marked hostility. However, one couple would soon peacefully unite these two worlds, trigger a wave of learning and understanding between them and impact lives on both sides of the Atlantic.

Matoaka, a young girl of about 12 years old, would have heard the dull, echoing thuds of mallet on wood as these new, pale-skinned settlers set about building shelters and repairing their ships. She was born in around 1595 and the English would later come to know her by the name Pocahontas. Her father was the Native Indian chief Powhatan, whom the English captain John Smith called 'The Emperor'. Smith described Pocahontas's father, whom he met in the summer of 1607, 'proudly lying upon a bedstead a foot high, upon ten or twelve mats, richly hung with many chains of great pearls about his neck, and covered with a great covering of racoon skins'. He remembered the leader was also accompanied by a group of women who wore necklaces made of beads and painted their heads and shoulders red. He had a natural grace and power, Smith said, sitting 'with such a majesty as I cannot express'.[4] Reports and letters show that Powhatan controlled a number of other local communities headed by chiefs under his command and had a reputation as a harsh and feared ruler.

Pocahontas's early life here in her father's village can be glimpsed in the records of Smith and the other early colonists. The Virginia climate was changeable, described as similar to Spain in the summer, while in winter, it reached temperatures like those in England or France. The area was prone to strong storms with thunder and lightning, although English settlers were grateful for the cool breezes that trickled across the landscape in the hottest weather. The world Pocahontas knew was shaped by hills and valleys intersected by rivers and brooks while tall oak trees reached into the sky. Settlers carefully recorded the creatures they encountered in Virginia that Pocahontas would have known such as wolves, raccoons, beavers, otters, turkeys and eagles.

The homes of the Powhatans consisted of long huts made by planting young trees in rows opposite one another and then tying them at the top to form a barrel-like frame. The sides were then lined with fabric, with a hole left at the top for smoke to escape from. Men wore their hair shaved on one side and long on the other, an effect created using the sharp edge of a shell to shear the hair close to the scalp. Clothing was made from skins or leaves. Englishmen also noticed the women's skin adorned with tattoos 'wrought into their flesh with black spots', and found them humble and 'very shamefast to be seen bare'.[5]

For their diet, they depended on what could be found locally. Corn was grown and made into bread and often spread with deer suet before being eaten. Meat and fish such as venison, oysters and sturgeon were boiled or roasted and dried fish was eaten in seasons when fresh meat was scarce. They also enjoyed fruits and nuts including walnuts, cherries, mulberries, strawberries, plums and beans. Pocahontas would have been familiar with the ceremonies conducted by priests to honour nature and the earth, but Captain Smith and the other devout Christians were stunned by them. Smith described one man wearing 'a great skin, his head hung round with little skins of weasels and other vermin, with a coronet of feathers on his head, painted as ugly as the devil' who howled, and cast food ingredients and tobacco leaves into the fire 'with strange and vehement actions'.[6] Smith's strong reaction to seeing these native practices of worship only show how different they were from the ordered and regulated Christian services he was used to in England.

Pocahontas would have known the homes of her father, one of which measured around 30–40 yards long and had a guard stationed on each of the four corners. He was always surrounded by advisors and was well guarded, with 'forty or fifty of the tallest men his country doth afford'. Captain John

Smith had numerous encounters with Powhatan and described him as 'a tall well-proportioned man, with a sour look, his head somewhat grey, his beard so thin that it seemeth none at all. His age near sixty; of a very able and hardy body to endure any labour'. Powhatan was fit and healthy, and 'esteemed as half a god' by his people. He used his appearance and power to full effect, Smith noting that, 'at the least frown of his brow, their greatest spirits will tremble with fear'.[7]

The young Pocahontas burst into the history books in December 1607 when Captain John Smith was hauled up in front of Powhatan and pushed onto a stone as a guard swung a club high above his head. Believing himself about to be executed, he credited Pocahontas with saving his life, taking his head in her hands and placing her upper body between Smith and the lunging weapon. He later remembered her as 'that blessed Pokahontas', who 'hazarded the beating out of her own brains to save mine'.[8]

A number of historians have doubted Smith's version of events. First, he has been widely criticised for only mentioning the rescue in his book, *The Generall Historie of Virginia*, in 1624, and in a letter written to Queen Anne of Denmark, James I's wife, in 1616. Surely such a hostile and dramatic event against one of James's diplomatic representatives would have deserved mention in one of his many reports back home. It is also interesting that the two sources that mention Pocahontas's heroism were created for Smith's own financial or social glory. We may never know if the event happened as Smith described, but we do know that he and Pocahontas were known to one another.

In his despatches to England, Smith recorded Pocahontas's efforts to help the English settlers despite her father's frequent anger towards them. She had served as an ambassador of sorts to the new English colony in the weeks and months before Smith's dramatic account, bringing the starving and despondent settlers fresh food and supplies. Smith also remembered a late-night visit when she brought intelligence of her father's impending attack on the colony. Smith and Pocahontas clearly formed a strong bond, but although it is sometimes told in terms of a love story, there is no evidence this was ever the case. It is more likely Smith saw Pocahontas as a pliable ally, grateful for her intervention and for prolonging the survival of his colony and contributing to his own success. Because of her efforts, the English community at Jamestown could take root. Smith's list of those who arrived in Virginia's 'first planting' of the colony included carpenters, labourers, a bricklayer, barber, surgeon and a blacksmith; professions vital to the building of a new, permanent settlement.[9]

Soon, others arrived in English ships, eager to start a new life in the lush, warm plains of Virginia. In 1609 Captain Smith sailed back to England, while a convoy of nine ships carrying another 500 settlers set sail for the American continent. Somewhere in one of these ships, tossed and turned by the bumpy waves, was John Rolfe.

Rolfe boarded a ship bound for Virginia with his heavily pregnant wife who gave birth to a daughter after the ship's arrival in Bermuda. The child sadly died shortly after she was baptised and was named after the islands. The early twentieth-century historian Lyon Gardiner Tyler believed that the Rolfes finally arrived in Virginia in May 1610, with John's wife also dying soon afterwards.[10] John therefore had to adapt to a new life in the colony without his wife and child.

It's believed John was the son of John Rolfe and Dorothea Mason, a family from Heacham in Norfolk. His baptism in that church is recorded on 6 May 1585, making him around 25 years old on his arrival in Virginia.[11] Like Pocahontas, specific details about his early life are sparse, however he becomes far more visible in the years following his arrival in the colony. Rolfe's letters show he was well educated, scientifically curious and morally sensitive. He was also well spoken, a natural problem solver and had a gift for recognising a commercial opportunity when he saw one.

It's not known exactly when Rolfe met his future bride; they had certainly met by the spring of 1613, the year she was captured by Captain Argal. With the deterioration of harmony between the English and Natives since Smith's departure back to England, Pocahontas stayed away from the colony. In April of that year, however, she was coaxed on board an English ship and held there to put pressure on her father to agree to the return of stolen goods and hostages, and to also agree to peace. To show that she was well kept, two of her brothers visited her and promised to return to Powhatan to convince him to resolve the situation. Master Sparkes and John Rolfe were sent to the chief to negotiate for the restoration of their goods and Pocahontas's release. They were met instead by Powhatan's brother, Opechancanough. According to Smith, as Rolfe negotiated for a cessation of hostilities with the Natives, he had already fallen for Pocahontas. The captain called Rolfe 'an honest gentleman, and of good behaviour', who was 'in love with Pocahontas, and she with him'.[12]

Rolfe was clearly anxious about his feelings for the 18-year-old Native. In a letter to the colony's deputy governor Sir Thomas Dale, he revealed that he was concerned over 'so mighty a matter' that his mind had 'a long time been so entangled'. He assured Dale that his love for Pocahontas was not driven by 'the unbridled desire of carnal affection; but for the good of this plantation, for the honour of our country, for the glory of God, for my own salvation, and for the converting to the true knowledge of God and Jesus Christ, an unbelieving creature, namely Pocahontas'.[13] Pocahontas and John Rolfe married on 5 April 1614 in Jamestown. The bride was given the English name of Rebecca although was still widely referred to in early Virginian documents as Pocahontas. Repeating their vows, they would have known that their marriage was the first of its kind, joining the Powhatan and English communities.

In his letter, Rolfe had urged that his marriage to Pocahontas was for the benefit of the plantation, a goal that was quickly achieved. Up until now, the settlers and Natives had lived together in erratic disharmony. The English settlement had now grown, with the establishment of three new Virginian towns in addition to their original base at Jamestown. However, thefts and kidnapping continued to take place, sometimes escalating into serious violence on both sides. English guns pointed stiffly from ships, while sharpened bone arrows silently took aim from tightened bowstrings. But from the moment John and Pocahontas were married, there was an understanding of peace. Smith later wrote that 'ever since [the marriage] we have had friendly trade and commerce, as well with Powhatan himself, as all his subjects'. He also noted that the union reconciled the English with the 'lusty and daring' Chickahominy tribe, who, on hearing of the wedding, promised from now on to be subjects of King James I of England.[14]

Sources, admittedly written by the English, maintain that Pocahontas willingly embedded herself in the settlers' culture and religion. This is sometimes explained as having come from a curious fascination with English life, as well as the love she had for her husband. Before their marriage, Rolfe wrote in a private letter that she possessed a 'desire to be taught and instructed in the knowledge of God … understanding, aptness and willingness to receive any good impression' and spoke of her 'own incitements stirring me up hereunto'.[15] Later, settlers would note how she had been 'taught to speak such English as might well be understood, well instructed in Christianity, and was become very formal and civil after our English manner'.[16] Pocahontas certainly seems to have fully adopted English customs, but it is not clear what may have motivated her to leave her old life behind. Writers have generally put this down to a fascination with the English, a wish to adopt the culture of her husband or a disillusionment of some sort with her Native community.

Whatever Pocahontas's motivation, the marriage brought a tentative peace to both sides. Colony leaders could now boast of a Native royal family member that had been converted to Christianity and integrated into English culture. In 1607 colonists endured animosity, illness, adversity and starvation, but seven years later it had its first interracial marriage and the promised obedience of Native tribes to the English king. A son, Thomas, cemented the couple's union. All that remained now was to make the colony a financial success.

Some of Pocahontas's earliest memories would have involved tobacco. Its smoke curled up into the air in thick wisps during tribal ceremonies and the leaves were sprinkled into water and the earth. Burned to appease gods, it was also smoked as a mark of respect to welcome visitors and guests. Smith wrote that Powhatan offered him tobacco at one of his meetings, smoked in a pipe up to three feet long.[17] The Powhatan tribe carefully planted and harvested this sacred herb and Pocahontas, like any Native American, would have known a great deal about its use and cultivation.

It is significant then, that John Rolfe's commercial fame comes from making a success of the planting and sale of the very commodity Pocahontas and her community cherished. Modern historians have tentatively attributed Pocahontas with a role in her husband's success, even if it is not openly given in the historical record. Her influence seems certainly probable, even though Rolfe is commonly celebrated in his own right as the founder of the English tobacco industry in Virginia.

Rolfe's tobacco, however, was different to that smoked, scattered and grown by the Natives. He managed to obtain seeds from the Caribbean and grew them in Virginian soil, resulting in a sweeter blend that better suited the tastes of distinguished customers back home. In the summer of 1615, *The Flying Horse of Flushing* sailed from Virginia with Rolfe's new tobacco blend, heading for Portsmouth in the south of England. However, the crop was not yet to Rolfe's satisfaction. He wrote, the following year, of his tobacco that 'no doubt but after a little more trial and expense in the curing thereof, it will compare with the best in the West Indies'.[18]

Rolfe was diligent in evaluating and improving his crop. Experimenting with technique, he planted, harvested and smoked until the quality was satisfactory and sales could turn a profit. It is unthinkable that Pocahontas was not in any way involved in this process. As well as having more knowledge than anyone on the colony about cultivating and harvesting tobacco, she had already shown herself inquisitive and dedicated to Rolfe and his culture, and earlier to the success and longevity of the colony. It follows logically that this considerate, moral and intelligent woman with knowledge of the settlement's previous hardships would collaborate with

Above left: Cosimo de Medici, considered the founding father of the city of Florence and the Medici dynasty. His often-forgotten wife, Contessina, was his loyal business partner, advisor, personal assistant and confidante. (Cosimo de Medici the Elder, Unknown Artist, 1465–1469 (The Metropolitan Museum of Art))

Above right: An eighteenth-century view of Florence. Here, while Cosimo and Contessina de Medici conducted business, craftsmen debated new ideas in art and architecture in the piazza under the shadow of the cathedral's dome. (A Procession in Florence c. 1733–1755, Giuseppe Zocchi & Bernardo Sansone Sgrilli (Rijksmuseum))

This gilded winged sprite, made in 1432, once decorated a fountain at the Medici home in Florence, near Donatello's bronze sculpture of *David*. The couple filled their home with fine art inspired by classical antiquity. (*Sprite*, Sculptor close to Donatello, 1432 (The Metropolitan Museum of Art))

Left: The introduction of the printing press in England had huge consequences for late medieval society and beyond. The marriage of Edward IV to Elizabeth Woodville, brought about and furthered its foundation at Westminster in the 1470s. (Earl Rivers presenting his book and Caxton, his printer, to Edward IV. Charles Grignion, 1717–1810 (Yale Center for British Art))

Below: Edward IV commissioned the grand rebuilding of St George's Chapel inside the grounds of Windsor Castle. He and Elizabeth Woodville were buried there. (St George's Chapel Choir, Windsor. Wenceslaus Hollar, 1663 (The Metropolitan Museum of Art))

Above: A painting of The Alhambra Palace in Granada, Spain, created in 1865 by Samuel Colman. Its capture in 1492 enlarged the territories of Ferdinand and Isabella. (*The Hill of the Alhambra*, Granada. Samuel Colman, 1865. (The Metropolitan Museum of Art))

Right: Ferdinand and Isabella's coat of arms, displayed on the queen's private book. The couple's union triggered political and geographical domination, as well as religious change. (Hours of Queen Isabella the Catholic, Master of the First Prayerbook of Maximilian and Associates, c. 1500 (Cleveland Museum of Art))

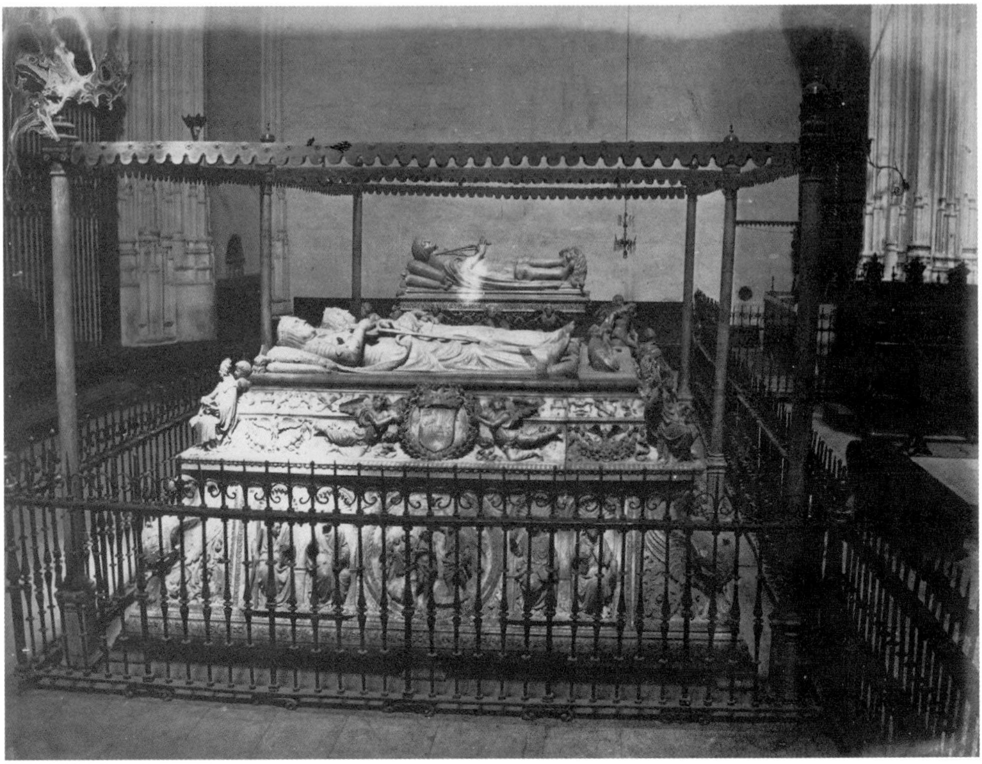

Above: Early twentieth-century photograph of the effigies of the Catholic monarchs, Ferdinand of Aragon and Isabella of Castile, in Granada. (Tomb of the Catholic Monarchs Isabella I of Castile and Ferdinand II of Aragon in the Chapel of the Cathedral of Granada, Spain. Attributed to C. Maufsaise, c. 1906. (Rijksmuseum))

Left: A depiction of St Sebastian, c. 1470–1490, by Francesco Bonsignori. His patron, Francesco Gonzaga, Marquis of Mantua, pushed the artist out of his comfort zone, at least once with the aid of a loaded crossbow. (*St. Sebastian*. Attributed to Francesco Bonsignori, Mantua, 1470–1490 (Rijksmuseum))

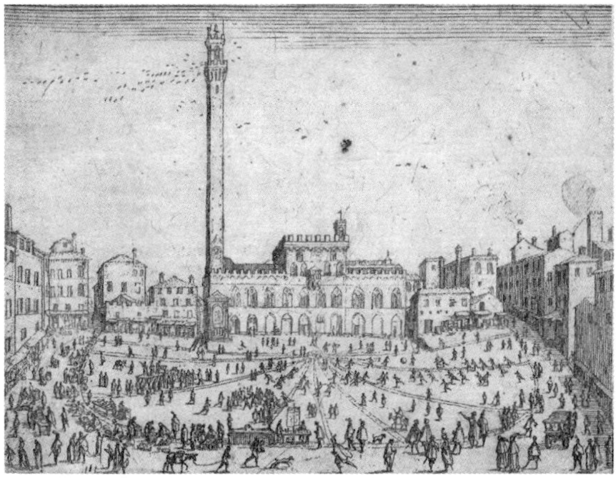

Above left: Margaret of Austria, illegitimate daughter of Habsburg Emperor Charles V. Literature written in her honour in the 1530s encouraged new debates on same-sex female love. (Margaret of Austria. Medal by Jacques Jonghelinck, 1567 (The Metropolitan Museum of Art))

Above right: Seventeenth-century depiction of the city of Siena, believed to have been the site of Margaret of Austria's first meeting with the Sienese poet Laudomia Forteguerri. (*Piazza del Campo in Siena*, c. 1675 by Melchiorre Gherardini (Rijksmuseum))

On her visit to England between 1616–1617, Simon van de Passe made an engraving of Pocahontas, a businesswoman, celebrity and campaigner. (Matoaka als Rebeka, Daughter of the Mighty Powhatan. Simon van de Passe, 1627 (The New York Public Library Digital Collections))

Above: A nineteenth-century imagining of the marriage of Native Indian princess Pocahontas and the Englishman John Rolfe in Virginia in 1614. Their partnership changed lives on both sides of the Atlantic. (*The Wedding of Pocahontas with John Rolfe*. George Spohni, c. 1867 (Library of Congress))

Left: Mughal Emperor of Hindustan Shah Jahan and his wife, enforced power with displays of public wealth, military might and ceremony. He was also a lover of European Renaissance art, demonstrated by the cupids that hover above him in this depiction. (Shah Jahan on a Terrace, Holding a Pendant Set with His Portrait, Shah Jahan Album. Chitarman, 1627–1628 (The Metropolitan Museum of Art))

The union of Shah Jahan and Mumtaz Mahal is memorialised in the Taj Mahal, today considered one of the Wonders of the World. (A View of the Taj Mahal by Oswald Lübeck, 1911. (Deutsche Fototek))

Below left: Catherine of Braganza, Charles II's Portuguese bride, as he would first have seen her, in 1662. She is often forgotten in discussions of Restoration Britain but contributed to the artistic, military and architectural identity of the realm. (Catherine of Braganza. William Faithorne the Elder, after Dirck Stoop, 1662 (The Metropolitan Museum of Art))

Below right: A seventeenth-century engraving of Charles II consulting advisors following London's Great Fire of 1666. His active collaboration with his wife in the aftermath of the event is less well-known. (Cartoon Showing Charles II and the Fire, Unknown Artist, seventeenth century (Yale Center for British Art))

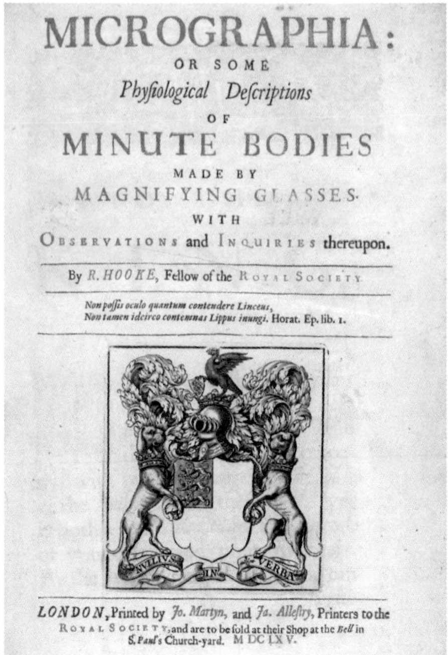

MICROGRAPHIA:
OR SOME
Physiological Descriptions
OF
MINUTE BODIES
MADE BY
MAGNIFYING GLASSES.
WITH
OBSERVATIONS and INQUIRIES thereupon.

By *R. HOOKE*, Fellow of the ROYAL SOCIETY.

Non possis oculo quantum contendere Linceus,
Non tamen idcirco contemnas Lippus inungi. Horat. Ep. lib. 1.

NVLLIVS IN VERBA

LONDON, Printed by *Jo. Martyn*, and *Ja. Allestry*, Printers to the ROYAL SOCIETY, and are to be sold at their Shop at the *Bell* in S. *Paul's* Church-yard. M DC LX V.

Above left: William and Margaret Cavendish, later Duke and Duchess of Newcastle, and their family in exile in 1656. Together they made significant progress to the arts, sciences and literature as well as to the roles of women in the seventeenth century. They can be seen seated to the right of the picture. (The Family of William Cavendish, Marquess of Newcastle-upon-Tyne. Peeter Clouwet, after Abraham van Diepenbeeck, 1656 (The Metropolitan Museum of Art))

Above right: Margaret Cavendish drew on the latest scientific discoveries in her work, now considered an early form of science fiction. In particular, she referenced Robert Hooke's research of a microscopic world in his *Micrographia*. (Title page from Robert Hooke's *Micrographia*. Robert Hooke, 1665 (Courtesy of Science History Institute))

While her husband Jan Miense Molenaer continued to find fame after his death, Judith Leyster's contribution to Dutch art was lost until the late nineteenth century. *The Serenade*, dated to 1629, is today considered one of her finest works. (A Lute Player, known as *The Serenade*. Judith Leyster, 1629 (Rijksmuseum))

her husband to create a new blend of tobacco to help secure their livelihood. In any case, the success of the plantation was in her personal interest now, too, as she had not only herself and her husband, but a young child to help support.

Thanks to the efforts of Rolfe, and likely also Pocahontas, Virginia was soon taken over by a tobacco-planting craze. Reports between 1615 and 1616 mentioned settlers' eagerness to plant the now-lucrative tobacco and their reluctance to grow any other crop for food. This threatened the future of the colony and Sir Thomas Dale issued an order requiring each man to 'set two acres of ground with corn, which doing they may plant as much tobacco as they will, else all their tobacco shall be forfeit to the colony'. Virginia's tobacco industry had begun and in 1616 twenty-five men were 'employed only in planting and curing tobacco' at West and Sherley Hundred, a plantation site established northwest of Chesapeake and on the James River.[19] By 1619 the Secretary of Virginia, John Pory, wrote that 'all our riches for the present do consist in tobacco, wherein one man by his own labour hath in one year raised himself to the value of £200 sterling; and another by the means of six servants hath cleared at one crop a thousand pound English'. Modern currency conversions are not straightforward, but as a rough guide for context, £1,000 in 1619 has an equivalent worth today of around £130,000.[20]

There is no doubt that both Rolfe and Pocahontas deeply respected the tobacco plant, albeit for different reasons, Rolfe's being primarily commercial, while Pocahontas' was cultural and spiritual. Perhaps though, these very different priorities resulted in the success of Rolfe's enterprise. He had been experimenting with the crop since at least 1612, before his marriage, and collaboration of some kind may have been under way soon after the couple's meeting in 1613.[21] Rolfe, it will be remembered, stated in 1614 that his marriage to Pocahontas was 'for the good of the plantation'. Between discussions of English law and religious doctrine, it's not unthinkable that the couple may have already dabbled in Rolfe's other passion of cultivation. He would therefore have already known, when he wrote the letter, that she could contribute towards the colony's success.

John Rolfe has been praised for his achievements in producing 'the first crop cultivated by an Englishman in America', and named 'the pioneer tobacco-planter of Virginia'.[22] Her husband may have taken all the credit on paper for the success of his tobacco blend, but Pocahontas would soon embark on an adventure that placed her at the forefront of England's high society.

On 12 June 1616 a wooden ship called *The Treasurer* limped into Plymouth, on the southwest coast of England.[23] This was Pocahontas's first glance at a country whose people, culture and customs had been part of her life since she was a young girl. She would have seen the cobbled paths of the city's Barbican, closely set with huddles of timber-framed and stone structures housing merchants, sailors and their families. Beyond the masts of ships, the tower of the church of St Andrew rose into the sky. Pocahontas was accompanied by her husband and son, along with Sir Thomas Dale, Captain John Martin and around twelve American Natives. Naturally, the holds of the ship were well stocked with Rolfe's 'exceeding good tobacco', as well as sturgeon, caviar, pitch, sassafras and other produce.[24]

The party made their way to London. It is generally believed that they settled into lodgings at the Belle Sauvage Inn on Ludgate Hill, a site also confirmed by Grace Steele Woodward in the book *Pocahontas*.[25] Originally named The Bell on the Hoop, the fifteenth-century inn stood on Ludgate Hill near St Paul's Cathedral. The building no longer survives, but drawings show that it was large, with three floors and further windows set into the eaves of the roof. Balconies were constructed on the two upper storeys and an archway led to the bustling London streets outside. Carts and carriages could turn in its courtyard and drop off guests and their luggage. They could then be taken to their rooms. There is a suggestion that the inn's name, which translates as 'Beautiful Savage', was later named to commemorate Pocahontas's visit there. However, records show that it already had this name in 1554, more than sixty years before her arrival, its origin in a local family name. It is possible, of course, that the image-savvy party chose the inn specifically to underline and draw attention to the exotic nature of its special guest. A series of the inn's tokens exhibited to the public after her visit, shown in the years 1648 and 1672, depicted 'an Indian woman holding a bow and arrow', although the date of their creation is not known.[26]

With its many rooms and corridors, the Belle Sauvage would have lodged the Rolfes and their entourage comfortably and it was here that visitors flocked to meet the American princess. The playwright Ben Jonson was one of those who met Pocahontas here, later acknowledging her in his play *The Staple of News*, first performed in 1626. He called her 'the blessed Pokahontas ... in womb of a taverne'.[27] Seventeenth-century playwrights were the communicators and content writers of their day and any mention of the colony or its glamorous and exotic resident gained the Virginia Company much-needed exposure and support. But the couple's stay was not a social one. She publicly represented the Natives of Virginia and her presence gave visible confirmation that they were, at least in principle, willing to adopt English customs, dress and religion. Dignified, smiling and patient in her meetings with dignitaries, she told stories of lush vegetation, a warm climate and fertile soil, all aimed to attract wealthy investors and future settlers to Jamestown.

One portrait survives of Pocahontas during her stay in London, engraved by Simon van de Passe. It is the only known likeness made of Pocahontas from life and shows her as she would have appeared to English aristocrats in London. A copy made after the engraving, in 1627, is today in the collection of the New York Public Library.[28] Pocahontas is depicted in a tall, brimmed hat along with pearl earrings, a stiff Jacobean lace collar and a delicately embroidered gown. In her right hand she gently holds a fan made from feathers. Her gaze is assured and confident, and her lips set firmly together with the faintest hint of a polite smile. The engraving identifies her as 'daughter to the mighty Prince Powhatan Emperor' and once again highlights her conversion to the Christian faith. Like her visit, the creation of this portrait was deliberate. Able to last long after she had returned home, it served as a reminder of Pocahontas's conversion and gave evidence of England's growing influence overseas.

One interesting exchange occurred during a visit to the Rolfes by Captain John Smith. Pocahontas had grown ill, something sometimes blamed on the pollution of London's smoky, tightly knit streets, but it could equally have been the exhaustion of her relentless socialising and mixing with strangers. She was moved to Brentford where Smith visited her, although he stated that he also saw her in London. Smith remembered that she was visibly upset on first seeing him, having believed he had died since leaving the colony in 1609. Seeing his wife becoming increasingly agitated, Rolfe helped manage the situation, encouraging those present to give her space to regain her composure, although it might not have been the 'two or three hours' that the ever-dramatic Smith claimed.[29] This event serves as another example of the couple's affection, with Rolfe prioritising the needs of his wife over the arrival of important dignitaries.

Smith, as a previous Deputy Governor of Virginia, would have known the social and commercial impact of placing Pocahontas in front of members of the royal family, in particular James I and his queen, Anne of Denmark. Funding and resources were important to the future of the settlement, but only James could dictate laws and charters to aid its growth. In his *Generall Historie*, Smith included a copy of the letter he wrote to the queen. In it, he underlined the service Pocahontas had willingly carried out for England as lifesaver, peacekeeper and supporter of the early colony at Jamestown. He argued that she possessed 'extraordinary affection to our nation' and was the 'first Christian ever of that Nation, the first Virginian ever spake English, or had a child in marriage by an Englishman'. She was also, he dangled, 'the ordinance of God to make her his instrument'. Failure to give the princess a royal audience, warned Smith, might 'turn to such scorn and fury, as to divert all this good to the worst of evil'.[30]

With James and Anne suitably praised, warned and persuaded, Pocahontas and a Native companion named Tomocomo were invited to the royal court at Whitehall to attend Twelfth Night festivities on 6 January 1617 with the king and queen. Cecily, Lady de la Warr, the wife of the Captain General of Virginia, Thomas de la Warr, was appointed to accompany Pocahontas to the palace. There, Pocahontas danced with the earls of Buckingham and Montgomery.[31] If John Rolfe was present, he remained in the background. Smiling and conversing her way through feasts and dances she also watched a performance of Ben Jonson's masque *The Vision of Delight*. Smith later wrote that 'it pleased both the King and Queen's Majesty honourably to esteem her, accompanied with that honourable Lady the Lady De la Ware, and that honourable Lord her husband, and divers other persons of good qualities, both publicly at the masques and otherwise, to her great satisfaction and content'.[32] Pocahontas even publicly protested that returning home was 'sore against her will', which may have reflected her own opinion, but could equally have been a display of polite enthusiasm towards her hosts.[33]

The Rolfes had now been more than six months in England, continually selling the benefits of the settlement in Virginia to royalty, aristocracy and the country's prominent thinkers and businessmen. For Pocahontas, it was an intensive cycle of meeting and greeting while her husband, never far from her, enthusiastically spoke of the many goods that could be found there, including of course, his new blend of tobacco.

In March 1617, the couple prepared to travel back to Virginia. As they sailed along the English coast that May in a vessel named *The George*, a number of those onboard fell ill, including Pocahontas and her son Thomas. Pocahontas's health suddenly worsened and she died onboard. Her body was taken to nearby Gravesend, where she was buried in St George's Church near the River Thames. The burial register records: 'Rebecca Wrothe wyffe of Thomas [sic] Wroth, gent, a Virginia lady borne, here was buried in ye channncel'.[34] The mistaken identification of Thomas as her husband (the scribe perhaps confusing it with the name of her son) may relate some of the hurried panic and confusion of that tragic day.

Pocahontas's death was likely caused by a bacterial or viral infection, contracted through exposure to dozens of excited guests and exacerbated by exhaustion. Pocahontas and her entourage would have tackled infections in England against which their bodies had not had the chance to build a resistance. At least three of the Rolfes' Native American travel companions died in London the previous year, and some of the party on *The George* were ill at the same time as Pocahontas.[35] Two-year-old Thomas survived his mother, but was considered too ill to travel with his father and stayed behind in Plymouth. The decision to leave his son in the English city weighed on Rolfe's conscience and he wrote on his arrival in Virginia that he worried about being judged for this, a decision ultimately made by Captain Argyl. 'My wife's death is much lamented,' he wrote on 9 June 1617, 'my child much desired, when it is of better strength to endure so hard a passage, whose life greatly extinguisheth the sorrow of her loss, saying all must die, but tis enough that her child liveth.'[36]

John Rolfe remained in Virginia and died in 1622, killed during hostilities between the English and Native Americans after a breakdown in the peace initially established by his and Pocahontas's marriage eight years earlier.

Traditionally, Pocahontas and John Rolfe's marriage is seen in terms of a true love story. Rolfe's own words, written in his private letter to Dale, reveal that he was 'provoked' in his love for her, and she in turn showed 'great appearance of love to me'. Rolfe admired her willingness to learn and wrote of 'her own incitements' to attain knowledge and adopt English customs. He also stated that he would pray to God for his and her 'eternal happiness'. Even Smith, who met the couple, vouched for their bond, writing that 'the true affection she constantly bare her husband was much, and the strange apparitions and violent passions he endured for her love, as he deeply protested, was wonderful'.[37] Rolfe seems to have been genuinely bereft at his wife's death, writing in a letter to Sir Edwin Sandys that 'greate is my loss, and much my sorrow to be deprived of so greate a comfort … as in her whose soule (I doubt not) resteth in eternall happyness'.[38]

Despite their obvious cultural differences, the couple seem to have had many things in common. Both were strongly motivated towards the social and financial success of the Virginian colony. From her early years Pocahontas acted as a diplomat between the English and her father and eventually joined the English community. Rolfe was also dedicated to the future of Virginia, crafting and perfecting the cultivation of tobacco for profit and accepting a position of leadership within the Company of

Virginia. Both would later embark on their famous tour in England to help raise interest and funds for the future of the settlement.

There is also evidence that they heavily supported one another in their marriage. Although Rolfe has received most of the credit for the foundation of the tobacco industry, it is almost certain that Pocahontas instructed and advised her husband, drawing on information she had learned growing up in the Powhatan community. Similarly, Pocahontas remained the focus of the curious and adoring English public in 1616–17, but Rolfe was always present, even helping his wife to readjust in private after her emotional meeting with Captain John Smith.

It is impossible for us to really know the personalities of Pocahontas and John Rolfe, but there are hints that tell us more about their interactions as a couple. She is depicted in Virginia records as energetic and free spirited, although later displaying determination and independence as she secretly communicated with Smith. She was inquisitive, bold, eager to learn and brave in her decision to not only approach the settlers, but begin a new life with a culture and values that were so vastly different to her own. As for Rolfe, his writings reveal a man who was rigid, religiously devout, morally obedient and well educated. He was determined and prone to perfectionism, working to perfect his tobacco blend until he believed it a worthy commercial product. But he was also modest, willing to stand back and allow his wife to take the spotlight while he waited by her side. Eyewitness accounts of the couple agree that they were happy up until Pocahontas's death in 1617.

Their relationship altered the course of events on both sides of the Atlantic. First, their marriage secured a peace between English settlers and the Powhatan Natives which lasted for almost ten years. Although there were still isolated hostile events, lifespans on each side were lengthened, ensuring that the colony – and the Powhatan community – could grow unimpeded during those years. It also resulted in a ceasefire with the Chickahominys, an adjoining tribe who pledged loyalty to the settlers on hearing of the marriage. Neither peace could have been achieved without co-operation between Rolfe and his bride. By 1622, however, with Powhatan and Pocahontas both dead, tensions returned and the new Powhatan leader Opechancanough led a rebellion against the English, in which Rolfe was killed.

Both partners also played visible roles in the commercial and social growth of the Virginia plantation. John Rolfe worked as its secretary and member of the council. Through his tobacco cultivation he offered, for the first time, a chance for the settlement to become self-sufficient economically.

As discussed, although Rolfe achieved a sellable blend in 1612, real commercial success came after his marriage to Pocahontas. By May 1617, planting was well under way and there were real hopes that the crop might support the colony financially.[39] Soon afterwards, prices for tobacco were set and regulated and by the summer of 1618, growers were making comfortable profits. As the writer Alexander Brown stated regarding the period, 'tobacco was fast becoming better than a gold mine.'[40] Later, Virginia tobacco would become well known outside of the Americas and in England, leading to the growth of this and other related commercial industries, such as the production of tobacco pots and cases and, of course, pipes for smoking. In 1620 the Tobacco Pipe Makers Company received its incorporation in a charter from James I, subsequently confirmed by Charles I and Charles II. Its device was based on a tobacco plant sprouting out of the soil.

The couple's visit to London in 1616 brought another level of change. Rolfe packed a stash of tobacco to lure investors, but it was the exotic 'Indian Princess' that people flocked to see. Charming the English public, one observer wrote that she 'did not only accustom herself to civility, but still carried herself as the daughter of a King'.[41] Pocahontas, dressed in stiff Jacobean outfits and smiling demurely to England's aristocrats, headed a public relations campaign that had everyone with funds and ambition talking about Virginia. She impressed James I and Queen Anne so much, that in 1617 James ordered schools and churches to be built in Virginia 'for the education of the children'. His statement that the act was inspired 'in furtherance of the hopeful zeal of diverse particular persons of honour' may refer to Pocahontas herself, or at least, those she influenced during her stay.[42] The constant public references to her conversion to Christianity not only gave outward hope that other Natives might adopt the religion, but also implied that the settlement had some level of divine approval. As Smith wrote, those she met in London 'concluded they did think God had a great hand in her conversion'.[43]

After Pocahontas's death, more English settlers set sail to begin a new life in Virginia. By Easter 1619, numbers at the colonies had reached 1,000 and by 1622 3,570.[44] Gradually an attempt at forming a cohesive government in the growing colony was made, and ships began to sail more regularly between England and its new overseas communities. The couple's own names survive today in some of the placenames of North America, which include Rolfe, a city in Pocahontas County in the state of Iowa. There is also Jamestown, named after their royal host and the Virginia town of Pocahontas. The couple therefore shaped the development and establishment of the settlement of North America as we know it today.

Finally, the couple created the enduring legend of Pocahontas that rolled off the printing press shortly after their visit to London. Captain John Smith, the adventurer she met in 1607, wrote his *The Generall Historie of Virginia* in 1624, establishing in the historical record events such as the daring saving of his life, her role in preserving the early colony and her meeting with England's king and queen. Smith's account later inspired further historical fiction, music, poetry and art based on the princess. While the de Passe engraving is the only known contemporary likeness of Pocahontas, the couple were reimagined during the eighteenth and nineteenth centuries with painters depicting her baptism, meeting with James I and the couple exchanging vows at their wedding in Jamestown.

Pocahontas and John Rolfe were an unusual couple, born almost 4,000 miles apart, who would never have met were it not for the thirst for knowledge and exploration triggered by the Renaissance. Their lives were conducted during an explosive period of learning and development that enabled them to make lasting change, not only to their contemporaries, but to future generations. Advances made in England in the sixteenth century in shipbuilding and navigation led to the first plans for English settlements on American soil that later resulted in Rolfe's ship drunkenly lurching onto the North American shore in 1610. The printing press, so heavily patronised in the mid-fifteenth century, was crucial to spreading information about the Virginian settlement, pressing into legend the story of their meeting and marriage, as well as Pocahontas's likeness. They were a powerful couple in terms of status, Pocahontas through her links to Emperor Powhatan and his tribe, and Rolfe through his roles in local government and commerce. But they also demonstrated a tireless dedication to the success and quality of life in the English colony of Virginia, helping to assimilate cultural differences and defending their unique relationship. As public figures, they worked to change lives on both sides of the Atlantic geographically, socially, politically and economically.

Chapter 7

Shah Jahan and Mumtaz Mahal, Mughal Rulers of Hindustan

Today two tombs lie, one awkwardly off-centre, under the marble dome of the Taj Mahal monument in Agra, India. The structure, built in the mid-seventeenth century, is widely regarded as one of the world's 'wonders' with photographers, filmmakers and artists all eager to capture its delicate and magnificent form. However, it is the story of the two individuals buried underneath its pearlescent dome that reveal an often-neglected side of the Renaissance era.

Hindustan in thc 1600s was lively and colourful, a bustling community of local and foreign residents. The land contemporary travellers described in their reports and journals reveal the character and appearance of cities, towns and villages then under Mughal rule. The French visitor Jean-Baptiste Tavernier observed oxen lumbering down lanes and streets carrying bags of corn, rice and salt, riders on their backs steering them like horses. This was not without some danger, Tavernier noting with some horror at least one occurrence when an ox with large horns shook its head to repel flies and accidentally plunged a horn into the stomach of its rider.[1] Other commodities included wheat and cotton, while fine muslin cloth was produced and exported to Persia, Turkey and Poland. Visitors also reported the production of indigo, a natural pigment used to make a vivid, rich blue dye. Agate was mined and crafted into delicate ornaments, cups and knife handles, while saltpetre was made into gunpowder. Peter Mundy, an English observer, noted the production of opium from poppies and the seeds from the flower heads sprinkled over bread.[2]

Those lucky enough to be hosted at feasts held by Mughal emperors reported golden plates filled with raisins, almonds, sliced lemons and pistachios. Salads were served alongside roasted, fried or boiled meats, all washed down with cups of wine and brandy. Mundy also noted a wide variety of trees growing in different areas of the empire, their leafy branches heavy with mangoes, pineapples, figs, apples, limes and oranges.[3]

The intense heat of the region might have been good for growing sweet, exotic fruits, but it made travelling arduous, especially for foreigners. A long trip was often therefore conducted at night, when the air was cooler. Wealthier subjects journeyed a little more comfortably, in satin-covered carriages covered with adjustable sides and canopies. Servants could then walk alongside the carriage and reposition the canopy to provide more shade as the sun's position shifted throughout the trip.[4] Foreign travellers to the realm also noted the erratic weather conditions, which swung dramatically from intense heat to rainstorms and flooding.

Visitors were enthralled by the realm's wildlife, which included peacocks, crocodiles, snakes and rhinoceroses. Monkeys were a common sight and Tavernier noticed locals leaving food out to deter them from pulling the tiles off houses and raiding the contents for themselves.[5] A representative of the East India Company, Peter Mundy reported with shock 'a loose elephant near about the river', that was eventually caught and returned to its owner, while the English ambassador Sir Thomas Roe was alarmed to find a lion and a wolf entering his home in search of the household's sheep and goats.[6]

Not all the animals caused havoc, with the Mughal court proud of its well-trained creatures that took pride of place at public ceremonies. Elephants were tamed and trained to help hunt, clear woodlands and serve in the army as an intimidating and powerful line of defence against an enemy. In royal processions they wore chains, metal rings on their tusks and jewel-studded plates, with people riding high on their backs, gazing down at the assembled crowds. Roe was told that the Emperor Jahangir, who ruled between 1605 and 1627, owned a lion that 'went up and down amongst the people that frequented his court, gently as a dog and never did hurt, only he had some keepers which did continually wait upon him'.[7]

The leader we know today as Shah Jahan was born Prince Khurram in 1592 to the Emperor Jahangir and one of his women, identified by Jahangir in his memoirs as a daughter of Moutah Rajah. Khurram's father noted that the prince was possessed 'of the brightest intellectual endowments' and hoped that in the future he would 'prove uninterruptedly progressive, as he is in all things conspicuously discreet'.[8] While conducting state business, Sir Thomas Roe chose to interpret Khurram's discretion as arrogance, finding him distant, challenging and difficult to deal with. In one report of 1616, he called Khurram 'proud, subtle, false and barbarously tyrannous', concluding that he found the greatest honour in acts of war.[9] Roe became irritated by the prince's demands for expensive presents at each meeting and, in early October 1617, walked out of an audience with Khurram, after the prince requested to defer their meeting to sunrise. Roe stormed out of his presence, pausing to retort that he was not the prince's 'slave', but the ambassador of a king (King James I of England), which resulted in a much cooler reception by Khurram the following day. 'I made reverence to the prince,' Roe wrote sheepishly, 'but he would not once stir his head.'[10]

At the time, Khurram was married to Arjumand Banu Begam, born in 1593. Generations of her family had served in Mughal governments and so from a young age Arjumand would have heard relatives discussing politics, power tactics and their service to the royal family. Khurram, in line with custom, was permitted to marry multiple wives and Arjumand was not his only bride. His first wife was the princess Kandahari Begum, whom he married in 1609 with a daughter born to the pair in the summer of 1611. In 1612 he married Arjumand. He later took a third wife, the daughter of a nobleman with military connections, in September 1617.[11]

Legend states that Khurram and Arjumand's marriage was based on love, while his other marriages satisfied political or military aims. Arjumand was elevated to a public role above the other women and we know that she also travelled with her husband across the empire on state business. The distribution of the prince's children between his wives also reveals their heightened intimacy. Each of the prince's other wives birthed one child each, while Arjumand and her husband produced fourteen children between 1614 and 1631.

Shah Jahan would dominate history as a famous and fearful leader, descended from fierce heads of Mughal royalty. But Arjumand also came from a politically powerful family. Her father, Asaf Khan, served Emperor Jahangir and later, Shah Jahan. He was an indispensable figure in the emperor's government, negotiating with ambassadors and providing or denying access to the royal presence, as required. Asaf Khan's sister, Nur Jahan, was Jahangir's wife and queen. Their father, Ettemaud-ud-Doulah, also served Jahangir. Nur Jahan and her brother Asaf Khan found an opportunity to exert increased power during the reign of Shah Jahan's father. Reports suggest that the Emperor Jahangir's character was in marked contrast to his son's, showing him to be jovial, generous and fond of alcohol. As Jahangir slipped into a reliance on eating, drinking and women, Nur and her brother were able to steer the reins of government to their own ends. Thomas Roe called the family a 'powerful faction', who 'now govern all and dare attempt anything'.[12] Jahangir himself wrote in his memoirs a little more optimistically, that 'the whole fortune of my empire has been consigned to the disposal of this highly endowed family; the father being my diwan, the son my lieutenant-general, with unlimited powers, and the daughter the inseparable companion of all my cares'.[13]

Jahangir died on 28 October 1627 and after a brief struggle for power, Shah Jahan ascended the throne at Agra on 6 February 1628.[14] Arjumand, or Mumtaz Mahal as she was now named, performed her own role at the occasion, where her husband awarded her with a large quantity of cash, along with ten lakhs of rupees as her annual allowance (estimated as equivalent to one million rupees by Waldemar Hansen in *The Peacock Throne: The Drama of Mogul India*).[15] According to the contemporary account, the *Shah Jahan Nama* by Inayat Khan, she was also granted an extra eight lakhs to distribute among the royal family, in a public acknowledgement of her power and position as empress, but also as matriarch of the royal family.[16]

Both attended other celebrations and public appearances in the coming weeks and months. On 7 March 1628 she rode with her daughter Jahanara and the couple's other children to meet her sons that had been living at Jahangir's Lahore palace before his death. She was seen stopping at Bihishtabad, before advancing to the princes, with all present 'overjoyed' at their reunion.[17] A week later, Shah Jahan publicly presented his wife with more money, jewels and gems, while she and their children gifted him ten lakhs of rupees, the same amount as her annual allowance. She was also present at another ceremonial gift-giving in October of that year and attended the promotion of Shah Jahan's prime minister.[18]

The couple's support for one another was not restricted to smiling and presiding at public ceremonies as they relied heavily on one another for support and strength. While Shah Jahan raised Mumtaz to a position reflected in her given name once empress, 'Exalted One of the Palace', she in turn protected, advised and assisted her husband to power.

The most dramatic of these events was related by Peter Mundy, who was told the story while working for the East India Company in the early years of Shah Jahan's reign. On hearing of his father's death, the prince was at Deccan and could not travel without some risk from his enemies. A plan was soon hatched that he would pretend to be dead, leaving Arjumand playing the grief-stricken wife who wished to travel home with her husband's body to Agra. According to Mundy, 'by that means, in a coffin covered with black, he was conveyed out of their dominion, which was but three or four days' journey distant from his own … until he came to Agra'.[19] In carrying out this charade, Arjumand put herself in considerable danger, sneaking her husband out of the region, all the while keeping up the pretence that she was a widow. In addition, by ensuring his safe arrival in Agra, she paved the way for her husband to mount his own claim to the throne and seize power for himself and their family.

The couple were ambitious, brave and could be hostile when the situation demanded. Arjumand, who smiled sweetly behind carved screens at events and was a dutiful wife, was no stranger to war or planning revenge. The Venetian visitor Niccolao Manucci reported that the empress tried to persuade her husband into a military conflict with the Portuguese of Hugli, in retaliation for capturing two of her women some years before. Manucci stated that she had loudly and angrily wished the assailants to be 'cut into pieces after great tortures'.[20] She is also widely credited as having custody of the royal seal, with the power to oversee and manage state affairs. We also know Mumtaz interceded on behalf of officials that fell from imperial favour. Doubting the loyalty of a governor named Saif Khan, Shah Jahan dismissed him from his position and had him arrested. Because of the empress's intercession, he was later pardoned and released.[21]

A number of accounts reinforce the idea that Mumtaz Muhal and Shah Jahan were rarely apart during their marriage. This is supported by the number of children born to the couple and evidence of her continued presence while her husband was on political or military business. Shah Jahan may have been the enigmatic, stern and calculating Mughal ruler, but Mumtaz Mahal was his ever-present advisor, accomplice and facilitator, 'accompanying him in his wars, as she did all the time of his troubles'.[22] It is likely, considering her success, that Mumtaz had been influenced by watching and observing the actions of her father, aunt and grandfather, all central to the politics of the previous Mughal ruler.

The couple's personal devotion to one another and their joint accomplishments were elevated in the public sphere by grand demonstrations of power and strength. Their adopted names reinforced their importance and status. As well as 'Exalted One of the Palace', Mumtaz was also known as 'The Lady of the World', while Shah Jahan was 'King of the World'. The emperor's regal and dignified composure exuded an air of superiority. Thomas Roe wrote, 'I never saw so settled a countenance, nor any man keep so constant a gravity, never smiling, nor in face showing any respect or difference of men; but mingled with extreme pride and contempt of all.'[23] Shah Jahan's measured and aloof conduct at the royal court instilled in his guests a sense of fear and mystery, ensuring anyone admitted to his person would feel not only highly privileged, but suitably intimidated.

One aspect of the Mughals' power-posturing was not subtle or mysterious. Accounts describe the emperor's processions through his country accompanied by elephants, horses and an army, all twinkling in priceless jewels. Jahangir remembered one occasion when, as prince, Shah Jahan had 3,000 elephants in his train, 'arrayed in trappings of gold and velvet empowdered with pearl'. With them trotted 1,500 horses of three different breeds and another forty elephants behind the prince, with yet more horses and groups of attendants beating drums and sounding horns. As this impressive cavalcade passed, vast quantities of gold and silver coins were scattered to the public who had emerged from their homes and businesses to watch the procession.[24] Peter Mundy wrote in 1632 after witnessing one of Shah Jahan's processions, that 'all this together made a most majestical, warlike and delightsome sight'. He had also been told that the emperor owned 12,000–14,000 horses in his stables; another staggering show of wealth and force.[25]

If subjects did not stand aghast at the jewelled elephants, the thud of thousands of horses or impressive titles, then they would certainly be humbled by his throne. Later in his reign, Shah Jahan commissioned the construction of the Peacock Throne, a large seat with cushions and a jewelled canopy supported by twelve emerald-studded columns. Two heavily jewelled representations of peacocks were placed on the top of each column, the throne accessed by three steps that led the emperor to his seat. The throne was set with rubies, garnets, diamonds, emeralds and pearls obtained from the treasury and, according to the *Badshah-nama* by Abdul Hamid Lahori, took seven years to complete.[26] The royal couple's own possessions displayed similar abundance and prosperity. They drank from cups carved out of jade, rock crystal and agate, wore pendants that glittered with diamonds and peered out from delicately carved screens of marble, called *jalis*, from their gardens. Chests at the palace were inlaid with mother of pearl and brightly coloured carpets woven with velvets and silks.[27]

All these demonstrations of wealth had a hidden political purpose. Just like the couple's extravagant gift giving in 1628, the elephants, horses and armed forces that rumbled through the countryside on behalf of the emperor were a clear demonstration of strength and proof that they had access to seemingly infinite resources. This was reinforced more intimately by the precious stones that twinkled on the Peacock Throne and around the necks of the couple themselves. The coins tumbling into eager, cupped hands during processions was recorded as acts of benevolence by chroniclers and historians of his reign. But they also conveyed the message that this emperor – and by association, his empress – possessed unlimited funds that could be used to protect themselves and their kingdom.

The Mughal Empire in the early seventeenth century did not exist in isolation to the rest of the world. Travellers reported the presence of English merchants, as well as Portuguese and Dutch residents, including the prince's own Dutch jeweller.[28] Shah Jahan's father Jahangir was an avid art enthusiast and collector, personally owning copies of European paintings. He once marvelled at the work of English miniaturist Isaac Oliver and had portraits of 'French kings and other Christian princes' hung in his home. Some of the works owned by the emperor show European influences, with winged cherubs and angels hovering above portraits of courtiers.[29] Shah Jahan inherited his father's love of art. In 1616, after Sir Thomas Roe showed some paintings to Jahangir, the ambassador presented Shah Jahan, then prince, with a silver watch. Roe stated that he took the gift, but asked if he had any paintings like the ones he had shown his father, as those 'he would have better accepted than anything'.[30]

Shah Jahan's image was reproduced in manuscripts and histories of the reign by skilled artists. Depictions made in his lifetime are stylised, but incredibly detailed. Painters portrayed him standing or sitting, his body turned away from the viewer, his face in profile. He had a neat, trimmed beard and wore expensive, delicate fabrics with patterns, along with strings of pearls around his neck and torso. A number of portraits exist of the emperor in The Shah Jahan Album, in the collection of the Metropolitan Museum of Art and the Freer Gallery of Art. Portraits include the emperor depicted on horseback, but also in more intimate scenes, such as one showing him seated with his young son Dara Shikoh.[31]

In contrast, there are very few contemporary portraits of Mumtaz Mahal. Timeri N. Murari in *Empress of the Taj: In Search of Mumtaz Mahal*, links this to the custom that Mughal women were not permitted to be seen by men, limiting the opportunities for portrait painting.[32] On this basis, Mumtaz would have appeared in public wearing a long veil or seated behind a carved screen. Many portraits of the empress we see today are later in origin, painted in the nineteenth and twentieth centuries. However, there is an image of Mumtaz in the collection of the Lahore Museum in Pakistan that has been dated to the seventeenth century. Titled *Portrait of Mumtaz Mahal on Ivory*, it measures just four centimetres in diameter and is painted with watercolour. Depicting the empress wearing gold and blue clothing with a jewelled headdress, her dark hair hangs to her shoulders and forms curls at the ends. She stares determinedly into the distance. But while it is tempting to regard this as a true likeness on the basis of its date, we cannot be certain, based on Timeri N. Murari's information that the artist might never have seen her. The portrait is significant in any case as testament to the skill of the artist and the high standards of miniature painting encouraged during Shah Jahan's reign. It also shows Mumtaz Mahal as she would have wanted to be seen, rounded and lifelike, the tiny brush strokes conveying incredible detail and character.[33]

The couple influenced art outside of their realm, too. The Dutch painter Rembrandt, who lived in the Netherlands while the couple ruled, produced a series of sketches inspired by Mughal portraits. Among them were likenesses of Shah Jahan and his nobles. Rembrandt tweaked these depictions, adding dramatic light and shade and sometimes slightly adjusting the posture or rounding the shape of the face. Conveying a more three-dimensional, fluid and moving form, the artist built upon existing portraits and created something new and more typical of the styles of the European Renaissance. Created in the 1650s, these sketches are today in the collection of the British Museum and the Cleveland Museum of Art.[34] The culture the couple presided over therefore inspired the work and learning process of a painter now considered one of the greatest artists of the seventeenth century.

Mumtaz Mahal and Shah Jahan also had a deep respect for education and openly supported court poets. Inayat Khan records one performance at court, the emperor listening intently to two poets reciting ten Hindi verses by memory. The text also credited him with the creation of new astronomical tables in 1629 and his patronage of scholars, musicians and astrologers at court. According to Tavernier, Shah Jahan also studied mathematics and astrology. He commissioned histories of his reign to be written, including the *Padshah-Nama* by Aminai Kazwini, begun in the eighth year of his rule.[35]

Mumtaz, too, was a patron of literature. Rekha Misra, in *Women in Mughal India*, finds that not only did the empress understand Persian and write verses of her own, but also supported a favourite poet named Vandidhara Misra and recruited another poet, Satiunnisa, to be their daughter Jahanara's tutor. The princess Jahanara later went on to become a writer and capable stateswoman under the later reign of her father and that of her brother, Aurangzeb.[36] Jahanara's brother Dara Shikoh, according to Waldemar Hansen in *The Peacock Throne: The Drama of Mogul India*, admired the philosophy of Aristotle and Plato, further evidence that European Renaissance learning had reached the Mughal court and was actively encouraged by the couple.[37] Their decision to inspire their children in the arts from a young age also reveals that they considered cultural and academic appreciation, from outside the empire as much as from within, an important attribute for future Mughal rulers.

One of the best-known contributions made by the couple can be found in their building projects. Shah Jahan was a compulsive builder and used the latest seventeenth-century technology to create some of the most iconic buildings of the age, including pavilions, palaces, houses, forts and other monuments. Tavernier wrote of a town founded by Shah Jahan, named Jahanabad in his honour. The Frenchman stated that the emperor, tired of Agra's intense heat, decided to build a palace where he could be more comfortable in the summer months. It contained three courts, one said to have been large enough for nobles to enter while seated on elephants. The hall in which Shah Jahan appeared in front of his subjects contained thirty-two marble columns, although the emperor had intended it to be even bigger. Tavernier heard that Shah Jahan commanded that the hall 'should be enriched throughout by wonderful works in mosaic, like those in the chapel of the Grand Duke in Italy', adding that plans had to change on account of not being able to find enough stone for the project.[38] Shah Jahan was once again inspired by developments in Renaissance Europe, adapting its designs to reflect the empire's own cultural preferences.

The emperor is also well known as the builder of the imposing Red Fort at Agra and the Pearl Mosque (Moti Masjid), among others. Mumtaz embarked on building projects, too. Tavernier records a stay in a place named Tenara (he also calls it Atenara), 'one of the pleasure houses built by the queen, mother of the king who reigns at present' (at the time of his visit, Mumtaz' son Aurangzeb ruled as emperor). He noted its 'many rooms, opening on a grand square which is in front of the house, for the accommodation of travellers', and described courtyards, a veranda and beautiful gardens. It also contained small rooms where poor travellers could come to be fed each evening.[39] But while both partners altered the landscape of the realm with military, political and benevolent institutions, one building in particular will forever be associated with Shah Jahan and Mumtaz Mahal and has stood for four centuries as a mark of their bond.

In May 1631 Mumtaz Mahal was staying at Burhanpur, accompanying her husband on a military campaign as she had done so many times during their marriage. Heavily pregnant, she would have taken in the view of the area subsequently recorded by European travellers. Mundy, who visited Burhanpur in late 1630 when Shah Jahan and Mumtaz were there, noted a 'fine castle standing on a hill towards the rivers side', and the many entertainments held there for the royal party. There was also a lively marketplace or bazaar, stocked with 'all things from all parts far and near'. Her eyes would have flicked over the nearby stone sculpture of an elephant carved 'in such a posture', said Mundy, 'that it seems to the life'.[40]

Just weeks later, she would enter labour for the fourteenth time, giving birth to a daughter named Gauharara. Shortly afterwards, on 7 June 1631 Mumtaz Mahal died. Upon hearing the news, Shah Jahan fell into a passionate grief, refusing to be seen in public. *The Shah Jahan-nama* describes his emergence a week later, his eyes weak from crying and his hair and beard now one-third white.[41] He ordered her burial to take place, temporarily, in a grave near the Tapti River, while he set about building a permanent mausoleum in her memory.

Tavernier claimed to have seen the Taj Mahal completed from beginning to end. He stated that it took 22 years, 20,000 men and enormous expense, marvelling at the huge quantities of white and black marble in its construction as well as its famous dome covering the tomb of the empress.[42] While it is likely that Tavernier did indeed see construction work taking place, he is known for completing a number of travels rather than staying in one place for any long period of time and so probably did not see the entire process as he claimed. The Frenchman can be placed in France, Turkey, Persia and Italy on various trips in the 1630s and 1640s.[43] Nevertheless, other commentators also remarked on its extravagance. Peter Mundy, writing in 1632, reported that 'there is already about her tomb a rail of gold. The building is begun and goes on with excessive labour and cost, prosecuted with extraordinary diligence'.[44]

In line with Shah Jahan's other building work, the Taj Mahal is impressively vast, but also conveys a sense of purity and fragility. It was decorated with precious metals and stones, with delicate carvings and scripts painstakingly whittled by sculptors and calligraphers. Seventeenth-century spectators were in awe of the monument, which continues to enthral visitors hundreds of years later. Lilian Leland, an American who embarked on a journey around the world in the nineteenth century, called the Taj Mahal 'the most beautiful structure in the world', with a dome 'so perfect in proportion and outline, so dazzling in marble whiteness, as to seem to have been created by the hand of some powerful genii rather than raised by the laborious efforts of men'.[45] Another writer compared the impetus behind the structure to another Wonder of the World, an ancient tomb at Halicarnassus erected by the Greek ruler Artemisia to honour her husband Mausolos in the fourth century BC.[46] With the Mughals' evident love of Renaissance art and ideas, in turn resurrected from the ancients, it is possible that the Taj Mahal was erected with Halicarnassus in mind. However, although their origins are similar, this cannot so far be proven.

Shah Jahan lived the rest of his reign under a cloud of mistrust, danger and scandal as his sons rebelled and he slipped into old age and illness. He was imprisoned by his son Aurangzeb and died in captivity at the age of 75 on 22 January 1666. He was buried alongside Mumtaz in a vault underneath the Taj Mahal.

Mumtaz Mahal and Shah Jahan were a power couple in every sense. They produced fourteen children, of which seven survived into adulthood, securing the future of the powerful Mughal dynasty. They presided over public events with their family to reinforce their domestic bond and status. Well educated and lovers of culture, they provided their children with training in literature, philosophy and religion, and were patrons of scholars, jewellers, artists, architects and poets. There is plenty of evidence from surviving artwork that Shah Jahan, like his father, loved Renaissance art, and the couple presided over a court that took inspiration from its developments in Europe. Their subjects marvelled at outward displays of wealth, power and resources, from jewelled elephants that thundered through the countryside to the huge amounts of cash the couple exchanged publicly as gifts.

As a couple, Shah Jahan and Mumtaz Mahal elevated each other to power, Mumtaz by ensuring his secret escape to safely assume the throne and Shah Jahan by deliberately elevating Mumtaz to a higher state position above his other wives. Both influenced matters of state, although for Mumtaz this was done more discreetly. There is also evidence that she tried to persuade her husband to conduct wars and had some sway over state affairs. Mumtaz's angry response to the theft of two of her women reveals passion, while her devoted and active service echo that of her father and aunt, Asaf Khan and the Empress Nur Jahan. Shah Jahan was to visitors composed, aloof and imperious. He loved jewels and extravagant displays of wealth and is remembered as one of the age's most prolific builders. His visible grief on Mumtaz's death demonstrates the extent of the personal and emotional bond between these two rulers.

But what impact did their relationship have on the world and their time? The most obvious is the Taj Mahal monument that stands today in Agra. Created to house the remains of Mumtaz Mahal, it is not only an enduring symbol of their love and a recognition of the service Mumtaz gave to her husband, but an awe-inspiring example of Mughal architecture. Peter

Mundy stopped to visit while on business with the East India Company and was amazed to see precious materials such as gold and silver being added to the structure as if 'esteemed common metal'. He had even heard a rumour that the emperor was considering levelling the hills around the monument so 'they might not hinder the prospect of it'.[47]

This love story and the magnificence of the Mughal court related by commentators such as Manucci, Roe, Mundy and Tavernier attracted visitors to Agra to see the famous structure for themselves. Over the following centuries, artists captured its form on paper and canvas, in watercolours and oils. William Hodges was an early painter of the Taj Mahal, creating an atmospheric landscape viewed from across the river in the late eighteenth century. Thought to have been created in around 1780, the painting is currently in the collection of the National Gallery of Modern Art in New Delhi.[48] Modern writers have rightly put the grandeur of the Taj Mahal in its Renaissance context, including Waldemar Hansen in *The Peacock Throne*, who stated that it was 'a tomb unrivalled by any Medici'.[49] Timeri N. Murari in *Empress of the Taj* referred to another Italian great, saying that in building the tomb the emperor 'captured in marble what Da Vinci captured on canvas'.[50] There is a similarity between the balanced and ordered measurements of Leonardo's drawing of *Vitruvian Man* and the painstaking outer symmetry of the Taj Mahal. Today, the monument is visited by huge numbers of sightseers every year with tourists, royalty, world leaders and celebrities all keen to be photographed in front of its pearlescent marble dome.

The couple also altered the lives of their subjects. Ongoing building projects sustained the incomes of architects, labourers, sculptors and gardeners. Ceilings and walls were studded with precious stones purchased from jewellers, while water ran through specially carved channels in the bathhouse of the Sheesh Mahal, installed by the empire's plumbers and engineers. In addition, scholars were appointed to offer prayers at the Taj Mahal, while 2,000 soldiers were commanded to guard it.[51]

They were also generous to the poor, improving the quality of life of many of their subjects and visitors to the realm. Courtesy of the empress, weary travellers were fed in the gardens of Zahara Bagh. Coins were also freely scattered among crowds that gathered to see royal processions. During the famine of 1630–32, Shah Jahan ordered soup kitchens to be established at Burhanpur, Ahmadabad and Surat 'for the benefit of the poor and destitute'. He also gave 5,000 rupees per week for poverty relief at

Burhanpur and a further 50,000 rupees for Ahmadabad 'among the famine-stricken people' of that region.[52] Despite the emperor's tough and brutal rule, actions like these led Tavernier to conclude after Shah Jahan's death that the emperor governed his subjects 'like a father'.[53]

The couple's effect on the Renaissance movement was significant. Their court and wider realm bustled with residents from France, the Netherlands, England, Portugal and Italy, as well as Persia and Turkey. Artists under the couple's patronage carefully worked royal manuscripts and book pages with gold and vivid-coloured inks and gently covered their personal items in gold and silks. The couple's personal art collection included drawings and paintings featuring winged angels and cherubs, exactly like the *putti* that peer down from the ceiling of the Gonzagas' bridal chamber at Mantua or from within the Medici palace in Florence. From architecture and paintings to personal objects and ornaments, the couple's empire was a hive of cultural expression and a melting pot of techniques and skills developed from far beyond the Mughal Empire.

But they did not just receive the learning and skills of the European Renaissance. As tales of extravagant legends surrounding the Peacock Throne, the Taj Mahal and the queen's bathhouse at Sheesh Mahal reached foreign ears, curious minds desired to learn more about the customs and stories of this exotic land. The seventeenth-century Dutch master Rembrandt copied Shah Jahan's likeness in sketches, creating new 'Europeanised' versions of the emperor's image. In print, people read eagerly about this powerful and extravagant duo in publications such as Tavernier's *Travels in India*, published in 1676. Another Dutch artist, Willem Schellinks, produced an oil painting that conveyed the opulence of the Mughal court now in the collection of the V&A in London. His *Parade of the Sons of Shah Jahan on Composite Horses and Elephants* dates to the late seventeenth century.[54]

Discussions of power, influence and patronage during the Renaissance age often skip over Asia and the East, but there is ample evidence that political, social and cultural exchanges flowed between the Mughal Empire and the rest of the world. This did not travel only in one direction, with Shah Jahan and Mumtaz Mahal's union triggering further interest and fascination for their kingdom from creators in the west. During their lifetime, the couple contributed not only towards the Mughal legend, but also to the livelihoods of hundreds and thousands of craftspeople. They left an enduring legacy, and although the Taj Mahal is their most well known, it is far from the only reminder of their bond that survives today.

Chapter 8

Charles II and Catherine of Braganza, of England, Scotland and Ireland

As the 69-year-old Shah Jahan adapted to confinement in Hindustan 5,000 miles away, London was buzzing with rumours of a royal wedding. In February 1661, the English diarist and Secretary of the Admiralty, Samuel Pepys, wrote that 'the talk of the town now is, who the King is like to have for his Queen'. He wouldn't have to wait long. Just four months later, he was being briefed on arrangements to bring Charles II's young Portuguese bride over from Lisbon.[1]

England had been torn apart by civil war from the early 1640s, a result of Charles's father, Charles I, demonstrating an antagonistic attitude towards Parliament and enforcing relentless taxation on his people. He demonstrated an unwavering belief in the Divine Right of Kings, that his authority on Earth was given to him directly by God and was answerable to no one but Him. Parliament became increasingly frustrated with a monarch who refused to listen or compromise on state issues. The presence of his wife, the French Catholic Queen Henrietta Maria, further irritated his Protestant subjects. The state fractured into royalists who supported the king and parliamentarians who stood instead for their military leader Oliver Cromwell and demanded change. In the end, Parliament secured the victory, and on the chilly morning of 30 January 1649 Charles I was executed outside the Banqueting House in Whitehall, London.

At the time of his father's death, Charles, his eldest son, was 18 years old. Present for some of the earlier battles of the war, he fled to Europe for his safety, sailing to Jersey, Paris and The Hague. A brief return in 1651 saw him crowned King of Scotland, but also marked his disastrous defeat at the Battle of Worcester, where he escaped and fled through the dimly lit passages of one of the town's pubs, the King Charles House, which still survives today. He lived in Europe for almost a decade before the eventual failure of the Protectorate government at the end of the 1650s. In May 1660 he was asked to return to England as king and was crowned at Westminster Abbey as Charles II on St George's Day, 23 April 1661.

London was excited about who might be their new queen, but negotiations for the royal marriage had been under way since the 1640s when the future bride and groom were children. A politically driven match, it was now pushed forward with renewed vigour by the bride's mother, Luisa de Guzmán, Regent of Portugal after the death of her husband, King John IV. The marriage aimed to forge an alliance between the two nations, distributing and enhancing power, wealth and influence on both sides. As part of the arrangement, Charles received new trading rights in the Portuguese territories of Brazil and the East Indies and took ownership of two new cities: Bombay in India and Tangier in Morocco. Portugal sweetened the arrangement with the promise of a large dowry of £500,000 to swell the royal coffers. In return, England promised to provide naval and military resources to help bolster Portugal's own war efforts, particularly against Spain, and to protect their other worldwide territories. The new queen, the marriage agreement carefully stipulated, would also be free to worship as a Catholic on her arrival to England. Charles addressed Parliament at Westminster on 8 May 1661 announcing that he would marry Catherine of Braganza. He promised to make 'all the haste I can to fetch you a queen hither, who, I doubt not, will bring great blessings with her to me and you'.[2]

Catherine of Braganza was born on 25 November 1638, the daughter of John, Duke of Braganza, later King John IV of Portugal. She was said to have lived an especially sheltered life, 'carefully and piously educated' according to one historian of the period.[3] In a portrait created in 1660/61 by Dirk Stoop in the collection of the National Portrait Gallery in London, the young infanta is petite, her long dark hair fashionably crimped into shoulder-length waves. Gazing out at us with heavy-lidded dark eyes, rouged cheeks and a small barely there smile, she sports the unusual hairstyle commented on by diarist John Evelyn in 1662, when he saw her at Hampton Court with 'her fore-top long and turned aside very strangely'.[4] A style that failed to catch on in England, it involved combing a wide lock of hair at the front of the scalp and securing it in a broad loop across the forehead.

The nation was especially enthusiastic about this new royal wedding. Not only was it the first involving a ruling sovereign in almost forty years, but it followed decades of internal strife, bloodshed and a revolutionary dismantling of traditional power. Castles standing since the time of William the Conqueror had now been reduced to rubble, while memories of battle stayed fresh in subjects' minds. It was hoped that the union between these two young royals would bring a strong leadership, as well as prosperity and security to the realm. Predictably, writers deliberately pushed the couple's joint legitimacy to the throne, Charles possessing 'all the royal blood of Europe', while Catherine's English lineage was also stressed. Historians busily published papers linking her to Edward III's son John of Gaunt as well as to the early medieval courts of Castile and France.[5]

On the continent, news of the couple's marriage was less happily received. Unsurprisingly, Portugal's enemy Spain sought reasons to end the marriage and Charles's influence in the war. They were rightly concerned. The army that Charles had provided to Portugal achieved a noted victory over Spain in the summer of 1663. In 1664, the Spaniards haughtily demanded ownership of England's new territory of Tangier. Charles responded pointedly that Spain 'had no more to do with the possession than it had with Plymouth'.[6]

Catherine arrived at Portsmouth on 13 May 1662 and the couple were married just over a week later on 21 May. Charles was pleased with his queen, 'for she has wit enough, and a most agreeable voice'. He added, in a letter to his advisor Edward Hyde, Earl of Clarendon, 'You would wonder to see how well we are acquainted already. In a word, I think myself very happy, for I am confident our two humours will agree very well together'.[7]

What Catherine couldn't have known before she arrived among the tangle of masts at Portsmouth harbour, was that a sense of unease was already growing among those close to the king. On 10 May, while the infanta was heading towards England on the *Royal Charles*, Pepys nervously wrote that 'my Lady Castlemaine do speak of going to lie in at Hampton Court; which she and all our ladies are much troubled at, because of the King's being forced to show her countenance in the sight of the Queen when she comes'. Barbara Palmer, Lady Castlemaine, was Charles's chief mistress at the time of his marriage and brazenly chose the red-bricked Tudor palace to await the birth of her illegitimate child with the king. This, along with a very public refusal to light a bonfire outside her door to celebrate the queen's arrival as the rest of the court did, was a pointed attack against Catherine's authority. Even Pepys, on 31 May, feared Castlemaine's reaction more than the queen's, worrying that the queen's presence 'will put Madam Castlemaine's nose out of joint'.[8] The newlyweds' first few months of married life had its obstacles, as Pepys had suspected. Catherine's mother, battling Spanish armies from her base in Portugal, was unable to pay the full marriage portion she had promised, offering some of the outstanding balance in cash and the rest in sugar, spices and other goods. Catherine also objected to her husband of Castlemaine's visible presence at court. Tensions grew, arguments were fought and the couple appeared visibly angry with one another. Over time, however, Catherine seems to have reluctantly accepted life with her husband's mistresses and the other 'beauties' of the court, even though, as the Count of Grammont noted on a visit, 'you could not look anywhere without seeing them'.[9]

Catherine's decision to tolerate the presence of her husband's mistresses was almost certainly deliberate and calculated. An interesting account from Pepys in October 1662 helps to explain the queen's mindset. Pepys had been told of a conversation between two physicians at court, one of them Catherine's own. This physician revealed that 'the Queen do know how the King orders things, and how he carries himself to my Lady Castlemaine and others … but though she hath spirit enough, yet seeing that she do no good by taking notice of it, for the present she forbears it in policy'.[10] Around this time, we see glimpses of the queen appearing more relaxed. She cheekily joked with her husband about a pregnancy and was even said to gingerly pause before entering her dressing room in case the king was there with another woman.[11] Among the mistresses the queen had to share her court with were Moll Davis, Nell Gwyn and the French aristocrat Louise de Kerouaille. There was also her husband's ever-growing illegitimate brood, all created dukes, earls and countesses by their royal father. By the autumn of 1662 Catherine realised that she needed Charles's assistance and not his animosity. This was the only way she could hold any influence as a consort and govern at his side. Grammont also observed that Catherine was a 'woman of sense' and, despite noticing that she was less glittering than the many beauties she shared her court with, considered that 'in the end she was pretty successful'.[12] Catherine's change in attitude, although frustration would still occasionally surface, eased the couple's immediate domestic tensions and by the middle of December 1662 the grateful Charles remarked that Catherine was 'one of the best women in the world'.[13]

With relations between the royal couple now more cordial, there was another problem. Despite Charles fathering at least twelve illegitimate children with his mistresses, the royal cradle remained empty. The queen did fall pregnant, but suffered with miscarriages. The poet Richard Flecknoe, on hearing of Catherine's pregnancy, wrote triumphantly 'now 'tis done, and Carolus has an Heyr, briefly obtain'd by Catharina's pray'r'. After her miscarriage soon afterwards, he wrote another poem, this time taking a cautious but optimistic tone, thanking God for his 'assurance that an Heyr will come', but the queen must 'iterate her pray'r'.[14] No doubt

Catherine did pray, but there was no sign of an heir and doubts began to surface that she would ever bear children. As early as 8 February 1664, Pepys related that Charles now expected his eldest illegitimate son James, Duke of Monmouth to succeed him. There was even talk of divorce, in the hope that the king would then marry 'a fruitful lady'.[15] In the late 1670s though, the couple encountered a true test of their marriage when a priest from Rutland in the East Midlands arrived at the palace with serious and dangerous allegations that brought public doubt on the couple's trust of one another and their loyalty to the realm.

Talk at court in the summer of 1678 was of betrayal, conspiracy and murder. The prime suspect was Queen Catherine. Titus Oates, a priest who had travelled to London from Rutland, claimed to know of a plot in which the queen's physician was offered £10,000 to poison the king. He also conveyed murky allegations that her household had been involved in the recent murder of Sir Edmund Berry Godfrey, a Protestant magistrate found strangled and stabbed.

Catherine had, as per the terms of her marriage agreement, been permitted to practise Catholic worship since her arrival in England in 1662. However this, along with the presence of a number of Catholics who were also regulars at Charles's court, triggered fear in some of his subjects of a full return to Catholicism in the country. There were also concerns about the religion's influence over the king, with his brother James, his mother Henrietta-Maria and mistresses also members of the faith. Catherine held services at her chapel in Somerset House, where she had lived since the 1670s, and this also became a focus for Protestant anger, alleged to be the location of plots and murders carried out with the queen's knowledge. Charles listened to Oates's accusations and immediately conducted an investigation, concluding afterwards that it was fictitious. Still, anti-Catholic hysteria resulted in heightened anxiety at court that led to the establishment of the Test Act, banning anyone of the Catholic faith from serving in Parliament, an effort to try to appease Charles's anxious subjects. The country was rife with panic and hatred and yet no proof was found of the 'plot' Oates had insisted was true. Eventually, even his supporters had to agree that the allegations were unfounded and Oates was imprisoned. He was sentenced to be hauled out to a pillory five times a year to be whipped in public.

The anti-Catholic hysteria created another threat to the couple's security and status. Supporters of the Duke of Monmouth, Charles's eldest illegitimate son, claimed that the king had been married to Monmouth's mother Lucy Walter before marrying Catherine. If true, this would remove Charles's Catholic brother James from the succession, making Monmouth, conveniently, next in line to the throne. It would also render his marriage to Catherine void. In March 1679 Charles vehemently crushed the rumours, issuing a proclamation that he had not been married to 'the Duke of Monmouth's mother, or to any woman whatsoever, besides the now Queen'.[16]

Although the Popish Plot of 1678 was one of the greatest adversities faced by the couple, their joint reaction was steadfast, swift and firm. As Lillias Campbell Davidson has pointed out, if Charles was dissatisfied with his queen, he could have discarded her and remarried, simply by standing back and allowing the hysteria surrounding the plot to run its course. He even had additional grounds for an annulment on the basis that the financial part of the marriage agreement had not been satisfied by Portugal. And yet he publicly defended his wife, arguing that he would 'not suffer an innocent woman to be wronged', even at the expense of an heir to his kingdom.[17]

Catherine was grateful for her husband's support and she wrote to her brother Pedro in 1680 about a dreaded journey the couple were to make, but added that she would accompany the king 'as I always do', and that 'his troubles give me more anxiety than my own'.[18] This is evidence that the couple did indeed share and discuss one another's problems and she later expressed gratitude for his protection. They remained at one another's bedsides through illness, maintaining public shows of strength, Charles even banishing his own mistresses from court if they did not show Catherine appropriate respect. He also seems to have felt some regret over his treatment of her, asking for her pardon as he lay dying in the winter of 1685. The diarist John Evelyn noted dryly that the king's remorse was 'not without cause'. After he died, Catherine went into full mourning, receiving visitors in a chamber with 'ceiling and floor, hung with black' appearing visibly grieved.[19]

At first glance, the timid wife and philandering husband that we know from the history books do not seem a likely power couple that were united in their aims. But there are plenty of examples of their combined efforts, working towards the good of the realm and maintaining respect for one another as rulers. It is important to remember that their marriage was conducted for purely political and dynastic reasons, not the result of a romance. Charles may have found companionship in his many mistresses, but Catherine worked with him as an agent of the state, meeting ambassadors from around the world and corresponding with foreign rulers. Catherine's pious, thoughtful and more rigid personality complemented Charles's affable and approachable character. They remained resilient despite challenges and worked as advisors and diplomats on behalf of one another to drive revolutionary change. In this respect, the 'odd couple' of Restoration Britain were actually well matched. While Charles is often praised for his contribution in terms of politics, arts and sciences, Catherine's is less well known. She tolerated mistresses at court sparkling with jewels bought by her husband and smiled politely at the many ambassadors who knelt to kiss her hand. However, she was far more interested in affairs of a military nature.

On 26 October 1664 a new warship was launched at Woolwich, *The Royal Catherine*, named after the queen. Built by Christopher Pett, it boasted all the latest technology of seventeenth-century shipbuilding, along with eighty-four guns. Charles 'did very much like the ship,' wrote Pepys, who was present at the launch, the king declaring it to have 'the best bow that ever he saw'.[20] Charles was a keen sailor, owning a pleasure yacht of his own and a library stocked with books on travel, an 'abundance of maps and sea charts' and various works 'relating to the Navy'.[21] Catherine, too, was eager to make the trip to Woolwich. Charles wrote to the Earl of Sandwich, 'my wife is so faraide [afraid] that she shall not see the fleet before it goes', requesting arrangements be made to have the ships ready for her arrival. Despite her worries, the queen arrived on time and proudly watched the launch of the ship named in her honour.[22]

Catherine's interest in the couple's new warship – and ships in general – was genuine. As Sophie Shorland, in *The Lost Queen: The Surprising Life of Catherine of Braganza, Britain's Forgotten Monarch*, points out, she was from a 'seafaring nation'.[23] Portugal enjoyed historic trading relationships with India, the Americas and elsewhere in Europe and talk of sailing and navigation would have been common during her childhood. She also knew from an early age that she would, in adulthood, become queen of an island with a rich maritime history. Her mother, Luisa de Guzmàn, was a tenacious and intelligent ruler who influenced her husband's rise to the Portuguese throne and governed as regent after his death. In many ways Catherine displayed similarities with her mother's personality in the manner she conducted business and was far from the meek, understated character of historical legend.

Catherine also had a political motivation to be interested in England's shipbuilding developments. Their marriage agreement promised that military support would be provided to Portugal and it is logical that she would want to keep updated with the latest technological advances made in her new realm. Proud of the alliance her marriage had created, Catherine was loved back in Portugal and would have felt a personal responsibility to ensure the terms of the marriage agreement could be carried out to protect her people. She attended other nautical occasions, too. In May 1671 the royal pair stood to greet the English fleet returning following a battle with the Dutch and in 1681 they witnessed the launch of the newly built ship *Britannia*.[24] Both Charles and Catherine owned their own yachts, Catherine's the 86-ton vessel which she named *Saudados*, built in 1670. She was even reported to have fired a gun at its launch in front of spectators. In 1673 admiralty records reveal that the queen's ship was ordered to be strung with silk pennants and gilded, and was later used for carrying soldiers and as part of a defensive convoy for merchant ships.[25] Catherine also knew the captain of her yacht by name, recommending his services to her brother Pedro in Portugal in 1687.[26]

A painting of *The Royal Catherine* by H. Vale survives in the collection of Royal Museums Greenwich. Painted in the seventeenth century, the work depicts the ship firing a salute while strewn with pennants and flying a Union Jack. At its stern is a full-size carving of the queen, the initials CR and KR carved underneath.[27] To anyone seeing the ship docked in waters around the world, the vessel was a display of the couple's combined political and military power. The initials of the pair, along with the imposing size of the ship, reinforced their combined power and strength. There is another enduring example of Catherine's love of the sea, emphasised every time she sent personal correspondence. An image of her seal, today in the Royal Collection Trust and made between 1705–1750, bears an image of her husband Charles driving a horse-drawn chariot through the waves, a visual representation of their perceived command of the seas.[28]

The Restoration years were spent on military, political and social restructuring, but it was also an era of rapid expansion in learning and scientific enquiry. Soon after arriving from exile, Charles founded the Royal Society where geologists, mathematicians and astronomers could meet to share and increase their collective knowledge of the world around them. The society had existed less formally since 1646, but it was Charles II who on 22 April 1663 granted the organisation its charter. In the document the king declared that he had 'long resolved within ourself to promote the welfare of arts and sciences, as well as that of our territories and dominions, out of our princely affection to all kind of learning, and more particular favour to philosophical studies'. He stressed the need for 'solid experiments' when investigating scientific queries, along with a wish that 'the learned world may acknowledge us to be, not only the defender of the faith, but the patron and encourager of all sorts of useful knowledge'.[29]

Two of its earliest members had links to Catherine's household. Its first president, the king's 'trusty and well-beloved' William Brouncker, was the queen's chancellor, while Samuel Tuke was the husband of one of her prominent ladies, Mary Sheldon.[30] Brouncker was present on 3 May 1661, when members of the society showed the king planets and their orbiting moons through 'his Majesty's great telescope'. Charles visited the Society a number of times, signing its charter book during a meeting of 11 January 1665, when John Evelyn, another courtier known to both the king and queen, was also an early member.[31]

Charles's founding of the Royal Society was hugely significant. Details of some of its experiments are preserved in the minutes of the society and reflect its members' eager curiosity. In one experiment held on 24 July 1661 members made a circle out of some powdered unicorn's horn spread out on a table. This powder, usually ground from a horn such as that of a narwhal, was believed to prevent poisoning during the medieval period. The aim of the experiment is not clear, but a spider was placed in the middle of the circle and observed. To begin with, the spider ran out, but eventually the members recorded, 'The trial being repeated several times, the spider once made some stay on the powder'. In another, on 25 March 1663 they stared intensely at a different heap of powder ('viper-powder'), to see if 'vipers would be produced out of that powder'. However, it was also here that the society listened, on 8 February 1672, to Sir Isaac Newton's groundbreaking conclusion that light consisted of 'different rays ... and that colours are produced', so that 'whiteness is nothing but a mixture of all sorts of colours'.[32]

Now fully established with a charter, permanent meeting place and royal backing, members of the Royal Society triggered a revolution in evidence-based, scientific reasoning. As well as Isaac Newton, whose theories on physics form the basis of theories today, another notable member was John Flamsteed, who mapped stars in the king's newly built observatory in Greenwich. According to John Evelyn in 1676, the observatory was 'furnished with the choicest instruments', ensuring that planets and other celestial bodies could be viewed and recorded with the best tools the seventeenth century had to offer.[33] Joseph Moxon, 'Hydrographer to the King's Most Excellent Majesty', published *A Tutor to Astronomy and Geography, or, The Use of the Copernican Spheres* in 1665, while in 1684 John Wilkins proposed the possibility of a 'habitable world in the moon'. Other subjects were also discussed at meetings, from the history of the silkworm to the eruption of Mount Etna.

Catherine seems to have left much of the business of the Royal Society to her husband, but there is some evidence that she shared Charles's fascination and interest in the cosmos. On 16 December 1664 Charles and Catherine sat up late together to watch a comet trail across London's night sky, an event grumpily recorded by Samuel Pepys, who squinted up at thick cloud the following night and saw nothing.[34] It is significant that the king chose to spend this moment with his wife and not one of his mistresses and it is just possible, judging from her interest in the sea, that she shared his enthusiasm for the night sky. Sailors used the position of stars to navigate across the blackness of the ocean, noting any unexpected celestial events with interest.

The London that sprawled underneath the couple as they sat up watching the sky that night in many ways resembled the late medieval and Tudor city. Timber-framed houses huddled into tightly packed lanes and winding streets, their upper storeys leaning unsteadily towards one another. Londoners piled into old churches that had stood for centuries, while the tall medieval spire of St Paul's Cathedral stood proudly in the sky. In the summer of 1666 much of this would be lost forever.

The Great Fire of London, believed to have started at a baker's house in Pudding Lane, spread throughout the city, rapidly burning homes, shops and places of worship. The fire quickly blazed through lanes and streets, destroying structures such as London Bridge, St Paul's Cathedral and other buildings along the River Thames, including a number of smaller parish churches. Charles was incredibly proactive in trying to save the city, ordering individual houses either side of the fire to be pulled down in an attempt to stop it spreading. He and his younger brother, James, Duke of York, also ventured into the streets to help the panicked citizens and issue commands. The fire resisted and by the time it was extinguished, houses, churches, offices and shops lay in smouldering, ashen ruins.

The event was catastrophic, but after the initial shock had passed, it was seen as an opportunity to rebuild a more modern London that fitted the growing needs of the later seventeenth century. Wider streets that ran parallel to one another were proposed, replacing the cramped and disordered narrow lanes. This would make it easier to navigate the city via horse or carriage, a popular method of transport and often mentioned by Samuel Pepys in his diaries. Cramped, medieval streets were also replaced by fashionable and spacious squares where people could meet and discuss news. Wharfs along the Thames were made larger and more efficient to help with travel and trade on the riverside, and the old spire of St Paul's Cathedral made way for the domed cupola that we see today. This building of a new London was carried out under Charles II's command, something the historian John Strype was grateful for in 1720, when he wrote of the more 'stately and uniform' appearance of the city, now built using durable, easily maintained and less flammable brick. Comparing the new layout of the city with that of Elizabethan London, he noted the 'the many Fields and Places that lay waste in those days, are now built into fair Streets, Lanes, Alleys and Courts'.[35]

John Evelyn, some years before the fire, wrote a book on the principles of architecture and presented it to the king. This inspired Charles who, on 27 October 1664 while 'casually in the privy gallery at Whitehall', led Evelyn to a window and asked if he had a crayon and some paper. Taking them from Evelyn's hands, the king sketched out plans for a rebuilding of the palace, unfurling the paper out on the windowsill as he drew. Later, as London lay in ashen ruins, Charles remembered Evelyn's architectural expertise and called on him in the autumn of 1666 to design a new city. On 13 September of that year, Evelyn 'presented his Majesty with a survey of the ruins, and a plot for a new City, with a discourse on it'. After dinner, Charles sent for him again, but ordered him to visit the queen's bedchamber, where Catherine and the Duke of York were waiting for him. 'They examined each particular,' wrote Evelyn, 'and discoursed on them for near an hour, seeming to be extremely pleased with what I had so early thought on.' Catherine, he noted, had been on her way out 'to take the air' dressed in her riding clothes and coat, complete with hat and feather.[36] Here, Charles intentionally sought Catherine's advice on London's proposed layout and she, with her brother-in-law, spent considerable time poring over Evelyn's plans. We can also see Catherine's involvement in another source, preserved in the Calendar of State Papers. In 1667 she responded to a petition addressed to the king, urging Lord Arlington to speed up his rebuilding of structures that had been damaged by the fire.[37]

Charles's actions during and after the Great Fire are well documented, but it is not often acknowledged that he called upon Catherine for her feedback on the rebuilding of London. It is impossible to ascertain the exact extent of her influence, any changes she personally made or whether any of her suggestions were carried out in the final commissions. Between couples, there is often little evidence of collaboration such as this, with conversations taking place during a shared dinner or while playing cards in private. However, thanks to a chance entry in Evelyn's diary and the queen's letter to Lord Arlington, the couple's active involvement together in the aftermath of the Great Fire has been preserved.

Towards the end of his life, Charles would have walked through the corridors of Windsor Castle and frequently visited the chapel built by his ancestor, Edward IV. On the ceiling of the Queen's Audience Chamber he would have looked up at a painting by the Italian artist Antonio Verrio, completed between 1675–1684. The work, *Catherine of Braganza in a Chariot*, owned by the Royal Collection Trust, demonstrates the art of trompe-l'oeil, mastered by earlier artists in Italy.[38] The painting deceives the eye, with the ceiling appearing to magically give way to ancient Italianate rails against a blue sky. Angels, gods and allegorical figures swell into the space twisting and lounging on clouds, offering crowns to the queen and placing foliage around the scene. And at the centre of them all, seated in a golden chariot, is Catherine of Braganza.

This work, with its expert use of perspective, anatomy, colour theory, geometry and space could not have been possible without the influence of Italian artists in the late fourteenth and early fifteenth centuries such as Michelangelo, da Vinci and Raphael. With its illusion of an opening in the ceiling and the lifelike figures that swirl beneath it, it is similar in basis to Andrea Mantegna's work undertaken for the Gonzagas at their Bridal Suite in Mantua 200 years earlier, except it is rounder, more dramatic and has heightened realism.

For two centuries, artists had been able to render a good likeness and execute shadow, depth and structure. It was now time to add a sense of drama and movement to the art form, eagerly encouraged by both Charles and Catherine. Not only did this sense of energy and emotion pair well with the nation's excitement for its newly restored monarchy, it also distanced itself from memories of the Civil War and the Interregnum period while Parliament ruled. Themes of excess, nudity and luxury were in opposition to many features of Oliver Cromwell's Puritan government, which prioritised restrictions and piety over indulgence. The arrival of Charles, and the return of the monarchy, was a cause for celebration. Bishop Gilbert Burnet noticed 'great disorders, and much riot everywhere', on Charles's accession, while Count Grammont, who arrived in England in around 1662, saw a nation that 'exhausted themselves in festivals and rejoicings' after the king's return to power.[39]

As public figures at the centre of this change, depictions of the royal couple were popular, and their likeness appeared on plates, bowls, mirrors and in textiles of the period. In one engraving by P. Stent in 1662 in the Royal

Collection Trust, the political agenda of this 'royal wedding' propaganda is unmistakable. Titled simply *Charles II and Catherine of Braganza* it depicts the couple standing between pulled back curtains as Charles gestures to a shield bearing the arms of England and Portugal. Similarly, a medal created in the same year by George Bower also in the Royal Collection Trust, *Medal Commemorating the Marriage of Charles II and Catherine of Braganza*, has the couple in profile, Catherine behind Charles, both staring determinedly and wearing what appear to be low-cut ancient robes.[40] Created in the early years of their marriage, these images not only conveyed hope for the end of conflict and excitement over the royal wedding, but projected the couple's legitimate power as rulers and the realm's new implied security, regardless of any domestic issues the couple faced privately.

One of the best-known artists of the royal court, Sir Peter Lely, painted portraits of both the king and queen, as well as many of the courtiers and nobles the couple would have known. Capturing the essence of the Restoration era, Lely posed his subjects reclining, twisting and propping themselves up on furniture, a move away from the stiffer, more traditional portrait style of earlier years. As a result, his subjects appear relaxed and sensual in billowing silks and tumbling curls, but they are also direct and confident. The well-known portrait of Charles II by John Michael Wright in the Royal Collection Trust is almost languid in its representation of such a solemn and ceremonial pose.[41] Thought to have been created in the 1670s, it shows Charles leaning back on his throne with his legs slightly apart. Clothed in silks and ermine, he loosely holds the sceptre and orb in each hand. He smiles slightly, regarding the viewer through heavy eyelids, with a direct and penetrating gaze. The portrait is as sensual as it is stately and reflects the character of Charles II's distinctly non-Puritan indulgent and pleasure-loving court.

Catherine, too, was an art lover and cultural trendsetter. As well as Lely, she was painted by Jacob Huysmans in various works including a depiction of her as St Catherine, painted between 1664–1670. Pepys was treated with a visit to Huysmans's studio on 26 August 1664, when he saw this and another portrait of the queen as a shepherdess. Soon, as Sophie Shorland in *The Lost Queen: The Surprising Life of Catherine of Braganza, Britain's Forgotten Monarch* has pointed out, other women were requesting to be painted as the saint, including Pepys's wife and the king's mistress Barbara Palmer, Lady Castlemaine.[42] Huysmans, who painted Catherine a number of times, was clearly trusted by the queen to convey her chosen public identity. Even as a shepherdess, in the portrait seen by Pepys and painted between 1662–1664, Huysmans portrays her bathed in light, her face soft, but challenging the eye of the viewer. She wears a silver satin gown with a sumptuously decorated red cloak, her long hair falling over one shoulder. Despite its humble subject matter, the painting exudes power, strength and confidence. Today, both these works are in the Royal Collection Trust.[43]

Through their patronage of chosen artists, Charles and Catherine shaped the identity of their reign and publicly promoted their own power and strength as a poster couple of a new era of monarchy and relaxed opulence. Like the women inspired to emulate the queen in depictions of St Catherine, other courtiers eagerly booked these royally approved artists to produce portraits of their own. Lely painted the Duke and Duchess of York, Edward Montagu, Earl of Sandwich, and Charles's sister, Henrietta, Duchess of Orleans among others. As for Verrio, his work at Windsor inspired others to employ him, including Lord Arlington, who commissioned the Italian to paint the staircase at Euston Hall near Newmarket.[44] Verrio, Huysmans and Lely excelled in their depictions of sumptuous and expensive fabrics, relaxed poses and sensual expression. Through their specific patronage, the couple shaped Restoration era art and promoted fashionable Baroque expression, a concept that was at its height during their reign. With its emphasis on motion, drama and realistic form, the style had first emerged in the early seventeenth century and went on to dominate the period until the early years of the eighteenth century.

Artists had not entirely suffered during England's uncertain years of civil war in the 1640s, as they had been able to take commissions from clients on both sides of the conflict. Conversely, the theatrical arts made popular under the Tudor and early Stuart rulers, experienced serious setbacks under Puritan rule. Playhouses were closed from the beginning of wartime and remained shut throughout Cromwell's Protectorate. On Charles's accession in 1660 though, the theatre business was not only able to recover, but thrived, assisted by the patronage of the eager royals.

On 21 August 1660 Charles issued a royal grant to Thomas Killigrew and Sir William d'Avenant giving them 'full power and authority to Erect two Companies of Players'. This led to the creation of the King's Company, which usually performed at the Royal Theatre in Drury Lane, and another company of actors at the Duke of York, based in Portugal Street in Lincoln's Inn Fields. In addition, the king had his own private theatre at Whitehall Palace.[45] Catherine and Charles were frequent visitors to all three of these London establishments and watched performances alongside courtiers, diplomats and the paying public. New opportunities were now available for actors, musicians, stage crew, and costume and set designers as Charles's grant in 1660 woke an entire industry from its slumber.

While they were popular, theatres did not always live up to audience's expectations. The King's Theatre in Drury Lane, established in 1663, was visited by diarist Samuel Pepys the day after it opened, who thought it was 'extraordinary good', but grumbled about the 'narrowness of the passages in and out of the pit, and the distance from the stage to the boxes, which I am confident cannot hear', adding optimistically, 'but for all other things it is well'. The building accordingly underwent a number of improvements in its first years, such as the widening of the stage, adding more candles for light and employing more experienced musicians.[46] Both the king and queen visited here, and were also seen taking in shows at the Duke's Theatre in Lincoln's Inn Fields and the Cockpit at Whitehall. Their unmistakable presence gave dignity to the industry and a much-needed boost to the profession. On days when the couple attended, audiences flocked to see them as much as the shows, eyeing their expressions and reactions to the actors' spoken dialogue through the candlelit darkness. On one trip to the Cockpit in December 1662 Samuel Pepys noted that during a particularly lacklustre performance of *The Valiant Cid*, attended by the king and queen, the spectators seemed to take no pleasure 'but what was in the greatness and the gallantry of the company'.[47]

With playwrights, poets and political writers keen to find their footing in this renewed craze, a wider variety of works began to be performed. Hosting the traditional tragedies, historical plays and romances, they also turned to a new and increasingly popular style of theatrical expression: Restoration comedy. Plotlines included satire, twisted storylines and saucy innuendo. Playwright John Crowne, in the introduction to his play *Sir Courtly Nice, or It Cannot Be*, stated that comedy was the king's favourite genre. With its love triangles, songs and displays of comic lewdness Restoration comedy set the stage for successful women actors to emerge for the first time, such as Nell Gwyn and Moll Davis as well as 'the fair and famous comedian' Roxalana that John Evelyn saw in January 1662. Women were writing plays, too. In February 1668 Evelyn recorded in his diary a performance of *The Tragedy of Horace*, written by 'the virtuous Mrs Philips', attended also by the king and queen. They are also recorded attending a ballet together at Whitehall in February 1671.[48]

The couple's support for the theatre extended to more than just turning up for a show and waving to their star-struck subjects. In the summer of 1664, not only did Charles lend one theatre his coronation robes for the actor playing Owen Tudor in a production of *Henry V*, but gave his brother James's suit to the actor playing the role of King Henry. It was a performance Pepys described as 'most noble'.[49] The king also influenced the genres of work written during his reign, suggesting to Crowne that he create a reworking of a Spanish play, *No Pudeser*, and adapt it for London audiences. In the introduction to *Sir Courtly Nice*, Crowne wrote that the king was 'he … who understood me and all Men, better than I only knew myself, encouraged by a Royal judgement that never was mistaken'.

Catherine also had links to the theatre, not only as a spectator, but through members of her household. The playwright Sir William Killigrew served as the queen's vice-chamberlain and was responsible for the efficient running of Catherine's court. His brother Thomas owned and ran the king's Drury Lane theatre.[50] The queen was joint patron of her and her husband's own troupe of actors and organised private performances at court. An enactment of *The Souldier's Fortune* was 'acted by their Majesty's Servants at the Theatre Royal' and the queen also hosted a masque at Whitehall in December 1674. Count Grammont related in his memoirs her enthusiastic and detailed planning of one masque where she appointed not only the dancers, but also specified the theme of the performance and personally decided on each of the dancer's costumes.[51]

In recognition of the couple's long-term support of their industry, playwrights included references to the king and queen in their plays. *The Souldier's Fortune*, first performed in 1681 and written by Thomas Otway, includes the line 'the old Cavaliers got such a trick of it in the Kings Exile', referring to Charles's earlier years out of the country following his escape from Worcester. Similarly, the preface to John Dryden's *Don Sebastian, King of Portugal*, published in 1690, mentions a character's link to 'Don John de Braganza, Father to the most Illustrious and most Pious Princess our Queen Dowager'.[52]

We can also find traces of Catherine's involvement in the early opera movement during the period. Giovanni Baptista Draghi was an Italian musician in the queen's household and in February 1667 Pepys recorded that he had written an opera in his native language, composing the score as well as writing the lyrics. Thomas Killigrew, who managed the King's Theatre on Drury Lane and was present with Pepys at their meeting, expressed a wish to produce the show. Draghi sung a spontaneous preview of his work in front of the men, who also included William Brouncker. Pepys thought Draghi performed 'most admirably, and the composition most excellent'. The Italian also worked as co-composer alongside another of Catherine's musicians, Matthew Lock. They both created the music for the opera *Psyche* in 1673.[53] It cannot be coincidence that two of the early pioneers of opera in England were both Catherine's musicians, who was also a lover of music and a champion of the theatrical arts. Catherine continued to love music later in her life and in 1699 had a harpist, violinist, organist and guitarist in her household.[54]

Like elsewhere, the new developments made during the Renaissance era in Charles and Catherine's realm were driven by communities. While particular individuals of the period have risen to historical prominence, they were only able to shape change through the support and interaction of patrons, collaborators, teachers, students, buyers, collectors and colleagues. The discussions that took place on Florence's piazzas between architects and mathematicians in the early fifteenth century were no different in their aims than the meetings of the Royal Society in London two centuries later. The finding of new discoveries and techniques fuelled communication, debate and validation as ideas were tested and new lines of enquiry undertaken. Looking for public, easily accessible places to gather, like-minded thinkers, artists and scientists flocked to institutions that offered a warm welcome, refreshing food and drink, and with the freedom to discuss theories and ideas.

In 1624 the English scientist and philosopher Francis Bacon reported on the use of a stimulating and reviving drink adopted as a custom by residents in Turkey. Ground into powder and mixed with 'water, as hot as they can drink it', it was consumed, he wrote, at 'coffee houses, which are like our taverns. The drink comforteth the Brain, and Heart and helpeth Digestion'.[55] Coffeehouses had already been established in England by the 1650s in Oxford, Cambridge and London, but under Charles II they reached a new level of popularity. Samuel Pepys made regular mention in his diary entries of visiting coffeehouses to meet clients relating to his work with the admiralty and to chase owed funds. During one visit to Covent Garden in 1668, he was loudly berated at a coffeehouse by Sir Philip Howard who criticised a speech Pepys had made to Parliament. Embarrassed, Pepys hastily left and went home to dinner.[56] Whether it was the comforting scent of freshly brewed coffee or the mind-focusing properties of the caffeine, these venues promoted lively debate and sometimes brutal honesty, as experienced by Pepys.

However, these establishments soon gained an undesirable reputation for encouraging laziness. One commentator complained that customers 'sit half a day, and discourse with all companies that come in of State matters, talking of news and broaching of lies'. They criticised the judgements of their social betters, spread gossip and magnified 'their own parts, knowledge and wisdom'.[57] Charles wouldn't have minded subjects refreshing themselves with a hot dish of coffee, or even the spread of education and learning, something we know he personally valued and encouraged. But what eventually rattled him was the potential of coffeehouses to promote what he called the 'Disturbance of the Peace and Quiet of the Realm'. In a declaration of 1675, the king called for the houses to be totally suppressed and shut down, arguing that they bred idleness, with subjects engaging in 'divers false, malicious and scandalous reports' that threatened the peace of the state.[58] Naturally, seventeenth-century coffee lovers fought back. Just days after his proclamation had been read out, Charles decided to withdraw it and in doing so, changed the lives of his subjects. Coffeehouses continued to host intellectuals, artists, poets, adventurers, scientists and politicians over the rest of the century and beyond. In 1674 a member of Charles's Royal Society, Dr Willis, approved coffee drinking, writing that 'being daily drunk it wonderfully clears and enlightens each part of the Soul, and disperses all the clouds of every Function'. The Astronomer Royal, John Flamsteed, also discussed business with his printer over a dish of coffee in the early 1700s. By 1683, a French historian estimated that there were 3,000 coffeehouses in London alone.[59]

As for Catherine, she is often claimed to have introduced tea to her adopted country. However, tea drinking in England pre-dates her arrival at Portsmouth by at least three years, with one coffee shop near the Royal Exchange in London said to have advertised it as 'all Physicians approved' in 1658. In June 1667 Pepys found his wife 'making of tea; a drink which Mr Pelling, the Potticary [Apothecary], tells her is good for her cold and defluxions'.[60] Tea was therefore already considered a health drink by 1658, although the queen was praised in her own time for making it fashionable in England. The poet Edmund Waller penned a rhyme called *Of Tea, Commended by Her Majesty*, to celebrate Catherine's birthday, containing the lines 'Tea both excels, which she vouchsafes to praise. The best of queens, and best of herbs, we owe'.[61] Soon after her arrival in England it was sold at coffee shops and played its own part in stimulating minds and fuelling conversation. Members of the Royal Society were known to hold meetings at Constantine Jennings' shop in Threadneedle Street, London, which provided tea, coffee and chocolate to guests in 1665.[62] Later in the century, they served as meeting places for auctioneers, who sold paintings and prints created 'by the best Masters' to the public, who sipped on warm dishes of tea and coffee as they bid. A surviving pamphlet advertises an art sale in 1691 'at Tunbridge-Wells, at the Auction Coffee-house, by the Lower Walks'. The caffeine-fuelled drinks would have been welcome, with the sale advertised as 'beginning in the Morning at Eight'.[63]

Charles and Catherine are not often considered a power couple of their time and yet it was through their combined efforts that significant changes occurred in their kingdom. The dependable Catherine is often sidelined by writers in favour of the more tantalising and thrilling relationship dynamics between Charles and his many mistresses. On evaluating the evidence, it does seem as if Catherine has been miscast. The timid, absent queen of the history books is at odds with what we have seen of the opinionated, gun-wielding, calculating, warship-loving advisor who was at the king's side for twenty-three years. Charles II, Count Grammont noted, was 'easy and affable' but 'his heart was often the dupe ... oftener the slave, of his engagements'.[64] During their marriage, Charles refused to curb his love of other women and it was natural that Catherine would be uncomfortable with this arrangement. In time though, she seems to have resigned to put her anger aside for the peace of the court and focused on her own political role as queen.

From the moment they were married, Charles and Catherine's partnership was viewed with hope. Perhaps deliberately, Charles's court was everything the previous Puritan regime was not. It was sumptuous, extravagant and theatrical, encouraged by the couple through artists and portraits that combined sensuality with confident, regal authority. Wielding new and significant geographical power through their marriage, they established links and territories in the Americas, Africa and India. Financial and military resources were also boosted by their union and officially underlined in the terms of their marriage contract. The couple's royal and military power at the beginning of their relationship was strong enough to even rattle Spain, its leaders anxious over Charles and Catherine's shared authority.

The change they triggered together was felt by all levels of society. Through shared interests, they encouraged a resurgence and reformation of the theatre, while the earliest operas were written by musicians in Catherine's household. The new Baroque style was introduced in music and art, building on the work of earlier Renaissance artists and transformed into a new and energetic genre. Scientists met to discuss ideas and experiments at the newly formed Royal Society, an organisation that still exists today, while artists, thinkers, poets and politicians collaborated in the coffeehouses of the nation over hot dishes of coffee and pots of tea. The couple ruled over a rapid burst of creative expression, scientific reasoning and political propaganda. The historian V. de Sola Pinto, writing in 1950 in *English Renaissance 1510–1688*, considered Charles II's 'the last English court which was a true focus of culture'.[65]

Their marriage survived almost continual adversity, fought in both public and private including the Great Fire, plague, foreign war and the visible and ongoing presence of Charles's mistresses at court. They also fended off accusations of Catholic plotting and calls for their divorce, a subject Charles refused to seriously consider, even if a new royal wedding could potentially secure the future of the succession. Both were involved in London's post-fire plans, although Catherine's contribution of 1666/67 is rarely acknowledged. Thrust together for the political benefits of their individual nations, they maintained a subtle and intimate power through supporting and defending one another during their marriage. Catherine accompanied her husband on his travels, took an interest in his hobbies and acted as advisor and confidante during his troubles and challenges. Charles defended her against her enemies, whether they objected to her nationality, her religion or the workings of her body. His preoccupation with protecting her suggests that she meant a lot to him, so much that he refused to abandon her despite leaving the realm with a succession crisis. Although, after ironing out initial differences, they treated one another with respect in public, we cannot know if they were ever truly in love romantically or simply resolved to work in partnership for the benefit of their states. Charles's sudden guilt over his treatment of Catherine as he approached death suggests that they at least had a fondness for one another and that he cared about her feelings. Equally, she tolerated difficulties at court for the sake of her marriage and role as queen.

Despite the positive changes they made to the realm, Charles and Catherine were unable to produce an heir to help stabilise the nation after Charles's death on 6 February 1685. His brother James II was proclaimed king. Rival claims to the throne and a rebellion soon followed, instigated by the Duke of Monmouth, Charles's illegitimate son. An unpopular king, James was soon deposed and in 1688 his daughter Mary and her husband William of Orange were invited to take the crown. During these events, Catherine continued to live in England as Queen Dowager, residing at Somerset House on the bank of the Thames. In 1692 she sailed to Portugal, writing her will seven years later as 'Catherine, Queen of Great Britain'. From 1705 she ruled as regent on behalf of her brother Pedro II, governing her home country during wartime, commanding a small team of ministers and Portugal's army. She therefore always had the ability to actively rule; it was just that in England, on account of her sex, religion and the demands of both the court and public, she was required to remain less prominent. Catherine died on 31 December 1705 at 67 years of age and was buried in the sixteenth-century church of Belem, near Lisbon.

Charles II would always be known as the 'Merry Monarch', his innovations to the kingdom celebrated in science and the arts. However, Catherine was quietly encouraging, advising or implementing many of these changes at his side. Edmund Waller composed a poem for the queen two years before Charles's death on New Year's Day 1683 when she was 44 years old and had served as queen for over twenty years. The couple would have listened, smiling, as Waller recited, 'What revolutions in the world have been, How we are changed since we first saw the Queen! She, like the sun, does still the same appear, Bright as she was at her arrival here!'[66]

Chapter 9

William and Margaret Cavendish, Duke and Duchess of Newcastle, England

In December 1593, a baby lay sleeping, swaddled in its cradle. Born to Sir Charles Cavendish and his wife Catherine, the boy was named William after his grandfather. At the time of his birth, he had a bold and formidable grandmother, Elizabeth (nicknamed Bess) of Hardwick, who had married Sir William Cavendish, a courtier and administrator of Henry VIII, in 1547. Sadly, Bess's husband died ten years after their marriage, although she would become famous in her own right for her acquisition of wealth and undertaking of building projects such as Hardwick Hall and Chatsworth House in Derbyshire. Bess married twice more after Cavendish's death and died in 1608 when the young William would have been a teenager.

Appropriately for a member of a locally powerful and well-connected family, William embarked on a Cambridge education at St John's College, although his real passion was horsemanship, which he practised religiously, along with fencing, dancing and music. In around 1612 he married Elizabeth Basset of Blore, the widow of Henry Howard, younger son of the Earl of Suffolk. The Bassets were a 'very honourable and ancient family in Staffordshire', and the lands Elizabeth brought to the marriage swelled William's own.[1] Their partnership was a happy one and they produced ten children, five of whom survived into adulthood.

Young, athletic and exuberant, William attracted the attention of the early Stuart kings James I and Charles I. In his mid-teens, he was made a Knight of the Bath and soon afterwards was created Viscount Mansfield and Baron of Bolsover, as well as Lord Lieutenant of Derbyshire. In 1628, Charles I made him Earl of Newcastle and ten years later, William was entrusted with the government of the king's eldest son, the Prince of Wales, the future Charles II. The royalist earl enthusiastically supported the king in the civil wars that followed, lending Charles I vast sums of cash and troops to help him regain control of the kingdom. In 1642 he was tasked with enforcing order and seizing supplies in the north, carrying out missions in Yorkshire, Northumberland, Cumberland, Westmoreland and Durham. His loyalty also extended to Charles's queen, Henrietta Maria, and William escorted her to York in 1643 under a substantial armed guard for her protection. He also gave her a gift of £3,000 in cash towards her cause.[2]

No one could deny that William was a generous and committed supporter of the monarchy, spending thousands of pounds of his personal funds on the war. Later estimated to have cost him a staggering £941,303, his contributions included loans and gifts to the king, personal war-related losses, legal bills and other expenditure. The accuracy of this figure has been doubted by writers, but C. H. Firth in the late nineteenth century did point out the similar amount of £918,000 spent by the equally patriotic Marquis of Worcester.[3] By 1643, however, it became clear to everyone that the royalists were losing the war and no amount of funds, troops or horses from rich supporters could save them. Even the enthusiastic William began to doubt that the Crown would emerge triumphant. With the death of his wife in April that year, along with Parliament's victory at the Battle of Marston Moor in July 1644, William cut his losses. Sensing the heavy glare of Parliament on his back, he gathered up £90 in cash and boarded a vessel bound for Hamburg in Germany, accompanied by his sons and a few close friends. Now a widower, William travelled throughout Europe, visiting Rotterdam, Antwerp, Mechelen and Brussels. While in Paris, he paid a visit to Queen Henrietta Maria, who had fled England with a reduced household and settled there. It was during one of these visits to the queen that he met a young, socially awkward brunette named Margaret Lucas.

Born near Colchester, Essex in 1624, Margaret was the youngest daughter of Sir Thomas Lucas and his wife Elizabeth. She enjoyed a close relationship with her siblings at their home at St John's, a medieval monastic building acquired by the Lucases after the Dissolution of the Monasteries in the sixteenth century. Margaret would have been familiar with parts of the original medieval abbey including its grand, turreted gateway and spacious grounds. Sadly, her father died when she was young and her mother took over the running of the home and the care of their five daughters and three sons. In later recalling her childhood, Margaret remembered that her mother preferred to discipline her children with reason and kindness rather than physical punishments. Ensuring they were always presentable and well dressed, Elizabeth Lucas raised them to be humble and compassionate and patiently indulged each of them in their individual interests. In Margaret's case, this was reading. Margaret acknowledged her 'overactive, unrestrained imagination' and that she had 'a poetical and philosophical genius even from my birth'. At the age of 12 she had already written a number of books, although promised that 'for want of good method and order' she would never release them.[4]

In 1643, while William Cavendish was propping up the royalist war effort in the north of England, the 19-year-old Margaret was begging her mother to allow to her to join the household of Queen Henrietta Maria, who she heard was residing in Oxford. No doubt attracted by the prestige of the position and the opportunity for her family to be recognised by the queen, her mother agreed. Margaret left the predictable comfort of St John's and travelled west, but on arrival bitterly regretted her decision. Her confidence melted away in crowds and she found it difficult to adapt to a busy court life away from her mother, brothers and sisters. Overly self-conscious and afraid of appearing 'dull' to strangers, she had a tendency to look down and shy away from conversation and socialising. Margaret had been used to the quiet structure of home life, with her family members ready to correct her manners or speech if necessary. Here, at Henrietta Maria's court, Margaret was alone. The strong, ambitious personalities that all vied for the queen's attention, along with the gossiping nature of the court, would have pushed Margaret further into the shadows. She wrote to her mother, asking for permission to return home, but was refused. Elizabeth, an ardent royalist, believed that Margaret's hasty departure from the queen's service so soon after joining would be disrespectful, and persuaded her daughter to stay. Dutifully, Margaret stepped on board a wooden ship with her royal mistress and other ladies and watched as the sails puffed with wind, the bow pointing towards the coast of France.

The gallant earl and the shy young woman met in April 1645 when Margaret was in her early twenties and William in his early fifties. 'He was pleased to take some particular notice of me,' Margaret later recalled, and the couple soon talked of marriage. According to Margaret their attraction was not 'amorous', but 'honest and honourable', and the pair, especially William, hoped one day for male heirs to add to the Cavendish brood. The couple were married in Paris, in the chapel of fellow royalist and English ambassador Sir Richard Browne.[5]

An image from the couple's period in exile gives us an idea of how they would have appeared in the early years of their marriage. *The Family of William Cavendish, Marquess of Newcastle-Upon-Tyne* in the Metropolitan Museum of New York shows the couple seated at a table with a group of men and women. Dating to 1656, we can see William and Margaret seated at the right of the composition.[6] William looks out at us, his arm slightly raised and finger pointed towards the others at the table as if he is about to stress an opinion. He has light-coloured hair curling in waves down to his shoulders and sports the moustache and bearded chin fashionable for the period. Margaret sits next to her husband, wearing a long gown, a tumble of curls trailing down her back, and listens intently to a man on her left. In many of her portraits, including this one, she is depicted wearing a short necklace of pearls. They are probably the ones William purchased for her as a gift in Antwerp in 1653, just a few years before this animated and busy scene was created.

Living abroad in exile, while a parliamentarian government ruled over England, the couple had a rocky start to their marriage. William and Margaret were now considered traitors and their lands were seized. William was therefore unable to obtain any income from his estates whether in sales, production or rents. To fund their lifestyle, he became a prolific borrower, negotiating loans from wealthy Europeans to purchase property and pay living expenses. Margaret's own account relates one occasion when they had no money to buy a simple dinner. William asked his wife if she could pawn some of her clothes to buy food, but realising she had nothing of any value, Margaret asked her waiting maid to pawn some 'small toys' she had given her, which the maid 'willingly did'.[7] In a letter of December 1653, William discussed the purchase of a pearl necklace for his wife, but Margaret cautioned him against spending too much on them. Writing to Lord Clarendon's secretary William Edgeman, he specified that Margaret had chosen the 'lesser size because they are so much cheaper'.[8] The pearl necklace Margaret is frequently seen wearing in portraits fits this description, being of a shorter length, hugging the throat. The couple's financial situation at the start of their marriage was, according to these accounts, uncertain and changeable. They were able to buy some luxuries, but could not access any of William's more secure income from England, with everything pawned or bought on credit.

At least this is what Margaret, in the biography she later wrote of her husband, wanted us to believe. There are other hints that the Newcastles did in fact enjoy a little more comfort during their years in exile. As well as the purchase of Margaret's pearls, the couple took a high-society carriage ride, bought and maintained a growing number of exotic horses and entertained aristocratic guests. In February 1658, the couple hosted members of the exiled royal family and fellow royalist supporters at their Antwerp home with dancing, singing and drinking. Margaret meekly called this a 'small entertainment ... such as his [William's] present condition was able to afford them', but an eyewitness account describes it as far more extravagant. There were recitations of Newcastle's poetry, costumes made out of black satin, bay leaf garlands and feathers, and four hours of dancing. A banquet was served 'in eight great chargers, each borne by two gentlemen of the court' while others brought in wines and other drinks.[9] The couple also lived in a relatively prestigious residence, once that of the painter Peter Paul Rubens who had died in 1640. Margaret even states proudly that the house, taken for their 'small family' was also for her husband's 'own content', making sure to point out, excitedly, that it was owned by the widow of the 'famous picture-drawer, Van Ruben'.[10]

Hosting lavish entertainments and choosing a well-known home do not sound like the actions of a couple who are unable to scrape enough money together to buy a dinner. Sarah Heller Mendelson, in *The Mental World of Stuart Women,* argued that the couple's hardships may have been later exaggerated by Margaret 'to prove to the world that Newcastle had been Charles's wisest, noblest and most loyal subject'. She further states that Margaret's decision to dedicate the work to Charles II was intended as a 'rebuke for his ingratitude' for neglecting to provide William with a position in government after his accession in 1660.[11] Of course, it is also possible that the Newcastles' financial situation improved and declined repeatedly over time and that they experienced periods of stability that alternated with those of poverty. It is also likely that William saw some of his expenditure as a social necessity, maintaining relationships with key advisors to Prince Charles and members of the royalist aristocracy in hope of future gain in the event of a return to power. This would support Mendelson's claim that Margaret showed some anger towards Charles when these overtures, paid for by the spiralling debts of the Newcastles, later went unrecognised.

By 1651 the couple were anxious about the future of their Cavendish estates back in England. William had charmed lenders and raised toasts to exiled royals on borrowed credit, but Margaret opted for a more proactive approach. Boarding a ship, she set sail for England to request the return of her husband's estates. Heading towards London with her brother-in-law Charles Cavendish, Margaret would have carefully considered how they might persuade the council to restore lands to a man now labelled a traitor. At the least, they hoped to secure some funding that would help sustain them in exile. Margaret and Charles received harsh, but predictable, news. They were told that William was 'the greatest traitor to the State', and that 'by reason I was married since my Lord was made a delinquent, I could have nothing'.[12] Adding insult, the pair then discovered that lands the Cavendishes had specifically wanted to retain had been sold in their absence, some of them even marked for demolition. These included the family's beloved homes of Bolsover Castle and Welbeck, although Charles Cavendish later managed to negotiate the purchase of the properties at an inflated cost. Dejected and defeated, Margaret was now missing William. She later remembered that she felt very 'melancholy, by reason I was from my Lord, which made my mind so restless, as it did break my sleep, and distemper my health'.[13] Leaving Charles in London to settle some of his own family business, she boarded a ship and headed back to Antwerp.

Margaret had also experienced adversities of her own relating to the civil wars, not limited to financial trouble. She lost four members of her family, including her beloved brother Charles and her family home of St John's was raided by soldiers, who took the Lucases 'goods, plate, jewels, money, corn, cattle and like, cut down their woods, pulled down their houses'.[14] William also mourned for those he loved. His own brother Charles, who had accompanied Margaret to London, died in 1654. The beheading of King Charles I, the man behind so much of William's rise and the husband of the queen that Margaret had served, would also have come as a shocking blow to the couple.

Both William and Margaret believed that monarchy was fundamental to a nation's stability. They were public champions of its political significance, but also respected its ancient ceremony. As Charles I's head tumbled from his shoulders on that cold morning at Whitehall, William must have looked back at his own service to the Crown. Considered a war hero during his lifetime, he had fulfilled political, military and household duties for the royals. In 1637 he was given a trusted and intimate position in the household, tasked with overseeing the upbringing of the Prince of Wales, the future Charles II. From around the age of 7, Charles would have received training from him in horsemanship, academic education and manners. William therefore had a hand in shaping the man who would later be king. Margaret later referenced her husband's influence on the prince, particularly in horsemanship. 'Being but 10 years of age,' she wrote of Charles, 'he would ride leaping horses, and such as would overthrow others, and manage them with the greatest skill and dexterity.'[15]

A letter William wrote to the young prince reveals some of his views on what constituted a royal education. There was a strong focus on study, although he told him, 'I would not have you too studious, for too much contemplation spoils action.' He advised Charles to have a knowledge of history to prepare him for the politics he would encounter as king, for in past and current events 'there is no alteration but in names'. He stressed the importance of prioritising culture, ceremony and an appreciation of the arts, and urged him 'to be courteous and civil to everybody', especially to the ladies of the court.[16] Katie Whitaker, in *Mad Madge*, noted that William and his royal pupil had some shared personality traits and explored evidence that Charles followed his governor's advice once king.[17] Both men loved women, were patrons of creatives and had an interest in science, and it is tempting to attribute these traits to William's earlier influence. Charles himself acknowledged Newcastle's impact on him early in his reign, in 1665. In the patent that granted him a dukedom in that year, the king referenced his role during his 'younger years' and vowed to 'always retain a sense of those good principles he instilled into us'.[18]

In the 1640s William fought tirelessly for the Crown and was recognised for his military impact. The writer Edward Hyde, Earl of Clarendon, in his *The History of the Rebellion and Civil Wars in England*, wrote that in battle he 'notoriously did sometimes change the fortune of the day'. The earl credited Cavendish with a strong reputation in the North, along with military victories which included rescuing the city of York from 'the Rebels, when they look'd upon it as their own'. Clarendon also praised his warm and generous nature which made him popular with his troops, but drew the line at praising William as a strong military leader. 'The substantial part, and fatigue of a General, he did not in any degree understand,' wrote Clarendon politely in his *Rebellion*, but chose to be far more direct in a private letter of 4 June 1650, calling Cavendish 'a very lamentable man, and as fit to be a general as to be a bishop'.[19]

Arguably, William's physical, financial and moral contributions helped to prolong the royalist fight during the 1640s. Even Clarendon had to admit that most of William's battles ended in 'Success and Victory' and he was known as fervent, courageous and fearless in war. He had ensured the safety of Queen Henrietta Maria and secured important strategic areas and ports for the king, such as in Scarborough and Hull. According to Margaret, he also repressed a mutiny in Durham in the northeast of England. And then there was Cavendish's lending, providing the king with thousands of pounds along with troops and horses. William was by no means the only wealthy royalist supporter who ploughed money into the war, but it is interesting to consider whether, without William's considerable financial, physical and strategic input, the government of Charles I might have crumbled earlier than it did.

Once married to Margaret, we find William still pulling the strings of royalist resistance in exile. *The Clarendon Papers* are full of references to actions taken by Newcastle to restore the monarchy to the throne of England during the late 1640s and 1650s, while Margaret, also a fervent royalist supporter, was by his side. In November 1645, now Marquis of Newcastle, we find him bringing a ship into the king's service. In April 1650 he was sworn into the Council at Breda, in the same month that he was lightly reprimanded for his habit of continually swearing. In August 1651 the papers reference William's canvassing of Frederick William, Elector of Brandenburgh, for military aid to back the future Charles II, and in February 1654 he presented a receipt for arms, ammunition and ordnance that he had purchased.[20] By mid-December 1659, William wrote to Clarendon assuring him of Charles's imminent restoration to the throne.[21] Just five months later, the Newcastles were making plans to return to England.

On 28 May 1660 William's leather boots thudded off the wooden gangplank of a ship and onto his home soil. Margaret, for the time being, remained in Europe as security for his debts. However, once the remaining £400 had been taken care of (with another loan) she followed William to London, and the two set about regaining and repairing their confiscated estates and homes.[22] Over the course of their marriage, the couple were responsible for restoring and modernising a number of buildings, including Bolsover Castle, a medieval fortress rebuilt by William's father in the early seventeenth century. The building had been partly demolished for its materials and ransacked for furniture by parliamentarian supporters. According to Lucy Worsley in *Bolsover Castle*, the couple built new staterooms, made repairs to the roof and added a new staircase.[23] In 1663 the ruined Nottingham Castle was added to the couple's estates, with rebuilding taking place between 1674–79 thus continuing after the duke's death.[24]

Welbeck, the couple's main residence in England, was a mansion with an impressive gateway, tiled roof and tall Tudor-style chimneys, all recorded in a depiction by Abraham van Diepenbeeck in an engraving now in the collection of the Royal Academy of Arts.[25] Once an abbey dating to the twelfth century, like Margaret's childhood home of St John's, it was dissolved by Henry VIII in 1538. It then passed through the hands of various courtiers and tradesmen before being owned by Elizabeth 'Bess' of Hardwick. From her, it descended to her son Charles Cavendish and then into William's hands. In William and Margaret's time, the property boasted a stable and riding house for William's beloved horses, along with staterooms, a gallery and kitchens with a well-stocked garden. Set in acres of land and near the sprawling oaks of Sherwood Forest, the couple entertained courtiers, playwrights, philosophers and poets within its stone walls. Richard Flecknoe, a visitor to the house, regarded it as a 'noble edifice' and a fine example of 'great mens Houses' while John Evelyn, visiting in 1654, called it 'a handsome and stately building', although his description of it as 'melancholy' perhaps reflects on the decay of the home during William's exile. Flecknoe, a friend of the Newcastles, was able to take a more intimate look at the property once the couple had settled back in. Writing a poem inspired by Welbeck, he noticed that, unlike those of other women, Margaret's closet contained 'nothing of vanity … excepting books, the mirrors of the mind'.[26]

The couple were prolific supporters of creatives and a long list of writers and artists established and furthered their careers as a direct result of their patronage. Henry Ten Eyck Perry, in *The First Duchess of Newcastle and Her Husband as Figures in Literary History*, has explored the couple's patronage and friendships with characters such as Ben Jonson, James Shirley and William Sampson, also noting that Margaret was present during discussions between her husband and the philosophers René Descartes and Thomas Hobbes.[27] The latter was a frequent visitor to the couple and Margaret remembered one conversation they had about the possibility of men flying with artificial wings, something the duke considered impossible due to the skeletal placement of human arms compared with the wings of birds.[28] William and Margaret also supported the careers of creatives while in exile. The Dutch artist Abraham van Diepenbeeck produced portraits of the pair and Margaret would later commission him to draw the striking images of her featured in her books. Their status as literary patrons and supporters was also celebrated, with Gerard Langbaine, in *An Account of the Dramatick Poets* of 1691, writing of William that 'No person since the Time of Augustus better understood Dramatick Poetry, nor more generously encourag'd Poets', while Flecknoe maintained that Margaret 'makes each place where she comes a Library'.[29] Working together, their patronage ensured not only the spread of art and culture, but also encouraged critical and scientific thinking in mid-seventeenth century England and Europe.

William and Margaret's literary interests went beyond simply encouraging and paying writers to create new work. William was also a keen author, writing plays and poetry, including *The Feign Innocence, Or Sir Martin Marall*, a collaboration with the writer John Dryden, and *The*

Humurous Lovers of 1667. Samuel Pepys and his wife watched *The Feign Innocence* in a packed theatre on 16 August that year, calling it 'the most entire piece of mirth', the diarist admitting that he 'never laughed so in all my life'.[30] In 1658 while in Antwerp William published his own work on horsemanship, *Methode et Invention Nouvelle de Dresser les Chevaux*. This was William's passion and personal field of expertise. A copy from the year of its publication in the collection of the National Sporting Library and Museum in the United States, contains several black and white drawings made by Margaret's preferred artist, Abraham van Diepenbeeck. In one, William glides into the air, seated on a winged horse as ancient gods and goddesses gaze down from a billowing cloud. Eleven horses surround William, each seated back on their hind legs in a bowing gesture. In another, William wears full armour as his horse rears up onto its hind legs in a dramatic pose, his page preparing to hand him his helmet. He is surrounded by angels and cherubs bearing his arms, blowing a horn and offering him a laurel wreath. Newcastle was considered a knowledgeable authority on horsemanship, or the 'Mannage', as he referred to it. He was able to perform 'tricks' on horses, such as training them to walk on their hind legs. In Antwerp, he remembered how 'Gentlemen of all Nations' visited to see him ride at his house there, among them Dutch, Italian, Spanish, Polish and French travellers. Once back in England, William penned a new work, *A New Method, and Extraordinary Invention to Dress Horses*, which contained everything from how to sit in the saddle to William's own advice on spurs. Published in 1667, it was intended to complement his first book, although he recommended the two be read together for best results. His work was viewed as groundbreaking, with the writer Gerard Langbaine calling it 'the most Magnificent, and withal the Best Book of Horsemanship, that was ever yet extant', adding that the French equestrian writer Jacques de Solleysel 'borrowed' William's chapter on the *Art of Breeding* and used it in his own work, with credit.[31]

With his interest in science, philosophy, the stage and horsemanship, William was the focus of his wife's hungry curiosity. She repeatedly credited her husband, whom she called her 'witty poet', with the role of a tutor. He was a willing teacher and she listened to his theories and tales with wide-eyed interest. Actively trying to understand the world around her, Flecknoe once noted that she carried 'a living Library in her brain'.[32] William later stated that she gained most of her knowledge from him, her brother and her brother-in-law rather than from scholars, but with so many meetings, dinners and social links between her husband and playwrights, poets, philosophers, political writers and scientists of the age it is difficult to imagine that Margaret was not inspired by them, too.

The wide range of subjects Margaret was interested in can be seen from the works she published. Her first book, *Poems and Fancies*, was published in 1653, quickly followed in 1655 by *The World's Olio*, where she ventured into discussing aspects of physics. Philosophy came next, in the same year, with *Philosophical and Physical Opinions*. In 1656 she released her own autobiography, a short story of her life, called *A True Relation of the Birth, Breeding and Life of Margaret Cavendish*, where she discussed her background, personality and aspects of her marriage to William. Three more books followed, this time dealing with observations of nature, romance and a book of plays, before *Orations of Diverse Sorts* in 1662. Here, Margaret offered a catalogue of speeches that could be used for funerals, deaths or to rally distressed soldiers. Margaret even included speeches a king could use, including one to calm rebellious subjects and another in case of a civil war. More philosophical work then followed, along with a biography of her husband called *The Life of William Cavendish*. The work received some harsh criticism during her lifetime, in particular from Samuel Pepys, who recorded in his diary that it was 'ridiculous', proving she was a 'mad, conceited, ridiculous woman and he [William] an ass to suffer her to write what she writes to him and of him'.[33] Although Margaret assured us that she had created a factual, historical biography of her husband, her depiction of him as a continually wise, capable commander serving a grateful and doting king betrays some bias. Pepys's reaction also suggests that Margaret's view of William was not shared by at least some of their contemporaries. However, the work is valuable for its biographical information, as well as an example of the perceived merits of a good soldier of the English Civil War period. It also reveals a touching and intimate commentary of William's life through Margaret's eyes.

The couple also collaborated, with William playing a vital role in the development of her writing career. Poems and statements written by the duke can be found in a number of her works and he also penned five scenes of her play, *The Lady Contemplation*.[34] He fiercely defended her work in print, responding to criticisms that she had not written them herself, but lifted ideas from the work of scholars. William wrote a four-page defence of Margaret's work in her *Philosophical and Physical Opinions* in 1655, which he titled *An Epistle to Justify the Lady Newcastle*. In it, he assured readers that she did author her own works, did not converse with scholars and produced her philosophical theories 'wrought out of her own brain'.

Of course, part of the problem was that Margaret was a woman, something the couple well knew and which William also addressed in his *Epistle*. 'But here's the crime,' wrote William, 'a Lady writes them, and to entrench so much upon the male prerogative, is not to be forgiven.'[35] But it was not just her sex that rattled the 'Gown Tribe', as William called them, but the fact that Margaret was also confident and unapologetic in her actions and behaviour.

Margaret was not the only woman writer of the Restoration period; Katherine Philips and Aphra Behn wrote poems, plays and prose in the seventeenth century. However, she not only tiptoed into the socially masculine subjects of science, philosophy and war, but was openly proud and ambitious in her writing and private life. Considered eccentric, Margaret became famous for her unusual fashions and ensured her name and full-length image were emblazoned on the frontispieces of her books. She dedicated her *Life of William Cavendish* to Charles II himself, admitting that it was a 'bold' thing to do, and daringly published her own advice on military conflict, taxes and how to rally troops, arguing that it was not 'inconsistent with my being a woman, to write of wars'.[36] Incidentally, Niccolò Macchiavelli had expressed this same sentiment in his introduction to *The Prince* the previous century, writing that it was 'presumptuous in me, a man of humble birth, to propose rules of conduct to those who govern'. However, he argued that only a citizen could 'judge properly of a prince' and this was perhaps the way Margaret saw her own contribution. As a woman who had lived through civil conflict, been exiled, had her family home ransacked and saw her own husband's attempts to claw back political and social power, she was in fact highly qualified to express her opinions on war.

Margaret also commented on seventeenth-century society, education, scholarship and science. She was not afraid to appear centre stage. Her readers would have turned the front page of *The World's Olio* in 1655 to find van Diepenbeeck's drawing of its author standing on a pedestal in the centre of the page, with two classical gods gazing at her on either side. The duchess looks out at us as if in a challenge, swathed in fabric, a hand resting self-assuredly on her hip.

In many ways, it is easy to understand why scholars resisted Margaret's rise as a non-fiction author. Here was a woman with no academic training, writing of atoms and Sir Isaac Newton's theory that colour was formed by broken rays of light from the sun. She understood tiny worlds, writing of minute 'creatures' and imagined a whole sub-atomic ecosystem in her poem *A World in an Earring*. She criticised writers, as well as those who criticised her, pointing out that they 'found fault that they [her works] were defective through want of learning, and on the other side, they said I had plucked feathers from out of the universities'.[37] If a woman from an unacademic background could understand, challenge and develop these notions on a public platform, what did it say about their own qualifications and authority? Even her fellow writer Katherine Philips recognised that Margaret's legacy would be appreciated more respectfully in future ages rather than her own. In a poem written before her death in 1664, Philips wrote of the duchess's 'boundless mind' and promised that in 'future-times authentick fame shall bring, Historians shall relate, and Poets sing'.[38]

In 1667 Margaret pushed the gender boundaries of scholarship even further, venturing into a space that had up until then been exclusively inhabited by men. On 30 May of that year, she was the first woman to attend a meeting of the Royal Society, the institution so heartily founded and encouraged by Charles II. The minutes reveal that Margaret had 'intimated her desire to be present at the next meeting', another example of her boldness. She was duly invited and various experiments were conducted in her presence, including the weighing of air, mixing of colours and 'two cold liquors by mixture made hot'. According to a nineteenth-century history of the Royal Society, its inviting of distinguished and well-known people was intended 'to promote experimental science' so that knowledge could spread, one of the original aims of the organisation.[39] By now Margaret had been an author for over a decade. Perhaps the Society believed that if she was to continue to discuss and publish works on science and philosophy, then she would benefit, in their eyes, from a demonstration of the more rigid and modern experimental approaches that they so vigorously endorsed.

Samuel Pepys was present at this meeting, but heard Margaret say nothing 'worth hearing, but that she was full of admiration, all admiration'. Later, after being shown more experiments, he wrote that 'she cried she was still full of admiration'.[40] There is a mocking note to Pepys' account, as if Margaret had not fully understood the experiments or could only reply in empty exclamations. However, what the diarist probably interpreted as emptiness was almost certainly the shyness and 'bashfulness' she often wrote about, that even with 'reason' she struggled to overcome, especially in crowds. Margaret, as a bold and confident woman, must have recognised the significance of her presence at the Royal Society, especially being among so many men who had criticised her work. Pepys recorded that there had initially been a lively debate over whether the duchess should be invited.

John Evelyn, on a visit to William and Margaret at their London home in Clerkenwell on 27 April, four weeks before her Royal Society appearance, found himself 'much pleased with the extraordinary fanciful habit, garb, and discourse of the Duchess' although Evelyn's wife was less impressed. Mary Evelyn found Margaret's conversation 'airy, empty, whimsical and rambling … terminating commonly in nonsense, oaths, and obscenity'.[41]

Despite these setbacks, with William's unwavering support Margaret soon became a pioneer for other women writers and thinkers of the mid-seventeenth century and beyond. Other civil war wives wrote and published biographies of their husbands, including Lucy Hutchinson and Lady Ann Fanshawe. Sarah Heller Mendelson, in *The Mental World of Stuart Women*, also highlights the duchess's probable influence on the work of Lady Halkett and Mary Rich, Countess of Warwick.[42] Another positive review came from somewhere Margaret and William must have least expected, the 'Gown Tribe' at the University of Cambridge. 'Hereafter,' they wrote, 'if generous and highborn men shall search our library for a model of a most accomplished general, they shall find it expressed in the Life, not in Xenophon's Cyrus, but in the Duchess of Newcastle's William.'[43]

Together, the couple raised the profile of women as creators and scientists in the mid-seventeenth century. As Margaret scribbled and William publicly defended her, they showed that a woman was capable of writing about science, war, history and philosophy. In his *Epistle*, he revealed the nature of their creative collaboration as a couple. Her work was created with his input as he shared his own knowledge and theories with her, while she interpreted them. He also boldly challenged his wife's critics to consider if her work offended them simply because of her sex. As a prominent military and political figure, his support lent credibility to her work, and he urged readers to encourage her. In her *Philosophical and Physical Opinions*, he wrote, 'Were the old Grave Philophers [sic] alive, How they would envy you', securing Margaret's place among those ancient thinkers so important to earlier Renaissance thought.[44] Margaret may have been writing, but William lit and kindled the flame behind her pen. As she wrote in *The World's Olio* in 1655, 'If I had never married the person I have, I do believe I should never had writ so, as to have adventured to divulge my works'.[45]

In 1666 with William as her loyal supporter, inspiration and champion, Margaret wrote one of the most fantastical works of her lifetime. It was to have huge consequences for the development of literature in the seventeenth century and beyond. She urged noble ladies to read the book, published as *The Description of a New World, Called the Blazing-World.* Heavy with feminine power, the story centres around a woman who finds herself in a new and unusual world and is quickly made empress of it. The reader is taken on a tour of this world through questions the empress asks of different members of society, finding out more about the domain she now rules. The women, although they are not permitted to take positions in the church or state, 'cause as much, nay, more mischief secretly, then if they had the management of publick Affairs' while the empress is driven in a carriage pulled by unicorns. Margaret's world has icy poles and two suns, as well as others that can only be seen with telescopes. Its residents are described in detail: geese-men that walk upright, men with a grass-green complexion, 'fish men' and others with blue, purple and orange skin. There is a city of gold constructed in the style of ancient Rome, while other cities are built with coral, amber and marble. Whole ships are made of solid gold, accompanied by engines that 'shoot forth Wind with a great force', to power them along the ocean. The people, predictably for Margaret, respect a monarchy that rules over them and dedicate themselves to learning subjects such as philosophy, chemistry, astronomy and mathematics. Robert Hooke's work *Micrographia* was published in the previous year and revealed a new world seen through a microscope lens. Hooke painstakingly illustrated and described everyday items in their magnified state, including urine crystals, vegetables, leaves and insects. Margaret's world took inspiration from this, with the empress observing a drone fly through a microscope with 'two hemispheres' for eyes, and the Plague 'a body of little Flies like Atoms, which go out of one body into another'.

Some of the references in *Blazing World* were more futuristic for seventeenth-century minds, such as Margaret's vision of souls moving in 'vehicles' made of air and stones that burst into flames when wet. Another emitted a light that allowed spirits to flit between worlds, and she described vessels moving underwater like modern submarines. Partly because of these references she has been widely considered one of the early pioneers of science fiction writing. As usual, William added his own public encouragement in a dedication inside *Blazing World*: 'your Creating Fancy, thought it fit, To make your World of Nothing, but pure Wit.'

Margaret and William exerted power and influence in political and artistic spheres. But is it possible to assess the nature of their personal relationship, 350 years after they lived? A look at the evidence suggests that they had a strong partnership throughout their thirty-year marriage. They each endured professional and personal criticism – William for his military actions and Margaret for her literary work – the merits of which were both hotly debated in the public eye. Their support and respect for one another in the face of this criticism was mutual and expressed publicly. William urged his wife to write and defended her place as an author, while in 1667 Margaret was seen crying out enthusiastic thanks from her box at the theatre to the actors in her husband's play *The Humorous Lovers*.[46]

They were a great support to one another in private, too. In her *Life of William Cavendish* Margaret related that her husband bolstered her spirits whenever she became despondent, particularly during their exile. 'He would gently reprove me, saying, I believed least, what I desired most; and could never be happy if I endeavoured to exclude all hopes,' she wrote.[47] She reflected, too, on their inability to have children, declaring herself 'barren', although stressing that her husband 'yet never did lessen his love and affection for me'.[48] Margaret similarly supported her husband during his exile, sailing to England to try to recover their estates and curbing William's extravagant spending in times of plenty with requests for restrained frugalness. Margaret explained in her *True Relation* that William was 'the only person I ever was in love with', while William maintained his affection for her throughout their marriage.[49]

It is especially interesting, considering their devoted loyalty to one another, to examine the striking differences in their personalities. William was a charismatic, jovial and charming cavalier, who, according to Margaret, was 'a great lover and admirer of the female sex'. He managed to charm his way into securing thousands of pounds' worth of loans in Europe and conversed effortlessly with people from all walks of society, doffing his hat to them as he chatted.[50] 'As for my humour,' wrote Margaret in *True Relation*, she was 'more taken or delighted with thoughts than in conversation with a society'. She preferred quiet contemplation over social visits, stating that she could 'most willingly exclude myself so as never to see the grace of another creature but my Lord as long as I live'.[51]

William's ease in company strongly contrasted with Margaret's self-proclaimed awkwardness which also shines in the diaries of her seventeenth-century commentators. She became tongue-tied at the packed meeting of the Royal Society, uncomfortable at the court of Queen Henrietta Maria and bodged even a simple curtsey among watching nobles. Sir Charles Lyttelton related in a letter of 7 August 1665 that at a gathering hosted in York by Sir George Saville, the duchess's behaviour was 'very pleasant, but rather to be seene then told', observing that she, 'instead of courtesies, made leggs and bows to the ground with her hand and head'.[52] These differences may have strengthened the couple's relationship. William joked, charmed and attracted patrons of all kinds to Welbeck. Margaret listened, learned and quietly processed information before setting down her interpretations on the page.

Despite their differences, the couple had much in common: a love of poetry, music and the stage as well as a thirst for knowledge and the sharing of it. In her own age Margaret was something of a celebrity, seen by her contemporaries as an eccentric aristocrat who loved to wear different fashions and styles of dress. On one occasion a horse-driven coach pulled up to the entrance of the royal court, and a woman stepped out wearing 'at least sixty ells of gauze and silver tissue about her, not to mention a sort of a pyramid upon her head, adorned with a hundred thousand baubles'. As those present wondered who this extravagantly dressed woman was, Charles II paused and eventually stated. 'I bet that it is the Duchess of Newcastle.'[53]

It wasn't the duchess on this occasion, but Margaret's reputation clearly preceded her. William seems to have doted on his wife and enjoyed her various expressions of personality and taste. The couple also experienced a degree of hardship while in exile, according to Margaret's *Life of William Cavendish*. As a couple they lived through adversity as well as success and were crucial to one another's development as personal and professional partners. Margaret Cavendish died at the age of 50 on 15 December 1673 and was buried in the North Transept of Westminster Abbey. William lived until the age of 84 and died on 25 December 1676, choosing to be buried beside Margaret. Their monument contains effigies of the couple, lying side by side in their formal robes. In the inscription, Margaret's writing is championed, reminding visitors to the tomb that she was 'a wise, wittie and Learned Lady, which her many Books do well testifie'.

The duke and duchess of Newcastle left a huge legacy on the lives of their contemporaries and in their contribution to the later Renaissance movement. Patronising artists, musicians, poets and playwrights, they also rubbed shoulders with leading aristocrats, leaders and diarists of the age. The couple counted René Descartes, Thomas Hobbes and John Dryden among their acquaintances and friends. They collaborated, commissioned, criticised and composed, encouraging the flourishing of art and science in England as well as in Europe. The genres that they contributed to were vast, publishing works on equestrian training, science, the theatre, poetry and philosophy. Together they also pioneered the new and mind-bending category of science fiction, and broke barriers in the acceptance of seventeenth-century women's writing. V. H. H. Green, in *Renaissance and Reformation – A Survey of European History Between 1450 & 1660*, believed one of the 'most significant' effects of the Renaissance was 'The formation of a new reading-public … to lead in its turn to the creation of an informed public opinion'.[54] The couple certainly embody this point. Both were authors of work aimed at the general reading public, created through collaboration, curiosity and ambition. But their legacy was not only literary. Politically, they each pushed the benefits of a seventeenth-century state ruled by monarchy and aided in its eventual restoration. For William, he may even have helped prolong the influence of Charles I and the objectives and leadership style of Charles II. Their trace can also be seen today in surviving structures of the homes they restored and renovated after their return to England in 1660. Nottingham Castle, Bolsover Castle and Welbeck Estate can all be visited today, although they are vastly different since Margaret and William walked their corridors.

Chapter 10

Jan Miense Molenaer and Judith Leyster of the Netherlands

Around the time William and Margaret Cavendish were cutting deals with creditors in Antwerp, 100 miles to the north a city just outside Amsterdam thrived with commerce, trade and social activity. A painting by Gerrit Berckheyde in the collection of the National Gallery in London offers us a glimpse into its past. Dating from 1674, *The Market Place and the Grote Kerk at Haarlem* shows the cathedral towering over other buildings in the square.[1] The butcher is open for business and residents hover in groups at the fish market. A couple walk their dog, while a man to the right of the painting squints to read a sign pasted onto a stone column. Huddles of people wearing hats and cloaks share news and greet one another in shadows cast by the sunlight. Berckheyde's depiction is not one of a dramatic, world-changing event involving political leaders, but a comforting and intimate glimpse of everyday life in the Netherlands.

Judith Leyster was born in the summer of 1609 to a working-class family in the city of Haarlem. She lived with her parents and siblings, although there is evidence that the family experienced some financial problems. On 18 December 1625 when Judith was in her mid-teens, her father Jan Willemsz Leyster, a former brewer, appeared in court stating that his creditors had taken all of his goods in payment of what he owed to them and he now wanted to 'distance himself' from the rest of his debts for the good of his family.[2] This source suggests that the family's hardship was long term, rather than a one-off failure to pay a bill. It is likely then that this financial uncertainty had an effect on the young Judith, who would have seen creditors entering the home and taking the Molenaers' treasured possessions based on their worth rather than any sentimental value. During her adult life Judith demonstrated resilience and determination as well as a motivation towards hard work. Later, sources also reveal that she had a sound understanding of financial and legal affairs. It's possible that these traits and skills were developed during observations of these uncertain years of her family's hardship in the 1620s.

A keen painter at a young age, Judith had embarked on an art career by the age of 20. Two of her most well-known works were completed in 1629, *The Jolly Toper* and *The Serenade*, both now in the collection of the Rijksmuseum in Amsterdam.[3] Approaching her work with serious and deliberate professionalism, she designed a monogram with which she signed her paintings, comprising of her initials, 'J. L.', with a star. A play on her surname, which translates as 'leading star', it was clever and unique. Underneath her signature she added the date of the work's completion. During these early years Judith had already achieved some fame. The writer Samuel Ampzing in his 1628 book *Descriptions and Praises of the City of Haarlem*, gave her a special mention, placing her in the workshop of the painter Franz Pietersz de Grebber. Grebber, wrote Ampzing, was 'an impressively good painter' specialising in the depiction of the human figure, exactly the genre Judith practiced and would become known for.[4] Her interactions with Grebber would have equipped her with not only a greater knowledge of the use of art materials and painting technique, but also some experience in running a business. It also connected her with the busy community of painters already working in Haarlem. Later, in a 1668 inventory of goods at her home, one of Grebber's works was listed suggesting that she continued to admire the artist long after she had finished her initial training with him.[5]

A number of writers have also speculated that Judith was a student of another Haarlem painter, Frans Hals, who was one of the most well-known artists in the city, creating scenes of laughing figures drinking and making music. Active in the earlier years of the seventeenth century, his work was prized by the time Judith joined Grebber and their styles are very similar. However, claims that Hals was Judith's tutor usually rest solely on comparisons of each artist's work rather than solid evidence. Markedly similar in subject matter, style and colour, many of Judith's paintings would later be mistaken for those of Hals and his influence can be clearly seen, but there is currently no proof that she was ever his student. She was known to the artist, however, and it is possible that Judith did train with him. Hals has also been linked as an instructor to other emerging artists of the time, including Gerrit Berckheyde and Adriaan Brouwer. Alternatively, Judith may have studied Hals's works privately, observing his work and emulating his style, which would explain the lack of surviving documentary evidence.

As an artist, Judith was viewed by her contemporaries as a trailblazer. The writer Theodorus Schrevelius championed her as a woman working in a male-dominated industry. Referring to 'the admirable Judith Leyster', he wrote, 'There are also in our city women painters ... still famous in our age who can compete with men in graphic art.'[6] Judith was not the only woman painter during the Renaissance. Artemisia Gentileschi was a successful artist in Italy, working in the mid-seventeenth century, while Lavinia Fontana also worked in Italy in the late sixteenth and early seventeenth centuries. In England, the miniaturist Levina Teerlinc created tiny portraits for the Tudors in the sixteenth century. However, women working as artists in their own right were still rare and often needed to deploy a heightened sense of ambition and independence to be seen in a world that was dominated by men. Judith was dedicated and determined and knew the power of a community. She forged links with other artists within the Dutch art scene and didn't hesitate to protect her business interests when challenged. In 1635 she issued a legal complaint when a student of hers named Willem Wouters left her tuition to join the workshop of Frans Hals. As well as underlining her business-like attitude, the episode is also evidence that she was teaching and encouraging other budding artists to join the city's vibrant art scene. Professional success came for Judith in 1633, when at the age of 24 she became the first woman to join Haarlem's Guild of St Luke as an artist. Judith's rise was swift. In just five years she had taken formal tuition in her craft, established her own business as a painter and was welcomed into the city's guild.

By the time she challenged her student for leaving her tuition, she had met another Haarlem painter, Jan Miense Molenaer. Like Judith, Jan was a skilled artist and heavily active in the community. They both shared similarities in style as well as a passion for genre painting: the depiction of people from lower social classes in animated, spontaneous scenes. The development of Dutch art is sometimes treated outside of its Renaissance context, but it had been busy learning and expanding since the time of Cosimo and Contessina de Medici. In the fifteenth and sixteenth centuries the country produced astonishingly lifelike portraits by artists such as Jan van Eyck and Hans Memling. It also gave the world the terrifying fantasy landscapes invented by Hieronymous Bosch, depicting humans, otherworldly creatures and strange structures in the unsettling triptych *The Garden of Earthly Delights*.[7] Through his paintings Bosch warned viewers of the frightening consequences of a sinful life, painting a tranquil garden scene alongside another with hellish beings and suffering. Later in the sixteenth century came the dramatic, regal portraits of Antonis Mor and Pieter Bruegel the Elder's depictions of peasants working in fields against dreamy landscapes.

By the opening years of the early seventeenth century, a new style had surfaced. Building on the realism of Mor and the subject matter of Bruegel, artists were motivated to replicate scenes of humble domestic life with increasing realism and movement. These were pushed forward by artists such as Rembrandt and Rubens, who painted women as they appeared in life with dimples on their skin and round bellies, with an emphasis on dramatic shadow and light. The stiff, formal portraits of the earlier period had given way to a more spontaneous, carefree depiction that was relatable to all social classes. Art historian David C. Preyer saw Dutch art driven by an 'honesty of purpose; for a dramatisation of the commonplace, with shades of beauty in its simplicity; its aim not so much to please the eye as to reach the soul'. Preyer saw this shift as a reaction towards decades of Spanish conflict in the Netherlands and, under its regime, turbulent religious restructuring such as that seen under Margaret of Austria during the previous century. Artists now, he wrote, turned towards familiar subjects they were grateful for in the face of uncertainty and chaos: clean, all-weather landscapes heavy with billowing clouds and smiling mothers feeding their children.[8]

Born in 1610, Jan was only a year or so younger than Judith. They would have had plenty of opportunities to meet and get to know one another through their interactions with the city's art community and perhaps through the guild itself. Although regarded with less curiosity by contemporary writers, Jan was recognised for his talent and technical ability. Records show that he conducted business with a range of art dealers and a number of his works appear in an inventory of the Amsterdam art dealer Johannes de Renialme in April 1640, listed among others by Frans Hals and Rembrandt.[9]

Jan was especially skilled not only in conveying realism, but also allegory, a style that expressed hidden meanings through symbolic objects. These were usually moral in nature; for example, a skull or hourglass alluded to the fragility of life and time, while flowers conveyed love or fertility. One of his early works, *Allegory of Vanity* in the collection of the Toledo Museum of Art, demonstrates his skill in this genre.[10] Painted in 1633, the year Judith entered the guild, it shows a well-dressed woman having her long hair combed as she rests her feet on a skull, a grim reminder of our mortality and a warning that death comes to us all. Jan would continue to incorporate hidden moral messages in works during his career. With shared interests in preferred genres, a similarity in age and moving within the same social circles, it is not surprising that Jan and Judith became a couple. They married on 1 June 1636 at a ceremony in Heemstede, a town a few miles south of Haarlem.

A self-portrait painted by Judith survives today in the National Gallery of Art in Washington D.C.[11] Believed to have been created in around 1630, she looks out at us with brown eyes, her dark hair pulled back beneath a white headdress. A wide lace ruff has been secured around her neck and she wears a rose-coloured gown with a black bodice. Pausing to paint a violinist composition on her easel she turns towards us, resting one elbow casually on the back of her chair, a brush in one hand and a palette in the other. The violinist she is halfway through painting can easily be identified as one of the figures in her *Merry Company* of 1629 now in the Klesch Collection.[12] Jan, too, completed a self-portrait in 1640, now at the Alte Pinakothek art museum in Munich, Germany.[13] Holding a cloak to his chest with one hand, he rests the fingertips of the other on the forehead of a skull on the table in front of him, showing that even in a self-portrait he could not resist slipping in a moral lesson. He has wavy, thick shoulder-length brown hair, and a trimmed, light-coloured beard on his chin. His lips are slightly pursed, as if he is about to speak.

The newlyweds, both successful businesspeople, settled into new roles within their partnership. While Jan continued to complete a never-ending number of commissions, Judith's attention seems to have turned towards supporting their growing family. With the birth of their children, it is understandable that the new demands of the household, including those of their businesses, needed to be reallocated. However, Judith was not ready to hang up her painter's apron just yet. The art historian Cornelis Hofstede de Groot considered it likely that Judith worked alongside her husband during these years, sharing tips and giving feedback on his paintings. De Groot based this on the similarities between their styles and techniques, remarking that many of Jan's 'pictures show so close an affinity to the style of Judith Leyster that husband and wife seem likely to have collaborated'.[14] It is also possible to see Judith's influence in Jan's professional progression and development. During the course of their union, Jan's colourful, traditional realism, as seen in *Allegory of Vanity*, takes a turn into the darker-lit and more spontaneous form favoured by Judith. His later brushstrokes are less careful and more expressive, the subject matter growing increasingly humble as we can see in *Saying Grace*, a painting in the collection of the Rijksmuseum dating to around 1653. In stark contrast with Jan's earlier work, it shows a greater emphasis on the use of shadow and the thicker, rougher brushstrokes that we see in Judith's work.[15] With her previous experience as a teacher, she was used to providing critique and guidance and was able to offer Jan a fresh perspective while settling a child or working on household duties. This was in both of their interests. If Jan improved in technique and demonstrated a greater flexibility in his artistic range, a wider variety of commissions could be taken, leading to more income for the couple. Jan grew into an increasingly versatile painter throughout the 1630s and 1640s, painting wealthy subjects as well as those from poorer sections of society. He was able to switch easily between formal and informal poses and styles and was as comfortable painting elaborate interiors and expensive fabrics as he was torn linens and wooden barrels. Taking into account the determination and ambition she had already demonstrated, her close proximity to her husband while working and her previous role as an art tutor, Judith's collaboration in her husband's work seems incredibly likely. In addition, there is the evidence of similarities within their styles and techniques. Jan's willingness to implement any feedback he received would have aided in his development and allowed him to take on a wider range of commissions. Some of her contribution is thought to have been more practical. Writer Frieda Van Emden in a 1918 article titled *Judith Leyster, A Female Frans Hals*, acknowledged the possibility that Judith appeared as a model for some of her husband's paintings during their marriage, including *The Dentist* and *Breakfast*.[16] The woman overseeing the chaos in Jan's depiction of a tooth extraction does bear a strong resemblance to Judith's own self-portrait created in around 1630. However, the painting, now in the North Carolina Art Museum, is believed to have been painted in 1629 and pre-dates their marriage by seven years.

Jan and Judith were diligent business owners independently, but there is more evidence that after their marriage they approached their workload together. Frima Fox Hofrichter, in *Judith Leyster, A Woman Painter in Holland's Golden Age*, noted that while Jan worked on portrait commissions, Judith completed a series of small botanical illustrations in 1643, seven years into their marriage. According to Hofrichter, this indicates that not only did they divide the market between them in order to maximise their sources of income, but they also avoided competing with one another for similar work.[17] A small project illustrating tulips is likely to have been something that Judith could work on around the needs of the family, rather than any commitment to a large-scale portrait or group painting. Surviving letters between the sixteenth-century Marchioness of Mantua, Isabella d'Este, and the artist Pietro Perugino reveal how time-consuming discussing even the concept of a commissioned work could be, even before an artist reached for their brushes. It therefore makes sense that Jan took over this more complex side of the business, while Judith assumed lighter projects or more advisory roles behind the scenes. One painting demonstrates this point. Jan's *Self Portrait with Family Members* in the Frans Hals Museum dates to around 1635 and depicts twelve figures playing musical instruments.[18] Each assumes a different pose, gesture and expression along with detailed painted panels, props, furniture and carved wooden panelling in the background. A painting of this complexity would have taken a great deal of time to plan and complete.

Even though Judith appears not to have created any large-scale work after her marriage, she was still working. Dedicated and business-like during her early career, she had fought for her professional reputation and later, for recognition. It is unlikely that in June 1636 this enthusiasm and passion simply evaporated. As housewife, mother, business partner and advisor Judith continued to leave a trace in contemporary sources and not just as a part-time artist. In January 1655, the couple bought a house in Amsterdam with Judith completing the legal purchase. Three years later, she was back in the courts administering its sale.[19] That Judith confidently took over the purchase of a house worth a considerable 8,200 florins with specific conditions about interest, part-payments (some of which were paid in paintings) and shares belonging to different parties, shows that she was a capable administrator, organiser and communicator, and confident dealing with such large sums. It is possible that her exposure to financial hardship during her earlier years prepared her for this administrative role. Aged around 14 at the time of her father's court appearance in 1629, she would have been old enough to observe and understand family conversations about financial arrangements and administrative procedures.

The couple appear in a number of other legal documents during their marriage. Two weeks after they had exchanged vows at Heemstede, Jan won a legal case against a buyer, Jacob Pietersz, for non-payment of a painting. Two months later, Jan was sued for half an ox. In August, there were more complaints over debts, including some involving Jan's family to be paid to grocers and bakers. As late as 1652 Jan was sued for not paying for a shipment of wine he had received. The Molenaers' reluctance to settle accounts in these cases suggests that despite their joint success as artists, they struggled financially. They often offered creditors their paintings to pay off debts, amassed from the purchase of everyday items such as bread, wine and meat. On the other hand, Jan's paintings were in demand and had considerable monetary value. One unscrupulous art dealer in 1656 sold a work claiming it to be one of Jan's, insisting that he had seen him painting it. It was later discovered to have been the work of another painter.[20] With a considerable backlog of canvases and Jan and Judith's strong reputations as artists, the couple had a continuous source of payment leaning against the walls of their studios. It makes sense that they would offer these to pay outstanding accounts when the actual cost to the household for these paintings had been simply time, canvas and oil paint. Further maximising the opportunities for work, the couple also moved their family between homes in Amsterdam, Haarlem and Heemstede.

It is exciting, that for a couple for whom so little biographical evidence survives, we are able to piece together some of the more intimate aspects of their life together. Jan's brothers Claes and Bartholomaeus were both painters and Judith would have known her in-laws well. There is speculation that Judith and Jan trained with Frans Hals, but their two families are also linked in other sources. Jan was present at a tavern in June 1638 with Frans Hal's brother Dirck when a dispute over a lottery result ended up in court, while Judith had embarked on legal action relating to Frans Hals in 1635. The couple were also close to the Leiden portrait painter Jan Lievens and the landscape artist Frans de Hulst. According to Alfred von Wurzbach, both men are known to have stayed at the Molenaers' homes on occasion, Lievens in 1644 and Hulst in 1659.[21] An inventory of their goods shows that the couple's walls were hung with landscapes, portraits and religious works. They also enjoyed seascapes, paintings of ships and characters playing musical instruments and owned portraits of themselves and one of Jan's mother and father. A violin and flute were also recorded among their belongings, likely something they enjoyed playing, but also handy props for their models to pose with.[22]

In 1640, between voyages to India, Denmark and Russia, Peter Mundy visited the couple's home city of Haarlem, describing it having 'rising ground, many pretty groves and woods, fair long ranks of trees with pleasant walks between'.[23] He also noticed something unusual that he had not seen in other places on his travels. The Dutch people had a profound love of art, which spanned all social classes. He said that residents were occupied 'in general striving to adorn their houses, especially the outer or street room, with costly pieces, butchers and bakers not much inferior in their shops, which are fairly set forth, yea many times blacksmiths, cobblers, etc will have some picture or other by their Forge and in their stall. Such is the general notion, inclination and delight that these country natives have to paintings'.[24] Mundy's remark shows that by 1640 the nature of artistic patronage during the Renaissance had shifted. At the beginning of the era, politicians, aristocrats and the church looked eagerly towards creatives for their interpretations of ancient ideals that could visually promote power and the influence of the state and church. Now art was being bought and enjoyed by the lower classes. Red hot filings flew off the blacksmith's hammer past scenes of domestic ease, while bakers pulled trays of hot loaves from an oven, with one eye on a jolly tavern scene. Genre artists, with Jan and Judith among them, were paving the way for a new style of art and expression, and a new buying public that shaped art through their preferences. It was no longer down to wealthy bankers like Cosimo de Medici or noblewomen like Isabella d'Este to further the careers of emerging artists. Art now belonged to everyone, and they connected with new themes of comedy, allegory and moral enquiry. It is also possible to see here the Renaissance focus on humanism – the importance and significance of the individual – come full circle. In Judith's *The Jolly Toper*, a rosy-cheeked man smiles languidly at the viewer while draining a jug. In Jan's *The Dentist* a man grips onto a rosary while having a tooth pulled out by a well-dressed man. The dentist leans into the patient's mouth wearing a determined, comedic expression, clamping onto the affected tooth with a pair of pliers. The scene is rich in theatrical humour, but was also relatable to viewers. A trip to a seventeenth-century dentist would have been known and dreaded by Jan and Judith's contemporaries whether they were rich or poor.

Today Judith Leyster and Jan Miense Molenaer are considered pioneers of the Dutch Golden Age of art. They experimented with depictions of light and shadow and loose, spontaneous brushwork that gave an illusion of movement. Judith in particular was fascinated with depicting the effects of light, inspired by earlier artists such as Italian painter Michelangelo Caravaggio, who worked in the early seventeenth century. Jan's wide range of styles and subjects show a thirst for his own development and learning. He catered for wealthier clients, portraying them glancing out at us warily in shining silks and stiff ruffs. In others, he showed the grittier side of life, of socks falling down, jaunty violin playing and half-lit scenes at a tavern. Allegory, comedy, theatre, religion, history and portraiture were all created by his brush and completed with striking care and accuracy. Art historian Christopher Brown, in *Images of a Golden Past: Dutch Genre Painting of the Seventeenth Century*, praised Jan as one of the artists who demonstrated a move 'towards higher finish, greater elaboration of detail as well as a new interest in the meticulous depiction of interiors and accurate descriptions of domestic settings and social genres'.[25] Walter Armstrong wrote of Molenaer's 'figures being extraordinarily full of life and movement', and praised Judith's 'manipulative ability' in her lively depictions.[26] Both also managed to portray laughter, a notoriously difficult emotion to convey convincingly in art.

After their deaths, Jan continued to enjoy recognition, appearing in a 1691 sale catalogue of 'valuable and inviting' pieces 'made by the greatest Masters'.[27] He has been noted for his influence on the styles and subjects of other Dutch artists, including the couple's contemporary Abraham van der Heck and the eighteenth-century painter Sebastiaen Heemskerk.[28] Judith though, was quickly forgotten, many of her works instead attributed to the man she was influenced by, Frans Hals. Her deliberately painted signature went either unnoticed or passed off as a different version of Hals's mark. It is interesting to wonder therefore whether later artists who claimed to have been influenced by Frans Hals were not mistakenly gazing in admiration at one of Judith's works during this period. In 1893, however, there came a turning point. One of her paintings, *The Duet*, became the subject of high-profile legal action. The painting had hung at Audley End House in Essex and was sold as a Frans Hals work for a considerable sum. Judith's 'star monogram' was later discovered on the painting and queried. Historians began to piece together Judith's life and her contribution to seventeenth-century Dutch art. The loss of Judith's story between the late seventeenth and the late nineteenth centuries, along with its resurgence, captivated supporters of the feminist movement. In 1918, as suffragettes campaigned for the right to vote in elections, Frieda van Emden called her 'a remarkable figure in the world of art and one to which her sex can point not without pride'.[29]

Judith Leyster and Jan Miense Molenaer were both successful and renowned artists before their marriage. Working as partners, they tackled the Dutch art scene with a pragmatic and business-like approach. Allocating roles, providing support and moving the family home they worked and made decisions that would maximise their family income. Similarities in their techniques hint at collaboration and Judith may even have modelled as characters for some of Jan's paintings. Judith continued to work part-time, prioritising her family and the couple's administrative and legal affairs. They both defended their businesses legally, adapted to commercial demands and remained resilient and marketable in an increasingly competitive industry. Depictions of Greek and Roman gods and legendary heroes were prized at the beginning of the Renaissance era, while images of peasants, tipsy and rosy-cheeked, were in demand by its end. Patrons now included blacksmiths and bakers, who exchanged their cash for art that was funny, thought-provoking and relatable.

Judith and Jan's twenty-four-year relationship was only ended by death. Both were recorded as desperately ill on 6 November 1659 when they made their wills at home in Heemstede. The couple agreed that the household possessions should not be sold by the surviving partner and that partner should also undertake the care of the children. It seems that Judith never recovered fully from her illness. She died in early 1660 and was buried in Heemstede although her grave has since been lost. Jan lived for another eight years, dying on 15 September 1668 in Haarlem. He was buried in the Grote Kerk in Haarlem's marketplace, leaving their two surviving children, a daughter, Helena, and a son, Constantijn.

After Jan's death, an inventory was made of the possessions in the family home at the request of the couple's adult daughter Helena. Taken in October 1668, it detailed a number of items expected to be found in the home of a working artist, such as sketchbooks, frames and a handful of unfinished works. There were also paintings by a number of artists including Grebber, the man who had overseen Judith's early training, along with works by Pieter Bruegel and the landscape artist Jan van Goyen. Among his other possessions were some of Judith's works. Poignantly, years after her death, Jan was reminded of his wife every day. The inventory stated that in the hallway of Jan's home hung an oval portrait of Judith herself.[30]

Conclusion

As celebrations rang in for the New Year of 1700, the world was a vastly different place than that of three centuries before. The many generations that lived through the era had witnessed the dismantling of rigid medieval concepts along with reorganisation of the social classes. They were also present for one of the most significant cultural and intellectual revolutions in history.

Of all the couples we have examined, the only partner still alive in 1700 was England's often-forgotten queen, Catherine of Braganza. Now back in her homeland of Portugal, she was overseeing the building of a palace at Bemposta, where she planned to retire, ordering the arms of England to painstakingly be whittled into the stone. While construction was under way, she stayed at the coastal area of Belem, in the south of the country near Lisbon. As she looked back at her life, the 66-year-old must have considered the enormity of events she had overseen, the challenges she had overcome and the relationship she had with her husband, Charles II, and their subjects.

The world was now smaller, with ships lumbering unsteadily towards the shores of new and strange lands. Increasingly detailed maps were unfurled before investors, sailors gesturing excitedly about their research into new trade routes and navigational passages. Isabella and Ferdinand of Spain celebrated their acquisition of parts of the Caribbean, inspiring the first Tudor king, Henry VII, to follow a few years later. His actions led to the arrival of John Rolfe in Virginia in the early seventeenth century. Two strangers who would never have met in 1400 – an Englishman from Norfolk and a princess in North America – formed a partnership that triggered consequences for both their homelands through culture, commerce and society. Catherine of Braganza also helped secure wider geographical power for England, her marriage contract specifying that she would bring the custody of Tangier and Bombay to the Crown. This alliance also established England's links with Portugal, an associated seafaring nation with its own growing influence in India and in the Americas.

The era is well known for its tense political atmosphere. Residents shielded themselves physically, politically and financially from war. Traditional modes of government were abolished and new leaders presided over unexpected shifts of power. Authority, no matter how it was obtained, was fragile. In the Mughal Empire, elephants decorated with chains and jewels thudded around the countryside in forceful shows of strength, but it did not stop Shah Jahan being brutally deposed by his own son. Edward IV and Elizabeth Woodville battled to retain their power in the uncertain climate of the Wars of the Roses. Threatened with warfare and conspiracy, their regime succumbed in 1470 when their opponent Henry VI returned to the throne. To regain his power, Edward murdered, fought and banished his enemies. Isabella and Ferdinand of Spain also encountered civil war while working towards the unification of the kingdoms of Spain, while Isabella d'Este and Francesco Gonzaga trod carefully to navigate the tetchy political atmosphere of the fifteenth- and sixteenth-century Italian states. Despite all their efforts, Francesco was still captured and held captive by his enemies. In England, the premise of monarchy was entirely dismantled under Charles I of England and Scotland, despite the efforts of wealthy royalist supporters. Eleven years later, it was restored with the accession of Charles II, leading to mass celebrations from within the kingdom. Even in Florence, that was ruled as a democracy, Cosimo de Medici employed cautious displays of power to avoid triggering a political uprising. The Florentine banker must have considered his father's dying words urging restraint, as he languished in an 8-feet-wide cell, imprisoned by enemies. People of all social classes were affected by these shifts in authority and the uncertainty of civil and foreign war. They responded with uprisings, fought in battle for their lords or experienced significant changes in rule, religion and customs. In some cases, authority was exerted forcefully, and permanent change was made to countless families who lost loved ones to war or were banished for their religion.

It was also a period of ambition and a thirst for the acquisition of wealth. Early medieval merchants traded with foreign lands, but we see a more fervent approach to commercial activity during the Renaissance years. The Bardis and Medicis were among Europe's greatest banking families who negotiated vast loans to kings and politicians. Their union strengthened financial opportunities for both families and led to greater political and social power. For the first time, the world's merchants docked ships at new and fascinating lands, rolling barrels and sacks of medicines, food ingredients and gold onto heavily laden vessels. In the seventeenth century the lucrative

Virginian tobacco industry was born and was so successful that growers on the settlement were pointedly told that they should also grow food to sustain their communities. If we could stand at the ports and markets of Shah Jahan and Mumtaz Mahal's empire, we would notice the warm air filled with Portuguese, Dutch, English, French and Hindi, as diplomats and merchants bartered for mangoes, limes and indigo. A greater understanding therefore developed between foreign lands and within cultures, while merchants built luxurious homes in their towns and villages, high on the success of these new opportunities for commerce.

A sense of community was vital to the development of culture and learning during the period. Sailors discussed the potential of new lands, among the tangled masts of harbours, while architects pondered theory in the piazzas of Florence. By 1450, the Italian city had become a hive of learning and expression, attracting other courtiers from foreign courts to study, debate and acquire new texts paid for with Medici money. On their return, they brought this new education with them, influencing residents and leaders of their own states and nations. Merchants, bankers and aristocrats introduced one another to their favourite craftsmen and artists, who in turn benefitted from a steady income and local prestige. Two men in the court of Catherine of Braganza sat down to write and produce one of England's first operas, while Florentine artists travelled together to gather inspiration from ancient Rome. They also taught one another mathematics, perspective and geometry, all subjects that impacted architecture, art, sculpture, astronomy and travel. And yet couples pushed these changes forward. Direct collaboration within them resulted in the production of new plays, philosophical works, collections of antiques, poetry and paintings. It also triggered two important aspects of English culture still seen today: the fashion for drinking coffee and tea. Intellectuals, thinkers and celebrities packed into late-seventeenth-century coffeehouses to share news, debate opinion and sip on a hot caffeine-fuelled drink.

Printing houses of the fifteenth century pulled pages wet with ink from wooden presses and bound them together, endorsed and encouraged by the industry's first patrons. Soon, a wide range of works was quickly, cheaply and easily accessible to a new era of readers. In Siena, intellectuals read with curiosity about a female poet's 'love' for a young Habsburg princess and explored how same-sex relationships could be celebrated and admired. New poetry was also created, inspired by the pair, while traditional romances and tragedies were neatly placed onto bookshelves. In India, Mughal princes read newly printed classical works while their paintings and buildings showed Italian influences and ambitions. Eager readers soaked up Captain John Smith's dramatic story of the birth of the Virginian settlement and Pocahontas's brave actions in saving his life. Her portrait, created while she was in England, was also circulated and viewed with interest almost 4,000 miles away from the place she was born, to thousands and since then, millions of people. As a result of this ease in the spread of knowledge, new authors were inspired to create and print works on horsemanship, poetry, philosophy and the thrilling new genre of science fiction. Scientific papers were also published, debated and tested, while the Royal Society reported on astronomy, the properties of chemicals, the weighing of air and the effects of light. This wider range of works appealed to a growing number of readers, sparking further debate, research and newer theories about how the world works.

Change was also made through brutality, and the period is famous for its ruthlessness in the search for power. In Italy, men with bold political ambitions were dragged lifeless and punctured from the river, while in London, the stabbing of a magistrate was blamed on a religious conspiracy. Men were cut to pieces on the battlefield or quietly assassinated by dagger, strangling or poison. Others were swiftly deposed, with carefully curated classical antiques removed from their palaces and discarded. Couples in leadership roles attempted to enforce total control over the states they ruled, imposing religious conformity and obedience, resulting in executions, interrogations and terror among the public. Slavery was in full force, too, and while Isabella of Castile seems to have paid attention to its moral aspects, people were still removed from their families, led onto ships and sold in foreign lands. It was the era of Machiavelli, whose name has become synonymous today with describing a calculating, unforgiving and manipulative form of leadership. The political writer praised some of these traits, judging the perpetrators less likely to be overthrown or face rebellion from their subjects. Consequences of this style of ruling trickled down to every social class, whose families ended up torn apart by political ambition, religious reform and war. Some, on the coasts of the Caribbean and Virginia, lined up to see strangely dressed newcomers wading towards their shores in search of glory and gold. Lives would never be the same for them, or their visitors.

The study of the Renaissance era is especially interesting in terms of women's history. Women appeared increasingly at the forefront of many of these changes and entered some of the more traditionally male-dominated areas of society. Not only acting as confidantes, counsellors and personal assistants to their partners, they marched unashamedly into power themselves. In the south of England, Elizabeth Woodville rose from relative obscurity to become queen, while Margaret of Austria, the illegitimate daughter of Emperor Charles V, organised armies, settled tensions and ruled as regent over the Netherland states. An armour-clad Isabella of Castile organised troops and raised morale during battle, while later, Margaret Cavendish argued that being a woman did not stop her advising on and writing about wars. Cavendish also wrote about politics, philosophy and science, receiving mixed reactions from her more unadventurous contemporaries. The Dutch artist Judith Leyster fought to gain recognition in the male-dominated Haarlem art community, while Isabella d'Este's tactful diplomacy and patronage of artists ensured the survival of many priceless statues and paintings. In her own time, these art pieces were studied, but also used to show wealth, resources and gain trust. A woman of letters and a meticulous organiser, Contessina de Bardi fulfilled business and personal roles, while influencing future generations of Medici women. Pocahontas, the Native American princess of the Powhatan tribe in Virginia, was hosted by the royals in London, and contributed to the successful settlement of the American colony in the early 1600s. Mumtaz Mahal, too, urged her husband to wage a war and accompanied him as he travelled through his empire. One militia-loving queen, Catherine of Braganza, was especially keen on naval developments, also influencing events in the aftermath of the Great Fire of 1666. All of these women received the support, praise and encouragement of partners, but it is important to acknowledge their individual contributions to the world around them in the context of these partnerships. This is even more important for those who have been sidelined or largely forgotten in histories of the time. And yet, the lesser-known partner of the pair was not always the woman. Care has been taken during the writing of this book to establish the contributions of often neglected or miscast male partners such as Francesco Gonzaga, William Cavendish and Jan Miense Molenaer. These men were crucial to the success of their more famous spouses, as well as of the partnership as a whole. Often found in the shadow of their wives' spotlight, their contributions can clearly now be seen.

It was also the age of the underdog. No one could have imagined at the time of their birth that Edward IV and Elizabeth Woodville would one day rule over a conflicted and turbulent realm. And yet they had a lasting effect on their age. Humble craftsmen, architects and artists were among the friends of powerful leaders such as the Medicis and Gonzagas. Rulers during the era rewarded hard work and service rather than promoting officials simply because of their birthright. During the Renaissance era, the higher social classes were filled with in-laws of monarchs, government officials and royal mistresses and their offspring.

Of course, the most well-known development to have come out of the age is in arts and culture. The first artists to emerge as masters of their craft accepted complicated and substantial commissions from politicians, merchants and popes, gaining fame and recognition in the process. Inspiring other craftsmen, architects and artists of their own generations, their influence has also trickled down into later periods with their work still taught and imitated by artists and students today. Giorgio Vasari immortalised their personalities, work and lives in the sixteenth century, providing extensive biographies of many of the craftsmen employed by our power couples of the age.

But it was not just artists who were central to this process. Without patrons and buyers, they would have struggled to maintain a livelihood or gain popularity. Artists boasted political and royal connections, enjoying the support and protection of their patrons as they daubed ceilings, walls and easels with religious, political and classical scenes that favoured and flattered their patrons. Leaders clutched detailed and lifelike miniatures of one another as mementos and had their combined arms painted into private possessions. Art was used as a form of propaganda to enforce this joint power. From depictions of English, Portuguese, Spanish and Mantuan arms, to the royal memorabilia of the Restoration, these images enforced status, legitimacy and right. By the end of the period, a new buying public had emerged, now motivated to fill their homes and businesses with comedic, relatable paintings that depicted reassuring, humble scenes from everyday life.

Couples altered the skylines of the nations they ruled over, too. Palaces, castles, churches and homes were built and renovated, paid for by Medici, Plantagenet and Cavendish funds. There were renovations in Mantua and new communities settled in Granada and Virginia. Many of these buildings fulfilled political aims and were used as personal and meeting places by advisors, members of the family and their communities. People of the age walked through corridors, paid social visits or worked as servants, pausing to look out of the very palace, church or castle windows we are able to gaze out of today. One building in particular has special significance for the memory of one power couple. Stonemasons and carpenters chiselled and hammered in the intense Agra heat to create a marble dome to cover the tomb of Shah Jahan's empress, Mumtaz Mahal. This structure alone has inspired art, literature, histories and, in more modern times, film and photography.

Finally, it is impossible to miss the rise of the entertainment industry during the period. Old playhouses were reopened in London in the 1660s, while others were freshly built, their dimly lit stages resurrected and modernised after years of civil conflict and stifling Puritan rule. At Mantua, theatres were elegantly designed and used to entertain diplomatic visitors to the Gonzaga palace. The strict protocol of Mantuan court theatre was also praised, replicated and discussed as an example of quality Renaissance theatre. The industry was alive with playwrights, actors and set and costume designers contracted to produce a wide range of entertainments including comedy, opera and tragedy. For the first time women actors dominated the stage, singing and reciting the lines of bawdy new Restoration comedies. Theatre also discovered its first celebrities, with audiences flocking to playhouses to watch their favourite actors and actresses perform in shows enjoyed and endorsed by their king and queen. This celebrity craze reached new heights in the next centuries with the careers of theatre actors such as David Garrick and Sarah Siddons.

Power couples achieved and exerted their authority in different ways. For some, it was dynastic. As kings, emperors, queens and princesses, power was transferred from their relatives through legitimate (and sometimes illegitimate) bloodlines. Others held sway over the worlds of business and local government. Cultural power enhanced the age's creative output through talent, inquisitiveness and hard work. Power was not always equally balanced. The Medicis, Gonzagas and Stuart monarchs formed partnerships with those similar in status to themselves, as did the Molenaers. Isabella of Castile's kingdom might have been larger than her husband's, but Ferdinand was the legitimate heir to the Kingdom of Aragon, and, at the time of their marriage, King of Sicily. The union of Edward IV and Elizabeth Woodville was dynastically unbalanced, as at the time of their marriage Edward was a king and Elizabeth his subject. Equally, the admiration Laudomia Forteguerri expressed for Margaret of Austria was outweighed by status, wealth and international influence. John Rolfe, a citizen of England, married a member of the Native American royalty, while Shah Jahan had three wives. Two he married for diplomatic reasons, while his favourite, Mumtaz Mahal, was the daughter of a politician.

In cases where partners were thrust together for political or diplomatic reasons, it is possible to see a fondness and intimacy develop through their letters to one another over the course of their relationship. For others, there were challenges and disagreements. However, there were some partnerships that had origins in romantic love, such as Edward IV and Elizabeth Woodville, John Rolfe and Pocahontas, Shah Jahan and Mumtaz Mahal, the Cavendishes and the Molenaers. The emotional link between Margaret of Austria and Laudomia Forteguerri is still uncertain, although their contemporaries believed that they experienced a form of platonic love or intense bond of friendship.

Fascinatingly, many of these couples experienced links with each other. The Gonzagas received a letter telling them of Isabella and Ferdinand's discoveries in the Caribbean, while Edward IV entered negotiations, later discarded, to become Isabella of Castile's husband before her marriage to Ferdinand. One of Edward's officials, John Tiptoft, Earl of Worcester, visited Florence and learned from texts collected by the Medicis. Edward's grandson Henry VIII would have angrily cursed the Florentine bankers when their great-grandson Pope Clement VII ruled that the marriage he had been trying to annul, between him and his queen, Katherine of Aragon, was indeed valid. Incidentally, Katherine was one of the daughters of Ferdinand and Isabella. Margaret of Austria's father, Charles V, was close to the Gonzagas, paying visits to Mantua and supporting the political careers of the couple's sons. Margaret and William Cavendish were also known by Charles II and his queen, Catherine.

While history tends to award individuals with recognition of the achievements they made to their time, the contributions of partners, whether forged in romance, creative collaboration or business, must not be forgotten. Each of these power couples of the Renaissance era lived during a period of adversity, danger and conflict, emerging together to steer the world towards a cultural and scientific revolution that made its mark on the Renaissance era and into the next age of discovery: the Enlightenment.

Notes

Introduction

1. Via https://www.getty.edu/art/collection/object/103QS6
2. Tommaso Campanella, The City of the Sun, in Machiavelli The Prince, p170 and in Green, p54
3. Green, title page, and Sichel, pp229-230
4. Phillips, Katherine, p24

Chapter 1: Cosimo de Medici and Contessina de Bardi, of Florence

1. Ross, p6
2. Ross, p7
3. Russell, Ephraim, pp. 93-135. *British History Online* [accessed 12 June 2024]
4. Russell, Ephraim, pp. 93-135. *British History Online* [accessed 12 June 2024]
5. *Calendar of Close Rolls*, 'Henry VI: 1426-27', Volume 2, p375
6. Ross, p6
7. Machiavelli, *History of Florence*, pp175-176, 192
8. Ross, pp19-21
9. Ross, p21
10. Ross, pp21, 28
11. Machiavelli, *History of Florence*, pp189-190, 197
12. Machiavelli, *History of Florence*, p203
13. Quoted in Ross, p15
14. Ross, p47
15. Ross, p11
16. Quoted in Ross, p54
17. Quoted in Ross, p63

18. Quoted in Ross, p63
19. Ross, p61
20. Heywood, William. *Palio and Ponte: An Account of the Sports of Central Italy from the Age of Dante to the Twentieth Century*, Methuen and Co, London. 1904, p7-11
21. Vasari, *Lives of the Most Eminent Painters*, Volume 2, pp152-154
22. Vasari, *Lives of the Most Eminent Painters*, Volume 1, ppxiv-xix
23. Vasari, *Lives of the Most Eminent Painters*, Volume 2, pp139, 203
24. Vasari, *Lives of the Most Eminent Painters*, Volume 2, pp211-213
25. Vasari, *Lives of the Most Eminent Painters*, Volume 2, p227
26. Vasari, *Lives of the Most Eminent Painters*, Volume 2, pp261, 267-268
27. Vasari, *Lives of the Most Eminent Painters*, Volume 2, p245
28. Vasari, *Lives of the Most Eminent Painters*, Volume 2, pp251-252
29. Ross, p131
30. David, c1440 (bronze), Donatello, (c1386-1466), Museo Nazionale del Bargello, Florence, via Jones, p367
31. 'The Chapel of the Magi', *Palazzo Medici Riccardi* website, https://www.palazzomediciriccardi.it/en/the-magi-chapel/ [accessed 26 March 2025] Benozzo Gozzoli, c1459, fresco, Palazzo Medici Riccardi, Florence.
32. Vasari, *Lives of the Most Eminent Painters*, Volume 7, p81
33. Vasari, *Lives of the Most Eminent Painters*, Volume 2 p249 and Maguire, pp58-59
34. Ross, p7-8
35. Quoted in Ross, p173
36. Ross, p15
37. Quoted in Ross, p158
38. Sprite, sculptor close to Donatelllo, 1432, High-copper alloy, fire-gilt, brown natural patina where exposed. Metropolitan Museum of Art, New York. Via https://www.metmuseum.org/art/collection/search/207394
39. Ross, p130
40. Maguire, p59
41. Ross, p48
42. Vasari, *Lives of the Most Eminent Painters*, Volume 10, p71
43. Ross, p74
44. Machiavelli, *History of Florence*, p315 and Vasari, *Lives of the Most Eminent Painters*, Volume 2, pp223-224
45. Ross, pp32, 73
46. Machiavelli, *History of Florence*, p318
47. Jones, p13, p5

48. Portrait of a Man with a Medal of Cosimo the Elder, Sandro Boticelli, c1484, Tempura on panel, Galleria degli Uffizi, Florence. Via https://www.wga.hu/html_m/b/botticel/7portrai/04medal.html
49. Portrait of Cosimo the Elder, Niccolò de la Casa, after Baccio Bandanelli, 1544. Print. British Museum, London. Via https://www.britishmuseum.org/collection/object/P_1869-0612-368
50. Contessina de' Bardi, died 1473, Wife of Cosimo de' Medici il Vecchio, Antonio Francesco Selvi, c1740s, National Gallery of Art, Washington, via https://www.nga.gov/collection/art-object-page.103331.html
51. Machiavelli, *History of Florence*, pp176, 318
52. Quoted in Ross, p155
53. Staley, p49
54. Cartwright, volume 2, p117
55. Machiavelli, *History of Florence,* p316
56. Confirmed in an email from Basilica of San Lorenzo in Florence, 19 April 2025

Chapter 2: Elizabeth Woodville and Edward IV of England, Wales, Ireland and France

1. Tighe, p395
2. Cayley, p218
3. MacGibbon, p32; Higginbotham, p29; Licence, p104
4. Commines, pp394-395
5. MacGibbon, p33
6. Cust, p37
7. Baker, p198
8. De Sola Pinto, pp24-25
9. Tighe, p396
10. Commines, p187
11. William Caxton and Anthony Woodville, c1477. Dictes and Sayings of the Philosophers, vellum. Lambeth Palace Library, via https://images.lambethpalacelibrary.org.uk/
12. *Calendar of Patent Rolls 1467-1477*, p283 and *1476-1485*, p7
13. *Calendar of Patent Rolls 1467-1477*, p528
14. Kempling, p14
15. *Calendar of Patent Rolls 1467-1477*, p190
16. Calendar of Patent *Rolls 1476-1485*, pp72-73

17. Cayley, p231
18. Scofield, pp27, 337
19. Scofield, p447
20. Einstein, pp26-27
21. Lewis, Sander, pp178-179
22. Rivers, Prologue
23. Munro, Caxton, pp1-2
24. Blake, p90; William Caxton and Anthony Woodville, c1477. Dictes and Sayings of the Philosophers, vellum. Lambeth Palace Library, via https://images.lambethpalacelibrary.org.uk/
25. Maunder, Edward Walter. The Royal Observatory Greenwich, a glance at its history and work. The Religious Tract Society, London, 1900, p27
26. Nicolas; *Wardrobe Accounts*, pp125-126, 132, 142
27. Nicolas; *Wardrobe Accounts*, p125
28. Munro, Caxton p2
29. Scofield, p452
30. Munro, Caxton, p7
31. A Selection of Ordinances, Prince Edward, p28
32. A Selection of Ordinances, Edward IV, pp16-19, extensively explored in Licence, pp176-184
33. Licence, pp177-178
34. Bently, *Excerpta*, pp109-211
35. Nicolas, *Wardrobe Accounts*, p142
36. Quoted in Tighe, pp367-371
37. Cust, p35-36
38. *Calendar of Patent Rolls 1461-67* p495; *1476-85* pp34, 477
39. Visit to Tower of London, November 2024
40. Tighe, pp371, 376
41. Tighe, p378
42. Tighe, pp386-387
43. Tighe, p391
44. Sichel, pp229-230

Chapter 3: Ferdinand and Isabella of Aragon, Castile, Granada, Sicily and Léon

1. Commines, p333
2. Ellis, Volume 1, p152

3. Prescott, Volume 1, p108
4. Bergenroth, p365
5. Prescott, Volume 1, pp101-102
6. Machiavelli, *The Prince*, pp5-6
7. Prescott, Volume 1, pp101-102
8. Prescott, Volume 1, p115
9. Prescott, Volume 1, p172
10. Prescott, Volume 3, p446
11. Machiavelli, *The Prince*, p40
12. Quoted in Prescott, Volume 1, 195
13. Quoted in Prescott, Volume 1, p198
14. Prescott, Volume 1, p204
15. MacNutt, *D'Anghiera*, Volume 1, p66
16. Hare, *Wanderings in Spain*, p269
17. Prescott, Volume 1, pp240-249
18. Hare, *Wanderings in Spain*, p192
19. Machiavelli, *The Prince*, p93
20. Prescott, Volume 3, pp189-190
21. Banner with a Quartered Royal Arms of Spain and the Madonna and Child, 1500s. Cleveland Museum of Art, via https://www.clevelandart.org/art/1916.1885. Also Hours of Queen Isabella the Catholic, Queen of Spain: Fol 1v, Arms and Mottoes of Isabel la Católica, c1500 Master of the First Prayerbook of Maximillian and Associates. Cleveland Museum of Art, via https://www.clevelandart.org/art/1963.256.1.b
22. Bergenroth, p107
23. Gracián, p64
24. Bergenroth, pxii
25. Reported in widespread media but for example see: 'Spain Cracks King Ferdinand's 500-year-old Secret Code', BBC News website. https://www.bbc.co.uk/news/world-europe-42931940 dated 3 February 2018 [Accessed 8 January 2025]
26. Quoted in Prescott, Volume 2, p15
27. Bergenroth, p365
28. Prescott, Volume 2, p89
29. Quoted in Prescott, Volume 1, p171
30. Tremlett, p109
31. Prescott, Volume 2, p88 and Volume 1, p403
32. Columbus, *Journal*, p1
33. MacNutt, *D'Anghiera*, Volume 1, p57

34. Keen, pp9, 16-17
35. Columbus, *Journal*, pp8, 15
36. MacNutt, *de las Casas*, p6
37. Prescott, Volume 2, p496, also 'Spain: October 1500', in *Calendar of State Papers, Spain, Volume 1, 1485-1509*, ed. G A Bergenroth (London, 1862), pp. 243-247. *British History Online* http://www.british-history.ac.uk/cal-state-papers/spain/vol1/pp243-247 [accessed 12 January 2025]. For a further discussion of Isabella and slavery see Ashrafyan, K.E. (2021)
38. Prescott, Volume 3, p180
39. MacNutt, *D'Anghiera*, Volume 1, pp67-68
40. MacNutt, *D'Anghiera*, Volume 1, pp110, 119
41. MacNutt, *D'Anghiera*, Volume 1, pp124, 390, Volume 2, p27
42. Prescott, Volume 3, p472
43. Quoted in Prescott, Volume 2, p483
44. Bergenroth, pp26, 64-65
45. Prescott, Volume 2, p358 also quoted in Tremlett, in a slightly different translation of the Latin, p454
46. Gracián, p90
47. Bergenroth, pp362, 365
48. Bergenroth, p27
49. Machiavelli, *The Prince*, pp92-93
50. Figure quoted in both Prescott, Volume 3, p484 and also in Green, p63
51. Quoted in Prescott, Volume 3, pp175, 177-178
52. Prescott, Volume 3, footnote on p253

Chapter 4: Francesco II and Isabella d'Este, Marquis and Marchioness of Mantua

1. Cartwright, Volume 1, pp94-95
2. Via https://mantovaducale.beniculturali.it/it/camera-picta
3. Brinton, p97
4. Cartwright, Volume 1, pp12-13
5. Cole, p165
6. Hare, Northern Cities, pp305-312
7. Vasari, *Stories*, pp203-204
8. Vasari, *Stories*, pp138-139 also Camera Degli Sposi Via https://mantovaducale.beniculturali.it/it/camera-picta

9. Via https://pinacotecabrera.org/en/collezioni/collezione-on-line/lamentation-over-the-dead-christ/
10. Cartwright, Volume 1, p90
11. Cartwright, Volume 1, pp91-92
12. Cartwright, Volume 1, pp79, 125
13. Via https://mini-site.louvre.fr/mantegna/acc/xmlen/section_7_0.html and https://mini-site.louvre.fr/mantegna/acc/xmlen/section_8_0.html
14. Romano medal via https://www.metmuseum.org/art/collection/search/195048; Roman coin in author's own collection
15. Cartwright, Volume 1, pp171-173, 318
16. Cartwright, Volume 1, pp310-311 and Vasari, *Lives* Volume 3, p161
17. Cartwright, Volume 1, p376 and Vasari, *Lives* Volume 3, p162
18. Cartwright, Volume 1, pp329-333, Perugino, Le Combat de l'Amour el la Chasteté via https://collections.louvre.fr/en/ark:/53355/cl010059230
19. Cartwright, Volume 1, p69
20. Cartwright, Volume 1 pp76-77, Volume 2, p24; Vasari, *Lives*, Volume 6, p17
21. Cartwright, Volume 1, pp272, 274, 372, Volume 2 p136-7
22. Cartwright, Volume 1, pp183-185
23. Cartwright, Volume 1, p264
24. Arts and Culture, Google. Mantova Museo Urbano Diffuso. Torso of Francesco II of Gonzaga. https://artsandculture.google.com/asset/torso-of-franscesco-ii-gonzaga/DgEln7loW0yJSw?hl=en [Accessed 18 January 2025]
25. Sismondi, pp226, 240 243
26. Cartwright, Volume 1, pp105, 178
27. Simon, p130
28. Cartwright, Volume 1, pp84-86. 112-115, 147
29. Cartwright, Volume 2, p101
30. Cartwright Volume 1, pp248, 285, p152, Volume 2, p51
31. Cartwright, Volume 1, p209
32. Cartwright, Volume 2, pp136-138
33. Brinton, p102
34. Cartwright, Volume 1, pp115-116, 119-120
35. Cartwright, Volume 1, pp297-298
36. Sismondi, pp249-250
37. Cartwright, Volume 1, pp187-188
38. Cartwright, Volume 1, pp207, 227
39. Cartwright, Volume 1, pp228-229

40. Vasari, *Lives of the Most Eminent Painters*, Volume 9, p12 and quoted in Cartwright, Volume 1, pp231-232
41. Cartwright, Volume 1, pp236-p237
42. Brinton, p137
43. Cartwright, Volume 1, p53
44. Cartwright, Volume 1, p237
45. Cartwright, Volume 1, p288, Volume 2, pp85-86
46. Cartwright, Volume 1, p288
47. Cartwright, Volume 2, pp85-86, 102
48. Simon, pp157, 163
49. Cartwright, Volume 1, p144
50. Cartwright, Volume 2, pp154-155
51. Preyer, p50
52. Brinton, pp164, 170

Chapter 5: Laudomia Forteguerri and Margaret Habsburg of Austria, Duchess of Parma and Governor of the Netherlands

1. Rachfal, p7 states that Margaret travelled through Mantua on her way to Florence.
2. Rachfal, pp1-3
3. Rachfal, p6
4. Ross, *Florentine Palaces*, pp262
5. Rachfal, p14
6. Eisenbichler, *Sword and the Pen*, p101
7. Heywood, *Guide to Siena*, pp41, 46, 49
8. Heywood, *Guide to Siena*, pp112-119
9. Eisenbichler, *Sword and the Pen*, pp114, p116
10. Heywood, William. 'A View of Siena', published in 1574, Plate 1. In, The 'Ensamples' of Fra Filippo, A Study of Mediaeval Siena. Enrico Torrini, Siena. 1901.
11. Heywood, pp142-144
12. Via https://www.metmuseum.org/art/collection/search/209261
13. Heywood, *Guide to Siena*, pp148-150
14. Quoted here from Piccolomini (1541) but another translation is offered in Eisenbichler, *Sword and Pen*, pp116-117
15. Piccolomini

16. Bergalli, translation from the Italian, p76
17. Vasari, Lives of the Most Eminent Painters Sculptors and Architects, Vol. 7, pp245-246
18. Firenzuola, pp40-41 and also referred to in Eisenbichler, *Sword and the Pen*, p121
19. Rachfal, p27and Strada, p75
20. Via https://recherche.smb.museum/detail/871678/herzogin-margarete-von-parma-1522-1586
21. Strada, p76
22. Strada, p75
23. Rachfal, pp25, 160
24. Eisenbichler, *Sword and the Pen*, p160
25. Grattan, p85
26. Robin, pp149-150 and also expressed in Eisenbichler, *Sword and the Pen*, p134
27. Bergalli, p76
28. That some of Margaret's 'lost' letters may still exist in archives was discussed in an email with Konrad Eisenbichler on 18 February 2025. If found, they may provide more evidence about her and Laudomia's partnership.
29. Bell, ppiii, xii
30. Robin, pxxiv
31. Eisenbichler, *Sword and the Pen*, p163
32. Duchess of Newcastle, *The Description of a New World*, p92

Chapter 6: John Rolfe and Pocahontas, of Virginia, North America

1. Bergenroth, p89
2. Harisse, pp50-51
3. Hakluyt, volume 8, pp297-300
4. Tyler, pp48, 54, 134
5. Tyler, p100
6. Tyler, p51
7. Tyler, pp114-115
8. Smith's Dedication in *A Generall Historie* and Tyler, pp326-327
9. Smith, pp43-44
10. Tyler, p237

11. Tyler, p237
12. Tyler, pp309-310
13. Tyler, p241
14. Tyler, p310
15. Tyler, p242
16. Tyler, p325
17. Smith, pp60, 115
18. Brown, Alexander, pp225-226
19. Brown, pp228-229
20. Tyler, pp284-285.
21. Brown, p196
22. Brown, pp196 and Seelye, p285
23. Seelye, p259
24. Brown, Alexander p230 also 'America and West Indies: June 1616', in *Calendar of State Papers Colonial, America and West Indies: Volume 1, 1574-1660*, ed. W Noel Sainsbury (London, 1860), pp17-18. *British History Online* [accessed 16 June 2024].
25. Woodward, p174-175
26. Matz, pp61-71
27. Jonson, Ben. *The Staple of News*, Act 2 Scene 5. Ed., De Winter, Cook, Albert S. Yale Studies in English, Henry Holt and Company, New York 1905, p53.
28. Via https://digitalcollections.nypl.org/items/510d47da-c3cb-a3d9-e040-e00a18064a99
29. Tyler, p328
30. Tyler, pp326-p328
31. Cokayne, George. *The Complete Peerage of England, Scotland, Ireland, Great Britain and the United Kingdom*. Volume 3, George Bell and Sons, London. 1890, pp49-50, Seelye, p268
32. Tyler, p329
33. 'America and West Indies: January 1617', in *Calendar of State Papers Colonial, America and West Indies: Volume 1, 1574-1660*, ed. W Noel Sainsbury (London, 1860), p. 18. *British History Online* http://www.british-history.ac.uk/cal-state-papers/colonial/america-west-indies/vol1/p18b [accessed 16 June 2024].
34. Quoted in Seelye, p269
35. Brown, p248
36. Kingsbury, p71
37. Tyler, pp241, 244, 316

38. Kingsbury, p72
39. Brown, p241
40. Brown, pp254, 268
41. Brown, p246
42. Brown, p248 and 'America and West Indies: July 1623', in *Calendar of State Papers Colonial, America and West Indies: Volume 1, 1574-1660*, ed. W Noel Sainsbury (London, 1860), pp. 47-51. *British History Online* http://www.british-history.ac.uk/cal-state-papers/colonial/america-west-indies/vol1/pp47-51 [accessed 16 June 2024].
43. Tyler, pp329
44. Tyler, pp285

Chapter 7: Mumtaz Mahal and Shah Jahan, Mughal Rulers of Hindustan

1. Tavernier, p43
2. Tavernier, pp51, 63; Mundy v2 p247
3. Tavernier, p287; Roe v1, pp241, 256; Mundy v2, p309
4. Tavernier, pp125-126
5. Tavernier, pp63, 115, 125
6. Mundy, v2, p48 and Roe, v2, p402
7. Roe, v1, p198
8. *Memoirs of Jahangir*, p20
9. Roe, v2, pp280, 283
10. Roe, v2, p424
11. Inayat Khan, pp5-7; Mundy, v2, p212 (note)
12. Roe v1, p118; v2 p281
13. *Memoirs of Jahangir*, p27
14. Inayat Khan, pp5-6
15. Hansen, p87
16. Inayat Khan, p18
17. Inayat Khan, pp20-21
18. Inayat Khan, pp26, 32
19. Mundy, v2, p213
20. Manucci, v1, p182
21. Mundy, v2, p108; Misra, Rekha, p41
22. Mundy, v2, p212
23. Roe, v2, p329

24. *Memoirs of Jahangir*, p136
25. Mundy, v2, pp194, 53
26. Eliot, p49
27. *The Great Mughals: Art, Architecture and Opulence* exhibition at the V&A South Kensington, visited 11 February 2025
28. Mundy, v2, p11; Roe v2, p332
29. Roe, v1, p214, p240 and cherubs seen in *The Great Mughals: Art, Architecture and Opulence* at the V&A, 11 February 2025.
30. Roe, v1, p258
31. Via https://www.metmuseum.org/essays/the-shah-jahan-album
32. Murari, p39
33. Via https://artsandculture.google.com/asset/mumtaz-mahal/TAH1bJ2GEyp3Ew
34. Shah Jahan, by Rembrandt van Rijn, c1656-61, pen and brown ink, Cleveland Museum of Art, via https://www.clevelandart.org/art/1978.38 and at British Museum, Shah Jahan, Via https://www.britishmuseum.org/collection/object/P_Gg-2-262
35. Inayat Khan, pp33, 35, 55; Tavernier, p111
36. Misra, pp89-90
37. Hansen, p95
38. Tavernier, pp96-98
39. Tavernier, pp172-173, 300
40. Mundy, v2 pp50-51
41. Inayat Khan, p70
42. Tavernier, pp109-111 (Mumtaz is buried in a vault underneath)
43. Tavernier, ppxiii-xiv
44. Mundy v2, p213
45. Leland, Lilian, p134
46. *The Art World*, "The Taj Mahal", p5
47. Mundy, v2, p213
48. Via https://artsandculture.google.com/asset/the-taj-mahal-william-hodges/fAGVnNoQmt7pQQ?hl=en#
49. Hansen, p29
50. Murari, p59
51. Tavernier p110
52. Mundy, v2, p347
53. Tavernier, p343
54. Via https://collections.vam.ac.uk/item/O69124/parade-of-the-sons-of-oil-painting-willem-schellinks/

Chapter 8: Charles II and Catherine of Braganza, of England, Scotland and Ireland

1. Wheatley, volume 1, p322; volume 2, p52
2. Strickland, volume 5, p485, pp492-493
3. *Angliae Notitia*, p185
4. Via https://www.npg.org.uk/collections/search/portrait/mw01148/Catherine-of-Braganza; Evelyn, volume 2, p186
5. *Angliae Notitia*, pp74, 184
6. Davidson, p210, p213
7. Quoted in Wheatley, volume 2, in notes, p241
8. Wheatley, volume 2, pp233, 239, 248
9. Grammont, (1888), p122
10. Wheatley, volume 2, p373
11. Wheatley, volume 2, pp331, 429 and volume 4, p36
12. Grammont, (1888), pp124, 144
13. Wheatley, volume 2, p414
14. Flecknoe, pp1-3
15. Evelyn, volume 3, p26
16. Davidson, p334
17. Davidson, pp319-320
18. Davidson p341
19. Evelyn, volume 3, pp140, 148
20. Wheatley, volume 4, p275
21. Evelyn, volume 3, p54
22. Quoted in Davidson, p212; Shorland, p134. For the launch, see Wheatley, volume 4, p275
23. Davidson, p212; Shorland, p134
24. Davidson, pp278, 352
25. Tanner, volume 2, pp9, 97, 102, 108, 345
26. Davidson, pp405-406
27. Via https://www.rmg.co.uk/collections/objects/rmgc-object-15079.
28. Via https://www.rct.uk/collection/602766/the-seal-of-katherine-queen-of-england
29. Banks, pp18-19
30. Wheatley, volume 2 p305, and volume 3, p8; Banks, p21
31. Evelyn, volume 2, p168; Banks, p30
32. Banks, pp27-28
33. Evelyn, volume 2, p394

34. Wheatley, volume 4, p309
35. Strype, John, p2.
36. Evelyn, volume 2, pp260-261
37. Green, Mary Anne Everett. State Papers, 1667, p128
38. Via https://www.rct.uk/collection/408426/catherine-of-braganza-in-a-chariot
39. Grammont, 1888, p110
40. Via https://www.rct.uk/collection/602629/charles-ii-and-catherine-of-braganza; https://www.rct.uk/collection/443132/medal-commemorating-the-marriage-of-charles-ii-and-catherine-of-braganza
41. Via https://www.rct.uk/collection/404951/charles-ii-1630-1685
42. Shorland, p114; Wheatley, volume 5, p224
43. Via https://www.rct.uk/collection/405665/catherine-of-braganza-1638-1705
44. Davidson, p267
45. McAfee, p39
46. McAfee, pp59-60
47. McAfee, pp197-198
48. Evelyn, volume 2, p181, Evelyn refers to Katherine Philips on p285; Davidson, p263
49. Wheatley, volume 4, p216
50. Wheatley, volume 5, note on p26
51. Grammont, 1888 p143
52. Otway, Act one Scene one, and Dryden, John, p4 of Preface
53. Wheatley, volume 6, p171
54. Davidson, p497
55. Robinson, p56
56. Wheatley, volume 8, p55
57. Robinson, p163
58. Robinson, p166
59. Robinson, pp66-67, 187 and Maunder, Edward Walter. The Royal Observatory Greenwich, a glance at its history and work. The Religious Tract Society, London, 1900, pp54-55
60. Wheatley, Volume 1, p231 and Volume 6, p398
61. Waller, p94
62. Robinson, p121
63. Auctio Millingtoniana, A Collection of Extraordinary Paintings and Limnings. Auction pamphlet, Tunbridge Wells, 13 August 1691. Edward Millington. Via archive.org

64. Grammont, 1888 p113
65. De Sola Pinto, p93
66. Waller, p93

Chapter 9: William and Margaret Cavendish, Duke and Duchess of Newcastle

1. *The Life of William Cavendish*, p5
2. *The Life of William Cavendish*, p36
3. *The Life of William Cavendish*, p150
4. *The Life of William Cavendish*, pxlix
5. *The Life of William Cavendish* pp87, 288-289
6. Via https://www.metmuseum.org/art/collection/search/739125
7. *The Life of William Cavendish*, p88
8. *Clarendon Papers*, volume 2, p284
9. *The Life of William Cavendish*, pp121-122
10. *The Life of William Cavendish*, p97
11. Mendelson, p50
12. A True Relation, in *The Life of William Cavendish*, p298
13. A True Relation, in *The Life of William Cavendish*, p304
14. A True Relation, in *The Life of William Cavendish*, p290
15. *The Life of William Cavendish*, p120
16. *The Life of William Cavendish*, pp326-329
17. Whitaker, p69 and p233
18. *The Life of William Cavendish*, p180
19. Clarendon, *History of the Rebellion*, volume 2, p393; *Clarendon Papers*, volume 2, p63
20. *Clarendon Papers*, volume 1, p285; volume 2, pp53, 54; volume 2, p105, p319
21. *Clarendon Papers*, volume 4, p472
22. *The Life of William Cavendish*, p128
23. Worsley, p38
24. *The Life of William Cavendish*, p137
25. Diepenbeeck Abraham van. 1596-1675, *Nobilissimo Coursier Nappolitain,* Royal Academy of Art, Via https://www.royalacademy.org.uk/art-artists/work-of-art/nobilissimo-coursier-nappolitain
26. Flecknoe, pp10-13; Evelyn volume 2, p89
27. Perry, pp94, 99-101, 124-125

28. *The Life of William Cavendish*, p197
29. Langbaine, p386; Flecknoe, p13
30. Wheatley, volume 7, p69
31. Langbaine, p388
32. Flecknoe, p13
33. *The Life of William Cavendish*, pviii and also quoted in Perry, p6
34. *The Life of William Cavendish*, p203, note.
35. Epistle, pp3-4
36. *Life of William Cavendish*, plvi
37. *Life of William Cavendish*, pxlix
38. Philips, Katherine, p142
39. *Sir Joseph Banks and The Royal Society*, pp30-31
40. Wheatley, Volume 6, pp324-325
41. Evelyn, Volume 2, pp269, p271
42. Mendelson, pp61, 110
43. *The Life of William Cavendish*, pviii
44. Epistle, p3
45. *The World's Olio*, 1655, end of the first book; also quoted in Whitaker, p184
46. Wheatley, Volume 6, p269
47. *The Life of William Cavendish*, p114
48. *The Life of William Cavendish*, p88
49. A True Relation, in *The Life of William Cavendish*, p288
50. *The Life of William Cavendish*, pp205-206
51. A True Relation, in *The Life of William Cavendish*, pp310, 317
52. *Hatton Correspondence*, p47 and also quoted in Perry, p296
53. Grammont, 1888 p154
54. Green, V.H.H., p42

Chapter 10: Jan Miense Molenaer and Judith Leyster of the Netherlands

1. Viahttps://www.nationalgallery.org.uk/paintings/gerrit-berckheyde-the-market-place-and-the-grote-kerk-at-haarlem
2. Bredius, p9
3. Via https://www.rijksmuseum.nl/en/collection/object/The-Jolly-Drinker--6857f6c4108e6c76957270776cddd621 and https://www.rijksmuseum.nl/en/collection/object/The-Serenade--5b56863e2af8c41e0f4d27c4553ddc8f?tab=data

4. Ampzing, p370
5. Bredius, p6
6. Wurzbach, p41
7. The Garden of Earthly Delights, c1490-1500, Museo del Prado, Madrid. Via https://www.museodelprado.es/en/the-collection/art-work/the-garden-of-earthly-delights-triptych/02388242-6d6a-4e9e-a992-e1311eab3609
8. Preyer, p1, p3
9. Bredius, p13
10. Via https://emuseum.toledomuseum.org/objects/55289/allegory-of-vanity
11. Viahttps://www.nga.gov/collection/highlights/leyster-self-portrait.html
12. Via https://www.metmuseum.org/art/collection/search/892538
13. Via https://www.sammlung.pinakothek.de/de/artwork/PdxzEPQ4w5
14. De Groot, p6
15. Via https://www.rijksmuseum.nl/en/collection/object/Saying-Grace--93dbf1d805c7b721eee5b41063e24482
16. Van Emden, p502 Dentist, Via https://learn.ncartmuseum.org/artwork/the-dentist
17. Hofrichter, p18-19
18. Via https://artsandculture.google.com/asset/self-portrait-with-family-members-jan-miense-molenaer/LAG_zAV0faspzA?hl=en
19. Bredius, p17-19
20. Bredius, pp10-p22
21. Bredius, p11; Wurzbach v2, pp176-177
22. Bredius, pp2-9
23. Mundy, Peter. *The Travels of Peter Mundy in Europe and Asia* volume 4, p65
24. Mundy, Peter. *The Travels of Peter Mundy in Europe and Asia* volume 4, p70; also quoted in Brown, p63
25. Brown, Christopher, p83
26. Armstrong, pp51-52
27. Auctio Millingtoniana, A Collection of Extraordinary Paintings and Limnings. Auction pamphlet, Tunbridge Wells, 13 August 1691. Edward Millington. Via archive.org
28. Wurzbach, v1 pp652, 661
29. Van Emden, pp501, 503
30. Bredius, pp2-9

Bibliography

All modern equivalent currency values have been calculated using the National Archive's Currency Converter at https://www.nationalarchives.gov.uk/currency-converter.

Primary Sources

Ampzing, Samuel, *Beschryvinge Ende Lof Der Stad Haerlem in Holland*, Haarlem, 1628 via archive.org

Angliae Notitia, or the Present State of England: Together with divers reflections upon the Antient State thereof, London, printed by T.N. for John Martyn, 1669

Ball, V., *Travels in India by Jean Baptiste Tavernier*, Volume 1. London, Macmillan and Co. Ltd., 1889

Begley, W.E. and Desai, Z.A, ed., *The Shah Jahan Nama of 'Inayat Khan', an abridged history of the Mughal emperor Shah Jahan, compiled by his royal librarian*, Delhi, Oxford University Press, 1990

Bentley, Samuel, *Excerpta Historica, or Illustrations of English History.* London, Samuel Bentley, 1831

Bergalli, Luisa, *Componimenti poetici delle piu illustri rimatrici d'ogni secolo, raccolti da Luisa Bergalli. Parte prima, che contiene le rimatrici antiche fino all'anno 1575*, Published 1726, National Library of Naples via Internet Archive [accessed 14 February 2025]

Bergenroth, G. A., *Calendar of Letters, Despatches, and State Papers Relating to The Negotiations Between England and Spain,. Volume 1. Henry VII, 1485-1509*, London, Longman, Green and Roberts, 1862

Bergenroth, G. A. ed., 'Spain: October 1500', in *Calendar of State Papers, Spain, Volume 1, 1485-1509*, London, 1862 via *British History Online* http://www.british-history.ac.uk/cal-state-papers/spain/vol1/pp243-247 [accessed 12 January 2025].

Bodleian Library, *Calendar of the Clarendon State Papers Preserved in the Bodleian Library, Volumes 1-5,*. Oxford, The Clarendon Press, 1869-1970

Bredius, Dr. A., *Künstler-Inventare Urkunden zur geschichte der Holländischen Kunst des XVI, XVII und XVIII Jahrhunderts*, Volume 1, Martinus Nijhoff, 1915

Camera Picta, Palazzo Ducale, *Complesso Museale Mantova website* https://mantovaducale.beniculturali.it/en/camera-picta [Accessed 18 January 2025]

Cavendish, William, *Methode et Invention Nouvelle de Dresser les Chevaux*, Antwerp, Chez Jacques, 1658. Collection of the National Sporting Library and Museum, US.

Cavendish, William, Duke of Newcastle, *A New Method, and Extraordinary Invention to Dress Horses*, London, The Millbourn, 1667

Chronicle of the History of the World from Creation to Woden, with a Genealogy of Edward IV, Free Library of Philadelphia, https://libwww.freelibrary.org/digital/item/3310 [accessed 3 January 2025]

Clarendon, Earl of, Edward Hyde, *The History of the Rebellion and Civil Wars in England, Begun in the Year 1641,* Volume the Second, Oxford, 1704

Columbus, Christopher, Joaquin Miller, ed., *The Journal of Columbus' First Voyage*, Washington, The Inventors' Outlook, 1912

Craigie, W. A. ed., *The Maitland Quarto Manuscript containing poems by Sir Richard Maitland, Arbuthnot, and others,* Edinburgh and London, William Blackwood and Sons, 1920

Crowne, *Mr. Sir Courtly Nice: or, It Cannot Be. A Comedy as it is acted by Her Majesty's Servants*. London, 1703

Diepenbeeck, Abraham van, 'Nobilissimo Couriser Nappolitain', object number 03/1557, Royal Academy of Arts, https://www.royalacademy.org.uk/art-artists/work-of-art/nobilissimo-coursier-nappolitain [accessed 17 December 2024]

Dobson, Austin, *The Diary of John Evelyn*, Volumes 2 and 3, London, Macmillan and Co. Ltd., 1906

Drury, G. Thorn, *The Poems of Edmund Waller*, Volume 2, London, A. H. Bullen, 1901

Dryden, John, *Don Sebastian King of Portugal, A Tragedy Acted at the Theatre Royal*, London, 1690 via archive.org

Ellis, Henry, *Original Letters, Illustrative of English History*, Volume 1, Second Series, London, Harding and Lepard, 1827

Fanshawe, Lady Ann, *The Memoirs of Ann, Lady Fanshawe, wife of the Right Honourable Sir Richard Fanshawe*, London, John Lane, 1907

Bell, Clara, ed., *Firenzuola, Agnolo. Of the Beauty of Women. Translated from the Italian by Clara Bell with an Introduction by Theodore Child,.* London, James R. Osgood, McIlvaine and Co., 1892

Firth, C. H., ed., *The Life of William Cavendish Duke of Newcastle, to which is added The True Relation of the My Birth, Breeding and Life by Margaret Duchess of Newcastle,* London, John C. Nimmo, 1886

Flecknoe, Richard, *A Farrago of Several Pieces, London*, 1666. Internet Archive

Foster, William, *The Embassy of Sir Thomas Roe to India, 1615-1619*, Volume 1 & 2, London, The Hakluyt Society, 1899

Green, Mary Anne Everett, ed., *Calendar of State Papers Domestic Series, November 1667-September 1668,* London, 1893

Hakluyt, Richard, *The Principal Navigations, Voyages, Traffiques and Discoveries of the English Nation,* Volume 8. Glasgow, James MacLehouse and Sons, 1904

Hamilton, Anthony, Count, *The Memoirs of Grammont*, translated with notes by Horace Walpole, Philadelphia, Gebbie and Co., 1888

Hamilton, Anthony, *Memoirs of Count Grammont. Edited with notes by Sir Walter Scott,* London, George Routledge and Sons Limited, 1905

Hooke, Robert, *Micrographia: Or some Physiological Descriptions of Minute Bodies Made by Magnifying Glasses with Observation and Inquiries Thereupon,* London, John Martyn, The Royal Society, 1667

Irvine, William, ed., *Storia do Mogor, or Mogul India by Niccolao Manucci, Venetian 1653-1708,* London, John Murray, 1907

Jahangir, Emperor. Price, Major David ed., *Memoirs of The Emperor Jahangueir written by himself,* Holborn, J, Murray, 1829

Keen, Benjamin, translator and editor. *The Life of the Admiral Christopher Columbus by his Son Ferdinand,* New Brunswick, New Jersey, Rutgers University Press, 1959

Kingsbury, Susan Myra, ed., *The Records of the Virginia Company of London*, Volume 3, Washington, Library of Congress, 1933

Langbaine, Gerard, *An Account of the English Dramatick Poets,* Oxford, George West and Henry Clements, 1691

Leland, Lilian, *Traveling Alone. A Woman's Journey Around the World,* New York, The American News Company, 1890

Lewis, David, ed., Sander, Nicholas, *The Rise and Growth of the Anglican Schism*, London, Burns and Oates, 1877

Machiavelli, Niccolò, Rennert, Hugo Albert. ed., *History of Florence and the Affairs of Italy*, New York and London, M. Walter Dunne, 1901

Machiavelli, Niccolò, *The Prince, The City of the Sun by Tommaso Campanella, Essays by Ugo Foscolo, Essays by Guiseppe Mazzini, Recollections by Guiseppe Garibaldi*, The National Alumni, 1907

MacNutt, Francis Augustus, ed., *De Orbe Novo, The Eight Decades of Peter Martyr d'Anghiera*, Translated from the Latin with Notes and Introduction, Volumes 1 and 2, New York and London, G.P Putnam's Sons, 1912

Maguire, Yvonne, *The Women of the Medici*, London, George Routledge and Sons, Ltd., 1927

Moxon, *A Tutor to Astronomy and Geography, or, the Use of the Copernican Spheres*, London, 1665

Mundy, Peter, edited by Temple, Sir Richard Carnac, *The Travels of Peter Mundy in Europe and Asia 1608-1667,* Volume 2 1628-1634, London, The Hakluyt Society, 1914

Mundy, Peter, edited by Temple, Sir Richard Carnac, *The Travels of Peter Mundy in Europe and Asia 1608-1667*. Volume 4 1639-1647, London, The Hakluyt Society, 1925

Munro, John., ed., *The History of Jason by William Caxton*, Part 1, Early English Text Society, 1913, New York, Reprinted by Kraus Reprint Co., 1975

Newcastle, The Lady Marchioness of, *The Philosophical and Physical Opinions*, London, J. Martin and F. Allestrye, 1655. Internet Archive. Includes the Duke of Newcastle's *Epistle.*

Newcastle, Margaret.,*The World's Olio*, J. London, Martin and F. Allestrye, 1655. Internet Archive.

Newcastle, Margaret Duchess of, *The Description of a New World, Called the Blazing-World. Written by the Thrice Noble, Illustrious, and Excellent Princesse the Duchess of Newcastle*, London, printed by A. Maxwell, 1668

Newcastle, Margaret Duchess of, *Orations of Divers Sorts, Accommodated to Divers Places,* The Second Edition, London, A. Maxwell, 1668

Newcastle, Margaret Duchess of, *Poems, or Several Fancies in Verse: with the Animal Parliament, in Prose,* The Third Edition, London, A. Maxwell, 1668

Nicolas, Nicholas Harris, Esq., *The Privy Purse Expenses of Elizabeth of York: Wardrobe Accounts of Edward the Fourth*, London, William Pickering, 1830

Nichols, John, *A Collection of Ordinances and Regulations for the Government of the Royal Household, Made in Divers Reigns. From King Edward III to King William and Queen Mary,* London, The Society of Antiquaries, 1790

Otway, Thomas, *The Souldiers Fortune. A Comedy. Acted by their Majesties Servants at the Theatre Royal,* London, 1687 via archive.org

Philips, Katherine, *Poems by the most deservedly admired Ms Katherine Philips, The Matchless Orinda,* London, Henry Herringman, 1678

Piccolomini, Alessandro, *Lettura del. S. Alessandro Piccolomini Infiammato fatta nell'Accademia degli Infiammati,* 1541 via Google Books [accessed 14 February 2025]

Price, Major David, ed., *Memoirs of the Emperor Jahangueir, translated from a Persian manuscript,* Holborn, J. Murray, 1829

Public Record Office, *Calendar of the Patent Rolls, Edward IV, Henry VI A.D. 1467-1477,* London, Eyre and Spottiswoode, 1900

Public Record Office, *Calendar of the Patent Rolls, Edward IV, Edward V, Richard III A.D. 1476-1485,* London, Mackie and Co. Ltd., 1901

Public Record Office, *Close Rolls, Henry VI: 1426-27, in* Calendar of Close Rolls, Henry VI: Volume 2, 1429-1435, London, 1933

Rivers, Sir Anthony. Caxton, William, edited by William Blades, *The Dictes and Sayings of the Philosophers. A facsimile reproduction of the first book printed in England by William Caxton in 1477,* London, Elliot Stock, 1877

Ross, Janet, ed., translated by, *Lives of the Early Medici as Told in their Correspondence,* London, Chatto and Windus, 1910

Scoble, Andrew R., ed., *The Memoirs of Philip de Commines Lord of Argenton in Two Volumes,* Volume 1, G. London, Bell and Sons, 1911

Sichel, Edith, *The Renaissance*, London, Williams and Norgate, 1914

Smith, John, *Governor of Virginia. The Generall Historie of Virginia,* London, Edward Blackmore, 1632

Society of Antiquaries of London, *A Collection of Ordinances and Regulations for the Government of the Royal Household, Made in Divers Reigns*, London, John Nichols, 1790

Strada, Famiano, *Novar, Melchor de, ed., Guerras de Flandes. Primera Decada. Por Marcos-Miguel Bousquet y Compaña*, Biblioteca de la Universidad de Sevilla, 1748, via archive.org

Strype, John, *A Survey of the Cities of London and Westminster*, Volume 1 and Volume 2, London, A. Churchill, 1720

Tanner, J.R., ed,. *A Descriptive Catalogue of Naval Manuscripts in the Pepysian Library at Magdalene College, Cambridge*, Volume 2, Admiralty Letters, The Navy Records Society, 1904

Thompson, Edward Maunde, *Correspondence of the Family of Hatton, 1601-1704*, Volume 1, Camden Society, 1838

Tyler, Lyon Gardiner, ed., *Narratives of Early Virginia 1606-1625*, New York, Charles Scribner's Sons, 1930

Vasari, Giorgio, ed., Blashfield, E.H and E.W and Hopkins, A.A., *Lives of Seventy of the Most Eminent Painters, Sculptors and Architects, Volume 1 & 2,* George Bell and Sons, 1896 & 1897

Vasari, Giorgio, ed., Gaston Duc de Vere, *Lives of the Most Eminent Painters, Sculptors and Architects. Volumes 1-10*, London, Philip Lee Warner, 1912-1914

Vasari, Giorgio, ed., Professor G. Baldwin Brown, translated by Louisa S. Maclehose, *Vasari on Technique,* London, J.M. Dent and Company, 1907

Wheatley, Henry B., ed., *The Diary of Samuel Pepys, Clerk of the Acts and Secretary to the Admiralty, Volumes 1- 9,* London, George Bell and Sons, 1897

Wilkins, John, *A Discovery of a New World, or a discourse tending to prove that 'tis probable there may be another Habitable World on the Moon*, London, 1684

Wren, Christopher, *Life and Works of Sir Christopher Wren, from the Parentalia or Memoirs by his son Christopher,* London, 1903 via archive.org

Secondary Sources

Allen, Paula Gunn, *Pocahontas, Medicine Woman, Spy, Entrepreneur, Diplomat*, Harper San Francisco, 2004

Architectural Times, Sheesh Mahal – Legendary Palace of Mirrors, 29 April 2021 https://architecturaltimes.news/sheesh-mahal-legendary-palace-of-mirrors/ [accessed 14 August 2024]

Armstrong, Sir Walter, *The Peel Collection and the Dutch School of Painting*, New York, London Seeley and Co. Limited, 1904

Ashrafyan, K.E., 'The policy of Catholic Monarchs and Popes in the New World on the Christianization of the population and the policy of local authorities (1492–1513)', *Samara Journal of Science,*. 2021. Vol.10. N. 1. P. 230-236. doi: 10.17816/snv2021101208 C.C by 4.0

Bailey-Kempling, William, ed., *The Poets Royal of England and Scotland,* London, Chatto and Windus, 1908

Baker, Sir Richard, *A Chronicle of the Kings of England, from the Time of the Romans Government, to the Death of King James the First, with a Continuation to the Year 1660*, London, Samuel Ballard, 1733

Blake, N.F., *Caxton and His Worl,*. London, Andre Deutsch Ltd, 1969

Brinton, Selwyn, *The Gonzaga – Lords of Mantua*, New York, Brentano's, 1927

Britain Magazine, Burghley: House of Treasures, https://www.britain-magazine.com/features/burghley-house-of-treasures/ [accessed 10 September 2024]

Brown, Alexander, *The First Republic of America, an account of the origin of this nation, written from the records then (1624) concealed by the council, rather than from the histories then licenced by the crown*, Cambridge, The Riverside Press, 1898

Brown, Christopher, *Images of a Golden Past, Dutch Genre Painting of the 17th Century*, New York, Abbeville Press, 1984

Capilla Real de Granada, https://capillarealgranada.com/en/the-temple/the-royal-mausoleums-and-the-crypt/ [Accessed 12 January 2025]

Cartwright, Julia, *Isabella d'Este Marchioness of Mantua 1474-1539, A Study of the Renaissance,* Volumes 1 & 2, New York, E.P. Dutton and Company, 1915 edition.

Cayley, Arthur, *Memoirs of Sir Thomas More, with a New Translation of his Utopia, his History of King Richard III, and His Latin Poems*, Volume 2, London, Cadell and Davis, 1808

Cokayne, George, *The Complete Peerage of England, Scotland, Ireland, Great Britain and the United Kingdom,* Edition 1, Volumes 3 and 6, London, George Bell & Sons, 1895

Cole, Alison, *Italian Renaissance Courts: Art, Pleasure and Power,* Laurence King Publishing, London. 2016. p164-p199

Collison-Morley, L., *The Early Medici*, London, George Routledge and Sons Ltd, 1935

Cust, Mrs Henry, *Gentlemen Errant, Being the Journeys and Adventures of Four Noblemen in Europe During the Fifteenth and Sixteenth Centuries*, London, John Murray, 1909

Davidson, Lillias Campbell, *Catherine of Bragança, Infanta of Portugal and Queen-Consort of England*, New York, E.P Dutton and Company, 1908

De Groot, C. Hofstede, translated by Edward G. Hawke, based on the work of John Smith, *A Catalogue Raisonné of the works of the Most Eminent Dutch Painters of the Seventeenth Century*, Volume 3, London, Macmillan and Co Ltd., 1910

Duncan, E.A., *Keene's Handbook for Visitors to Agra and its Neighbourhood,* London, Thacker, Spink and Co., 1909

Einstein, Lewis, *The Italian Renaissance in England*, London, Macmillan and Co Ltd., 1903

Eisenbichler, Konrad, 'Laudomia Forteguerri Loves Margaret of Austria', in Francesca Canadé Sautman and Pamela Sheingorn (eds.), *Same-Sex Love and Desire Among Women in the Middle Ages*, New York, Palgrage, 2001, pp. 277-304.

Eisenbichler, Konrad, *The Sword and the Pen, Women, Politics and Poetry in Sixteenth Century Siena,* Notre Dame, Indiana, University of Notre Dame Press, 2012

Eliot, J.M., *Shah Jahan*, Lahore, 1875 via archive.org

English Heritage, History of St John's Abbey Gate, english-heritage.org [accessed 17 December 2024]

Faggioli, Sarah, 'The First Commentaries on Women Poets: Alessandro Piccolomini and Rinaldo Corso Critique Laodomia Forteguerri and Vittoria Colonna' in Mercedes Arriaga Florez and Stefano Santosuosso *(eds.), Women and the Canon*, Seville, Arcibel Editores, 2018

Fraser, Antonia, *King Charles II,* London, Phoenix, 2022

Gilbert, Kelly Ann, 'Medici power and patronage under Cosimo the Elder and Lorenzo the Magnificent' (2005). Senior Honors Theses and Projects. 103. Parts 1 & 2. https://commons.emich.edu/honors/103

Gracian, Lorenzo, *El Politico D. Fernando el Catholico. Juan Blaeu,* Amsterdam. 1659 (National Library of Naples)

Grattan, Thomas Colley, *The History of the Netherlands*, Philadelphia, Carey and Lea, 1831

Green, V.H.H., *Renaissance & Reformation, A Survey of European History between 1450 & 1660,* London, Edward Arnold Ltd, 1975

Gristwood, Sarah, *Game of Queens: The Women Who Made Sixteenth-Century Europe,* Oneworld Publications, 2017

Hale, John. R. and The Editors of TIME-LIFE Books, *Renaissance*, New York, Time Incorporated, 1965

Hansen, Waldema. *The Peacock Throne: The Drama of Moghul India,* New York, Holt, Rinehart and Winston, 1972

Hare, Augustus J. C., *Cities of Northern and Central Italy*, Volume 1, London, Daldy, Isbister and Co, 1876

Hare, Augustus J. C., *Florence*, London, Smith, Elder and Co., 1884

Hare, Augustus J. C., *Wanderings in Spain*, London, Strathan and Co., 1873

Harisse, Henry, *John Cabot, The Discoverer of North America and Sebastian his Son*, London, Benjamin Franklin Stevens, 1896

Heywood, William and Olcott, Lucy, *Guide to Siena, History and Art*, Siena, Libreria Editrice Senese, 1924

Higginbotham, Susan, *The Woodvilles, The Wars of the Roses and England's Most Infamous Family,* Stroud, The History Press, 2013

Historic Houses of the United Kingdom, 'Welbeck Abbey'. London, Cassell and Company Ltd., 1892

Hofrichter, Froma Fox, *Judith Leyster, A Woman Painter in Holland's Golden Age*, The Netherlands, Davaco Publishers, 1989

Jones, Jonathan, *The Loves of the Artists; Art and Passion in the Renaissance*, London, Simon and Schuster, 2013

Licence, Amy, *Edward IV and Elizabeth Woodville, A True Romance*, Stroud, Amberley Publishing, 2016. Chapters 8 to 11

Lucas, E. V., *A Wanderer in Florence*, New York, The Macmillan Company, 1914

Lumby, J. Rawson, ed., More, Thomas, *History of King Richard III,* London, Cambridge University Press, 1924

Matz, B. W., *The Inns and Taverns of 'Pickwick'*, London, Cecil Palmer, 1921

MacGibbon, David, *Elizabeth Woodville 1437-1492 Her Life and Times*, London, Arthur Baker Ltd, 1938

MacNutt, Francis Augustus, *Bartholomew de las Casas, His Life, His Apostolate, and His Writings,* New York and London, G. P. Putnam's Sons, 1909

Mauritshuis, *Abridged Catalogue of Pictures and Sculpture in the Royal Picture Gallery, The Hague,* National Printing Office, 1899

McAfee, Helen, *Pepys on the Restoration Stage*, New Haven, Oxford University Press, 1916

Medici Genealogical Tree, museumsinflorence.com [accessed 15 June 2024]

Mendelson, Sara Heller, *The Mental World of Stuart women: Three Studies,* Amherst, The University of Massachusetts Press, 1987

Misra, Rekha, *Women in Mughal India (1526-1748 A.D.),* Delhi, Munshiram Manoharlal, 1967

Murari, Timeri N., *Empress of the Taj: In Search of Mumtaz Mahal,* New Delhi, Speaking Tiger, 2019

National Gallery website, London. https://www.nationalgallery.org.uk

Perry, Henry Ten Eyck, *The First Duchess of Newcastle and Her Husband as Figures in Literary History,* Boston and London, Ginn and Company, 1918

Pinto, V. de Sola, *The English Renaissance 1510-1688*, London, The Cresset Press, 1950

Prescott, William Hickling, *History of the Reign of Ferdinand and Isabella, The Catholic*, Tenth edition, Volumes 1-3, New York, Harper and Brothers, 1845-1846

Preyer, David C., *The Art of the Netherland Galleries*, Boston, L.C. Page and Co., 1908

Rachfahl, Felix, *Margaretha von Parma, Statthalterin der Niederlande (1559-1567),* Munchen & Leipzig, 1898

Rijksmuseum website, particularly, 'Judith Leyster', https://www.rijksmuseum.nl/en/stories/dutch-masters/story/judith-leyster-10 [accessed 19 March 2025]

Robin, Diana Maury, *Publishing Women: Salons, the Presses and the Counter-Reformation in Sixteenth-Century Italy,* Introduction and Chapter 5, Chicago, University of Chicago Press, 2007

Robinson, Edward Forbes, *The Early History of Coffee Houses in England*, London, Kegan Paul, Trench, Trübner & Co., Ltd., 1893

Romero, Jo, *Forgotten Women of the Wars of the Roses, The Untold History Behind the Battle for the Crown*, Barnsley, Pen and Sword Books, 2024

Ross, Janet, *Florentine Palaces and Their Stories*, London, J.M. Dent & Co., 1905

Royal Museums Greenwich website. https://www.rmg.co.uk/collections/objects/rmgc-object-15079 'The Royal Katherine', accessed 30 August 2024

Russell, Ephraim, 'The societies of the Bardi and the Peruzzi and their dealings with Edward III', *Finance and Trade Under Edward III the London Lay Subsidy of 1332*, (Manchester, 1918), *British History Online* [accessed 12 June 2024]

Scofield, Cora L., *The Life and Reign of Edward the Fourth King of England and of France and Lord of Ireland,* Volume 2, London, Longmans, Green and Co., 1923

Seelye, Elizabeth Eggleston, *Pocahontas*, New York, Dodd, Mead and Company, c1879

Simon, Kate, *A Renaissance Tapestry: The Gonzaga of Mantua*, New York, Harper and Row, 1988 pp. 91-166

Singleton, Esther, Famous Women, 'Margaret of Parma, Regent of the Netherlands'. New York, Dodd, Mead and Company, 1904

Sir Joseph Banks and The Royal Society, London, John W. Parker, 1844

Sismondi, J.C.L.de, *A History of the Italian Republics*, New York, Harper and Brothers, 1864

South Asia Institute, The Lakshimi Mittal and Family, Harvard University. 'Lost & Found: Toward a Living Heritage', 10 March 2016 https://mittalsouthasiainstitute.harvard.edu/2016/03/lost-found-toward-a-living-heritage/ [accessed 14 August 2024]

Sparrow, W. Shaw, *Women Painters of the World from the time of Caterina Vigri 1413-1463 to Rosa Bonheur and the present day,* London, Hodder and Stoughton, 1905

Staley, Edgcumbe, *Famous Women of Florence*, London, Archibald Constable and Co Ltd., 1909

Sutton, Anne, F. and Livia Visser-Fuchs, 'A Most Benevolent Queen' Queen Elizabeth Woodville's Reputation, her Piety and her Books, www.richardiii.net [Accessed 12 January 2025]

Strickland, Agnes, *Lives of the Queens of England*, Volume 5, London, Henry Colburn, 1854

The Athenaeum Journal of Literature, Science, the Fine Arts, Music and the Drama. July to December 1893. John C. Francis. London, Chancery Lane.

Tighe, Robert Richard and Davis, James Edward, *Annals of Windsor, Being a History of the Castle and Town.* Volume 1, London, Longman, Brown, Green, Longmans and Roberts, 1858

Tremlett, Giles, *Isabella of Castile, Europe's First Great Queen,* London, Bloomsbury, 2017. Kindle ebook.

Van Emden, Frieda, 'March 1918: Judith Leyster, a Female Frans Hals', in *The Art World: A Monthly for the Public Devoted to The Higher Ideals,* Vol 3, Oct 1917-March 1918. New York, No 2 West 45th Street

'The Taj Mahal by Cooper', in *The Art World: A Monthly for the Public Devoted to The Higher Ideals,* Vol 3, Oct 1917-March 1918. New York, No 2 West 45th Street

Wagner, Heather Lehr, *The Medicis: A Ruling Dynasty,* Philadelphia, Chelsea House Publishers, 2006

Weller, Dennis P., *Jan Miense Molenaer: Painter of the Dutch Golden Age*, Raleigh, North Carolina Museum of Art, 2002, pp. 1-7

Whitaker, Katie, *Mad Madge; Margaret Cavendish, Duchess of Newcastle. Royalist, Writer and Romantic,* London, Chatto & Windus, 2003

Williamson, James A., *The Voyages of the Cabots and the English Discovery of North America Under Henry VII and Henry VIII,* London, The Argonaut Press, 1929

Woodward, Grace Steele, *Pocahontas*, University of Oklahoma Press, 1969

Worcester Art Museum, James A. Welu and Pieter Biesboer, *Judith Leyster – A Dutch Master and Her World.* In particular the chapter by, Ellen Broersen., 'Judita Leystar: A Painter of "Good, Keen Sense"',' pp. 15-39, Yale University, 1993

Worsley, Lucy, *Bolsover Castle*, English Heritage. 2000

Wurzbach, von., Dr Alfred, *Niederländisches Künstler-Lexikon Auf Grund Archivalischer Forschungen Bearbeitet. Mit Mehr Als 3000 Monogrammen Zweiter Band L-Z,* Wien und Leipzig Verlag von Halm und Goldmann, 1910

Index